18th CENTURY JAPAN
CULTURE AND SOCIETY

EDITED BY C. ANDREW GERSTLE

Sydney
ALLEN & UNWIN
Wellington London Boston

First published in 1989
Allen & Unwin Australia Pty Ltd
An Unwin Hyman company
8 Napier Street, North Sydney NSW 2059 Australia

Allen & Unwin Zealand Limited
75 Chuznee Street, Wellington, New Zealand

Unwin Hyman Limited
15–17 Broadwick Street, London W1V 1FP England

Unwin Hyman Inc.
8 Winchester Place, Winchester, Mass 01890 USA

National Library of Australia
Cataloguing-in-Publication entry:

Eighteenth century Japan: culture & society.

Includes index.
ISBN 0 04 380031 9.

1. Japan—History—Tokugawa period, 1600–1868. 2.
Japan—Civilization—1600–1868. 3. Japan—Social
life and customs—1600–1868. I. Gerstle, C. Andrew,
1951–   . II. Australian National University. Dept. of
Far Eastern History. III. Asian Studies Association of
Australia. (Series: East Asia series (Sydney, N.S.W.)).

952′.025

Library of Congress Catalog Card Number: 89-83594

Set in 10/11pt Times by Asco Trade Typesetting Ltd. Hong Kong
Printed by Kin Keong Printing Co Pte Ltd. Singapore

18th CENTURY JAPAN

FEH/ASAA East Asia Series

Contents

v

Contributors

Robert L. Backus, Professor of Oriental Languages, University of California, Santa Barbara, has published extensively on Tokugawa Confucianism and Heian fiction.

H. B. D. Clarke is Professor of Japanese at Sydney University. He specialises in linguistics (particularly dialects) and literature.

Maria Flutsch, Senior Lecturer in Japanese at the University of Tasmania, is currently researching Sōseki's Chinese writings.

C. Andrew Gerstle, Professor of Japanese at the Australian National University, is author of *Circles of Fantasy: Convention in the Plays of Chikamatsu* (1986).

Thomas J. Harper, Lecturer in Japanese at the University of Leiden, is an authority on the history of *Genji* criticism in Japan.

Mark Morris, Senior Lecturer in Japanese at the University of Adelaidl, has accepted a position at Cambridge University. He has published several outstanding articles on classical and modern Japanese poetry.

Nakano Mitsutoshi, Professor of Japanese Literature at Kyūshū University, is one of Japan's leading scholars of Tokugawa culture.

Hiroko C. Quackenbush, Professor of Japanese at Hiroshima University, has made Japanese linguistics her special field of research.

Teruoka Yasutaka, Emeritus Professor of Japanese Literature of Waseda University, is a renowned authority on Tokugawa literature.

Torigoe Bunzō, Professor and Head of the Drama Department of Waseda University, has published extensively on Tokugawa drama.

Illustrations

Acknowledgements

It is a pleasure to acknowledge some of the individuals and organisations that helped make this book possible. Andrew Fraser, as general editor of the monograph series, has guided the manuscript through all the stages leading to publication. Margaret Pollock of the Japan Centre at the Australian National University has typed most of the volume and prepared the final copy. Stephen Large's comments and support have been most appreciated.

Above all, we are most grateful for the support of the Australia–Japan Foundation and the Japan Foundation, which made possible the original 1982 Conference '18th Century Edo' at Sydney University from which this volume grew.

Introduction

Japan enjoyed many benefits from the long peace of the Tokugawa era. Earthquake, fire and famine occasionally took their toll, but by 1750 civil war was a distant memory. Literature, poetry and the arts flourished on a scale never seen before among the military class, let alone among the prosperous merchants and artisans of the great urban centres like Edo, Kyoto and Osaka. The outside world was a distant curiosity, but already through the Dutch, Korean and Chinese traders of Nagasaki foreign culture was seeping in, despite strict controls on personal contact and deep official hostility to the 'evil sect', as Christianity was termed. Literate, free, self-confident and complacent, urban Japan was able to turn in upon itself and savour to the full all aspects of its native tradition, selectively stimulated and fertilised by benign influences from overseas.

The result was a cultural flowering that even in its twilight stage took Europe by storm in the mid-nineteenth century. Whistler's *Westminster Bridge*, Monet's gardens, Van Gogh's copies of Japanese prints, Toulouse Lautrec's theatre posters are a few of the more famous examples of Japonisme which swept Europe in the second half of the nineteenth century. Later, Nō drama, Kabuki, architecture, ceramics and textiles too would serve as a stimulus to 'modern' European arts. Japan was to borrow much from the West after the opening of the country in the 1850s, but it was by no means a one-way exchange. In fact, particularly in relation to the arts, Tokugawa Japan did more to stimulate the outside world than vice versa. It certainly gained in technology, but until late in the nineteenth century owed little to the West in matters of aesthetics.

Even so, Meiji bureaucrats after 1868, in seeking to justify their hasty drive to transform Japan into a modern industrial state within a single generation, cast harsh aspersions on the previous regime, and were joined in this by many contemporary scholars and critics. Only recently has a new era of postwar peace and prosperity allowed a more leisurely and sympathetic view of Tokugawa Japan; its cultural riches are now esteemed and appreciated to a degree unknown before, both in Japan and overseas. Recent economic studies also paint a more complex portrait of growth and stagnation. Further, we now know that literacy rates in the mid-1700s were by no means inferior to those in contemporary Europe. A firm conclusion arising from recent research is that it is impossible to generalise about the two and a half centuries of Tokugawa Japan, features of which were cities among the largest in the world and wide regional diversity.

Much research up till now has focused on the political economy or the relationship between samurai administration and the peasantry. Literary studies, on the other hand, have tended to be ahistorical, often ignoring the fact that most art was a commodity produced for a price. Further, our understanding of the role of art in daily life—particularly in the larger cities, with their pleasure quarters and theatre districts, publishing houses and salons—remains rudimentary.

Recent critical theory has reminded us afresh that the production of art is very much a part of the dynamics of power in society. It is commonly assumed that most 'art' in the Tokugawa period was produced by townsmen for their fellows in the major cities. The introduction of commercial printing in the seventeenth century, as in Europe, transformed society as had no other technological advance since the invention of writing. Ordinary people were able for the first time to gain access to culture previously confined to the privileged holders of manuscripts in courtier or samurai households, or in Buddhist monasteries. The classics were literally up for sale. As a consequence, the economic ascendancy of merchants and tradesmen by the end of the seventeenth century gave rise to a new social hierarchy and popular self-awareness.

The 1700s thus saw the mature intertwining of two major strands of commoner culture, distinct though not necessarily antagonistic. The first was centred in the pleasure quarters and theatre districts of the cities. These 'carnivalesque' spaces were a Rabelaisian world of food, wine, sex and, in the theatre, of grotesque exuberance and symbolic violence: all part of a licensed subculture, with its own language and customs, essentially off limits to samurai. Here, outcast courtesans and actors reigned as sovereigns in a topsy-turvy society where the samurai were often the butt of jest. Within these spheres all were pulled down to the level of a common denominator—money. But as in Bakhtin's depiction of Renaissance popular culture, imagery and custom were double-edged. Out of the pleasure-quarter marketplace arose *sui*, an aesthetic ideal that contrasted sensitivity, genuine feeling, and gentleness with money, violence and power. In the theatre we see this ambivalence clearly; the 'rough' *aragoto* Kabuki actor was both outlaw and hero, both violent and gentle, both a samurai and an outcast. The Edo actor Ichikawa Danjūrō lorded over his world as 'hero' of the oppressed. Ranked at the bottom of the official Confucian social scale, urban merchants created in the theatre and pleasure quarter a world of their own to command.

Some merchants, however, began a conscious search for access to aristocratic culture. Ambitious citizens of this kind began an active appropriation of Japan's classical past. Until the advent of commercial printing, access to classical culture had been restricted for over 500 years to the Kyoto upper classes (courtier or samurai). For a commoner to attempt to be a *waka* poet and thereby be accepted as an equal by the aristocracy was a political act, because *waka* was their property. Bookshops and lending libraries gave the masses access to the cultural treasurers of the past as never before, but we know from courtier diaries in the seventeenth century that aristocrats remained disdainful towards even sophisticated commoners. As in any society during periods of rapid technological, economic and social change, class tensions arose. It was one thing for a commoner to read *The Tale of Genji*, another to publish treaties claiming that his reading was more sophisticated and more accurate than those of the aristocrats who possessed manuscripts dating to the eleventh or twelfth centuries, and who traced their lineage to Murasaki's own time. In the 1700s it was a radical claim that the past belonged to all, regardless of blood or class. As T. Harper's chapter shows, Motoori Norinaga and other scholars' desires to have their work accepted was not only a quest for academic respect. They sought to alter the rules of discourse, to remove status as an attribute necessary for possession of the 'right of knowledge'.

The demand to participate, and therefore to create 'high culture' in a commercial, non-aristocratic setting, however, had obvious limitations, especially if one lacked an independent income. Yosa Buson and Ueda Akinari among many others, in striving to produce art worthy of the best in the Japanese and Chinese tradition, found the ideals of earlier Chinese literati useful. The idea of artist as amateur, creating art for art's sake appealed to them as an ideology of resistance to the dominance of commercial publishers and wealthy patrons. Through salons of like-minded artists and sophisticated patrons, the literati were able gradually to achieve a measure of independence. Most artists nevertheless had to sell their work to support themselves and their families. Buson's letters, as analysed by M.

Morris below, give us a fascinating glimpse of one figure attempting to maintain integrity while continuing to meet the desires of patrons. Chinese aesthetics, particularly the contrast between high/elegant/ traditional (*ga*) versus popular/vulgar/modern (*zoku*) had been the guiding principle of high culture from the eighth century onwards. The long Tokugawa peace after 1600 inspired a renaissance of interest in this classical theory. S. Nakano's chapter pursues this matter in greater detail. *Ga* meant tradition, and tradition means the actual physical preservation of art objects: manuscripts, paintings, ceramics. In contrast, *zoku* is ephemeral by definition. The *ga–zoku* theory gave artists a framework to see clear distinctions between 'levels' of culture. In Bashō, the greatest poet of the Tokugawa age, we see a highly literate and tradition-conscious author making deliberate use of the *zoku* world as he travels about the countryside interacting with locals in the context of linked-verse gatherings. The notes and poems he collected served a future use in the carefully crafted poems for *ga* publications back in the city. In contrast, Saikaku, the famous poet– novelist, was proud of his commoner, live-for-the-moment Osaka background, unlike Bashō, who as a former samurai seems more conscious of his place in a tradition, though he too worked in the popular medium of *haikai*. The outrageousness of Saikaku's *zoku* is similar to that of Kabuki, that most popular and ephemeral of the arts, which consciously kept itself in the *zoku* sphere throughout the Tokugawa era by never publishing complete texts. Only the fleeting moment of performance was to matter. The pleasure quarters, too, left no record in the sense that the parties, antics, singing and lovemaking were, as a matter of custom, not to be remembered the next day.

These two strands of popular ideology: the rebellious folk culture of the quarters and theatre districts, and the movements to 'raise' commoners both into the traditions of the classical past and into the power structure are, at their extremes, in opposition. Those aspiring to the upper world were often critical of the excesses of the 'vulgar' *zoku* culture, as were many commoner thinkers like Nakai Riken and Yamagata Bantō. Most artists, of course, drew on both spheres for stimulus, though one can imagine the tensions inherent in a political and social system where wealthy merchants, officially at the lowest rung on the social ladder, virtually financed the samurai government; where actors and courtesans, officially below the four classes, were idolised as heroes and goddesses far above the samurai.

An era of tension in the hierarchical structure, the eighteenth century also witnessed the advent of regional rivalry between the Kansai (Kyoto/Osaka) area, with its traditional cultural and linguistic domination, and the newly risen political capital of Edo. The last third of the century saw Edo publishers (most of which were originally founded as branch offices of Kansai companies) begin to print works in the local dialect, an act that decisively altered the cultural balance of power. Edo would not pre-dominate culturally or linguistically until the end of the nineteenth century when it became modern Tokyo, but from the 1760s it began to exert cultural influence nationally that was commensurate with its political power.

One need not overstate the tensions in Tokugawa urban society. Compared to the wars and revolutions in Europe over the same period, Japan still appears stable. It was an age of gradual change. Nor should we overstate the 'threat' to samurai authority. The Kansei Reforms of the 1790s implemented by Matsudaira Sadanobu show clearly that the Edo government was still in control and could exert its power at will. Nevertheless, much social and cultural activity was stimulated by what we might term 'institutionalised' tensions, whether they be architectural in terms of walled districts for pleasure and theatre, social in a rigid class system, cultural in the *ga–zoku* ideology, or regional in the Kansai/Edo rivalry. The essays collected here, in examining the social context of 'commoner' culture, show urban life to be both dynamic and creative.

The first group of chapters examines urban entertainment, as centred on the pleasure quarters and theatres. Y. Teruoka presents a vivid account of the role of the pleasure quarters in popular culture, drawn from a wide range of original sources. The author, generally accepted as the doyen of this subject, argues that the seventeenth century was the golden age of high class pleasure-quarter culture when the famous *tayū* (first class courtesans) such as Yoshino and Yūgiri became symbols of ideal femininity in the popular mind because their reputations for beauty, taste and sensitivity reached far and wide through the novels of Saikaku and plays of Chikamatsu. He contends, however, that from the early 1700s the quarters gradually begin to lose their central place in urban culture. Nevertheless, they remained important throughout the eighteenth century: two notable examples being Shimabara's role as Kyoto's salon for literati (*bunjin*) artists, and the role of Edo's Yoshiwara in the development of shamisen music. The Kansei Reforms of the 1790s, however, put an end to Yoshiwara as a cultural centre.

Next, A. Gerstle looks at theatres, the other centre of popular entertainment, and examines the social role of Kabuki in the Edo metropolis, presenting it as an ongoing festival, an essential element in the rhythms of city life, and argues that Kabuki was not only important for merchants, but also served as a focus for high fashion, intellectuals, poets and samurai. In particular, he looks at the role of the *Danjūrō* actor as the symbolic guardian of Edo's citizens.

In the last essay in this group, B. Torigoe gives a history of the term *jōruri* from its origins in medieval storytelling, emphasising its nature as vocal music. In particular, he discusses the different Edo Jōruri traditions, and argues that though Osaka is rightly thought to be the home of Jōruri puppet drama (Bunraku), Edo Jōruri was important in the seventeenth century as an independent tradition. By the eighteenth century, however, the Osaka tradition had come to dominate puppet theatre and not until the second half of the century, when Osaka performers began to travel to Edo in greater numbers, do we see a second flourish of Edo Jōruri. In particular, the patronage of Mitsui Jirōemon (d. 1799), the owner of the Mitsui business, encouraged the 30-year burst of Edo playwriting from the 1760s by Hiraga Gennai and others.

The second group of essays considers Edo language: its development in the eighteenth century and its eventual evolution, in the nineteenth, into 'standard' Japanese. H. Clarke outlines the various lineages of the hybrid Edo dialect which began to mix from early in the 1600s. He finds much similarity between the Edo language as depicted in the early Rodrigues treatise on Japanese (1604–08) and that reflected in Edo fiction some 200 years later. As in Edo Jōruri discussed in Torigoe's essay, late eighteenth century Edo fiction writers (like Shikitei Sanba) were acutely conscious of their own linguistic heritage distinct from Kamigata (Kyoto–Osaka), and give us a sharp picture of the spoken language. H. Quackenbush in 'Edo and Tokyo Dialects' narrows in on two significant phonetic changes to give insight into the ways in which both linguistic and social factors contribute to the development of a standard language.

The third group of papers moves from the world of commercial or 'popular' art into the sphere of 'high' culture. M. Morris opens a window into the daily life of Buson, the most famous poet-painter of eighteenth century Japan. Morris lets Buson's letters to his patrons bring to life the dilemma of a man striving to live the code of a literati amateur artist while nevertheless needing to sell his works to make a living. The letters show his attempt 'to negotiate the compromise that would allow him to be both artisan and artist'. We see Buson the astute, subtle dealer ingratiate himself to patrons, and at the same time play one off against another—increasing the value of his work. We see also, however, that Buson was not free to paint entirely as he wished; most of his works were commissioned.

Scholarship on classical Chinese and Japanese literature also flourished at this time. T. Harper describes how *The Tale of Genji* (and by extension all traditional court literature) ceased to be the exclusive realm of Kyoto aristocracy. He contends that, though the methodology of Motoori Norinaga and other non-aristocrat scholars was not significantly different from that of courtiers, these men were consciously creating 'new' criticism and subtly claiming classical Japanese literature as the heritage of all Japanese. Next M. Nakano, in a somewhat polemical essay, contends that the terms *sui* (elegance in the pursuit of pleasure) and *tsū* (connoisseurship) had their origins in the official pleasure quarters at a time when the quarters had a genuine aesthetic life (until late in the eighteenth century), but that their influence was limited. He postulates a need for reassessing the importance of 'high' or 'elite' culture, as expressed in the traditional Chinese-inspired *ga–zoku* (elegance–vulgarity) dichotomy. His theory, that all levels of society aspired to emulate this 'higher' aesthetic, offers a fresh perspective on this important middle period in the Tokugawa era.

The final essay by R. Backus conveniently closes the century and the volume, because the Kansei Reforms (1790s) instigated by Sadanobu set a new—and, many would contend, a decisive—stamp on Japanese culture. Backus uses Sadanobu's own lectures to show his 'conservatism' and desire to regenerate the government's power and prestige through strengthening of Bakufu finances, discipline of the bureaucracy and standardisation of the educational system. Backus argues that Sadanobu was the last defender of the old order who could act with confidence in his beliefs. The author's translations of Sadanobu's writings gives us a clear view of his ideas: we see a man rigorous in his pursuit of self control and scholarship, a leader consistently striving to make *bun* (scholarship) as essential and intense as *bu* (martial spirit) in samurai life.

Courtesans and actors, satirists, poets and painters, scholars and samurai bureaucrats—strange bedfellows indeed—are all players in the multi-layered drama that is eighteenth-century Japan. Much work yet remains to be done on other aspects of city life, and on how urban centres interacted with the countryside. These essays, nevertheless, show that though under a relatively rigid segregated class system, urban society was fluid and dynamic, with complex rules and conventions. Both as a precursor to modern Japan and as a fascinating era of its own, the eighteenth century rewards our attention.

Part I

PLEASURE QUARTERS AND THEATRE

1

The pleasure quarters and Tokugawa culture

Teruoka Yasutaka

In the Tokugawa era (1603–1868), courtesans were of two kinds: those who were under licence by the government and those who were not. The licensed courtesans were confined within a thick-walled enclosure, while the unlicensed ones were found scattered throughout the cities, the object of constant police surveillance and crackdowns. In contrast to 'unofficial' brothel areas, the Yoshiwara quarter in Edo (Tokyo), the city of the Shogun, was dubbed 'the licensed ward' (*gomen no ochō*) or just 'the ward'; in Kyoto and Osaka, the Shimabara and Shinmachi wards were also called 'the ward', signifying pride in being the quarters of higher-class courtesans rather than of common prostitutes.

Among the many licensed pleasure quarters under the Tokugawa, those in these three large cities certainly mirror the rise and fall of merchant culture and economic power. The aesthetics born from this high class merchant world—Kyoto and Osaka's *sui* (savoir-faire, gentleness and elegance as contrasting with force, money and coarseness) in early Tokugawa and Edo's *tsū* (connoisseurship) in its latter years—represent an era comparable with the elegance (*miyabi*) of the aristocratic Heian court of the ninth to twelfth centuries. Popular fashion in such things as hairstyles and clothes was also based on the aesthetics emanating from the licensed quarters, which became cultural centres as both the setting and the source for the urban arts of literature, theatre and music. First, let us trace their development in the three main cities.

The development of pleasure quarters

Until the end of the sixteenth century, prostitutes plied their trade freely wherever demand arose, such as in Kyoto, other urban centres and along the crossroads of important thoroughfares. Under Toyotomi Hideyoshi's regime in the late 1500s, prostitution was brought under control for the first time, mainly in the interest of military security, by gathering the dispersed brothels into a single area of Kyoto. In 1589 Hara Saburōemon, a retainer of Hideyoshi, set up the first licensed quarter in Kyoto. It was called Yanagimachi and was located in the three hectare area of Made no Kōji-dōri and Sanjōoshi no Kōji-dōri. Hideyoshi is known to have frequented this quarter himself in disguise with his retainers, as recorded in *The Great Mirror of the Way of Love* (*Shikidō ōkagami*, 1678).

Thirteen years later, in 1602, the year before Tokugawa Ieyasu officially established the seat of his government in Edo, Kyoto had grown greatly and the Yanagimachi quarter was moved to Muromachi Rokujō. Since this two-hectare area had three roads (*suji*), it was called Misujimachi, remaining lively for 40 years until 1639. Only one source shows us how Misujimachi quarter looked, the picture scroll *The Tale of Tsuyudono* (*Tsuyudono monogatari*, 1620s).

In 1640 the Kyoto magistrate was ordered to move the quarter to Shimogyoku Nishi Shinyashiki, where traces of it are still extant today. It was a block of 120 square yards, with a canal running through the middle. As for its name 'Shimabara', the most likely explanation is that its 'great gate' (*ōmon*)—the only entrance—was thought to have resembled the gate of the Shimabara castle in Bizen which had been retaken from rebels two years earlier. The renowned Osaka Shinmachi quarter (present day Shinmachi-dōri, Shinmachi Nanboku-dōri), like Kyoto's Misujimachi, had a predecessor. Before 1620, the Hyōtanmachi quarter had been in the Dōtombori district under the control of Kimura Matajirō, a Fushimi *rōnin* employed by Hideyoshi. In 1631, it was moved to the present site under an order from the Tokugawa government, and called Shinmachi. Gradually the courtesans from Sadoshimamachi, Tenma's Yoshiharamachi, and Kawaguchi's Sankenya were gathered together in the new quarter, which was completed by 1657. In contrast to Kyoto's Shimabara, which served upper-class and well-educated gentlemen, Shinmachi's guests were the local wealthy merchants or those from all over Japan who came on business to Osaka, the hub of national commerce. Even the novelist Ihara Saikaku, an Osaka native, found it too bustling and noisy as recorded in his *Great Mirror of Love* (*Shoen ōkagami*, 1684). Situated near the many daimyo storehouses and the bustling commercial port where wealthy merchants gathered, the facilities at Shinmachi were unrivalled throughout the land. As Saikaku says in *Life of an Amorous Man* (*Kōshoku ichidai otoko*, 1682), summing up the ultimate in a playboy's dream, 'A Kyoto courtesan with some Edo spirit (*hari*), meet up with her in Shinmachi, what could be better.'

This *hari*—the pride or stubbornness in not submitting to any force, whether physical, official or monetary—was a particularly important attribute for Yoshiwara courtesans in the 'rough' Bakufu city of Edo, with its population of more than half a million samurai, most of whom were transients from the provinces on the alternate-attendance system (*sankin kōtai*). There was also constant tension between city ruffians and lower-ranking officials.

The year 1618 is the accepted date for the opening of the Yoshiwara official quarter. The site selected by the Bakufu was Fukiyachō no Shita (present day Chūō-ku, Horidome 2 chōme). Between 1603 and 1618 there were several brothel areas in the new city of Edo: fourteen or fifteen houses in Kōjimachi 8 chōme, the same in Kamakura Kawagishi, and more than twenty in the Yanagimachi area of the castle gate at Jōbanbashi. The master of the Yanagimachi, one Shōji Jin'emon (rumoured to have been a descendant of the Odawara Hōjō family), in 1612 presented the following reasons to the government for the creation of an official pleasure quarter. These were to control:

1 thieves who steal their master's money in order to enjoy themselves;
2 villains who kidnap young girls and sell them into prostitution, or who get adopted by a good family and force their wives into prostitution; and
3 unemployed samurai of ill repute, ruffians or vagabonds.

The prime reason given was 'security' in this newly-established frontier city; the brothel owners pledged their support in the control of unruly elements. Five years later, in 1617, the Bakufu granted conditional permission for the building of the Yoshiwara pleasure quarter, with Shōji Jin'emon as head officer. The most important conditions were the following:

1 Prostitution is only to be allowed in the quarter. (Hereafter unlicensed prostitution became illegal and survived as a clandestine activity.)
2 Courtesans are not to leave the quarter.
3 Suspicious loiterers are to be questioned and their addresses checked. If suspicion remained, the city magistrates office must be informed.

These were recorded by the sixth head of Yoshiwara, the grandson of Shōji Jin'emon, Matazaemon Katsutomi, who was ordered by the city magistrates to compile a history of Yoshiwara (*Shin-yoshiwarachō yuisho sho*), later published in the book *Writings from the Bedroom* (*Dōbō goen*, 1721).

The Yoshiwara quarter remained at Chūō-ku Horidome from 1618 until 1657, the year of the Great Fire of Meireki. It is termed 'old' (*moto*) Yoshiwara; the post-1657 Yoshiwara, which was moved to the outskirts of Edo in the Nihon Tsutsumi area of Asakusa, is called the 'new' (*shin*) Yoshiwara to distinguish the two. We have only one source for the street names, houses, top-class courtesans (tayū), second-to-top courtesans (*kōshi*), courtesans' poetic names (*genjina*), ages, etc. This is *Tales of the East* (*Azuma monogatari*) published in 1642. Though it is a guide to a local district of the new city of Edo rather than an appraisal of courtesans (*yūjo hyōbanki*), when it was reissued the following year, four pages of reviews were added of the eighteen new *tayū* who had had their debut during the year. This second edition aimed to appeal to the massive increase of samurai entering Edo due to the previous year's (1642) order of alternate attendance for all Tokugawa vassal daimyo; it was unmistakably a guide to the Yoshiwara pleasure quarter and the forerunner of the courtesan critique (*yūjo hyōbanki*) genre.

The revised *Tales of the East* was, however, published to fill a sudden demand and did not have immediate successors, perhaps because the 'old' Yoshiwara had no outstanding courtesans of lasting fame. Only with the creation of Shin Yoshiwara after 1657 did Yoshiwara really become the cultural centre of Edo.

The rise and role of *tayū*

The crowning jewels of urban culture were the first-class courtesans, or *tayū*, a term used originally for theatrical performers. Next came the second-class *tenjin* (termed *kōshi* in Edo). *Tenjin* were back-ups or trainees; especially talented *tenjin* could become *tayū*, the most exalted rank in the quarter, and *tayū* might occasionally lose favour and drop down to the *tenjin* class.

Early seventeenth-century references to life in Kyoto suggest how the term *tayū* came to be used for courtesans. In the *Tales of Tsuyudono*, Tsuyudono is taken on a tour of Kyoto by the proprietor of his inn:

> Along Shijō Kawara, resthouses, small sideshows, and theatricals abounded, each behind drawn curtains. At one, where the customer-enticing-drums were pounding, Tsuyudono approached to have a look

at the notice board: 'From this coming fifteenth, Kanze Nō will be performed here. The *tayū* (performers) are Yoshino, Tsushima, Tosa, Teika, Onoe, Takashima, all famous actresses. Everyone is welcome to the show.' At another place was a sign for the 'Sadoshima Kabuki' where it said: 'A performance of Nō and puppets will be held. The *tayū* is Kawachi no Kami.'

This work is referring to the Kanze Nō performances at Shijō Kawara by Misuji courtesans in the early decades of the seventeenth century. The 'Yoshino' (Yoshino II, became *tayū* in 1620, retired from quarter in 1632) and others mentioned are later listed in the *Tales of Tsuyudono* as famous performers of the Misuji quarter. Since all were acting leading (*shite*) roles, they were called *tayū*, short for *nō-tayū* (actor).

Further, the Sadoshima Kabuki mentioned above also was a troupe of Misuji courtesans led by the girls of the Sadoshima House who performed *shibai nō*, a kind of song and dance courtesan Kabuki, at Shijō Kawara. The most talented actresses were called *tayū*. However, though the names were for stage acting and though it was called 'Nō' or 'courtesan Kabuki', the day performances were primarily advertisements (*kao-mise*) for the evening business. Women were eventually banned from the stage in 1629. Due to this quirk of fate, 'young boys' Kabuki, which had been driven into obscurity by the women troupes, was returned to the limelight.

The reference in *Tale of Tsuyudono* to a talented courtesan being called a *tayū* is corroborated in the *Great Mirror of the Way of Love*:

> From around 1620 'Women Kabuki' began, and soon after, 'Courtesan Nō' also began to be staged. The first troupe was Sadoshima Kabuki followed by other actors such as Dōki, Nakajorō, etc. Among the many courtesans, those with acting talent were called *tayū*. From then on this became the term for them.
>
> Long ago *tayū* simply had to be talented, and even if their appearance wasn't perfect, they would be called *tayū*; but recently even if a woman is extremely talented, if not also a real beauty, she won't become a *tayū*. Only if one of the ten best of a hundred, can she do so.

How elite were these *tayū*? The earliest record of 'old' Yoshiwara *Tales of the East* (1643) lists the total number of courtesans as 987 and the *tayū* as being 75 of these. Even so, this source notes, 'There were three classes of *tayū*.' The classification was still undeveloped, and proprietors as yet have the intention of making a few *tayū* supreme in the quarter. Any talented courtesan was made a *tayū*.

By the 1650s, however, a very small number of *tayū* presided over a rigid elitist hierarchy in each of the three great cities. In Shimabara there were thirteen *tayū* in 1655; in Shinmachi there were eleven *tayū* in 1656; and in Yoshiwara there were seven *tayū* in 1669.

In the Genroku period (1688–1704) total figures compared with the number of *tayū* shows their supremacy. Shimabara had thirteen *tayū* out of a total of 329, while there were seventeen *tayū* in Shinmachi, which had a total of 983 courtesans (from *Guide to the Quarters of the Land* [*Shokoku irozato annai*, 1688]). Yoshiwara had three *tayū*, from a total of more than 2780 courtesans (from *Great Map of Yoshiwara* [*Ōezu*], 1690).

Just over a decade later, the figures were as follows: Shimabara—thirteen *tayū* (total 308); Shinmachi—37 *tayū* (total 800+); Yoshiwara—five *tayū* (total 1750+) (from *Courtesans and Erotic Shamisens* [*Keisei iro jamisen*, 1702]. Since the low-class prostitutes are omitted from the total, the figure should be about the same as for the figures above).

By the end of the seventeenth century, Edo was probably the largest city in the world with a population of approximately one million, half of which was classed as samurai. Furthermore, with an overabundance of males even in the *chōnin* class, it is no wonder Yoshiwara had the largest number of courtesans—nearly 3000. Next was the merchant capital of Osaka with a population of 350 000; Shinmachi courtesans numbered nearly 1000. Kyoto, with a population comparable to Osaka, preferred higher quality and fewer numbers, in keeping with its aristocratic tradition. In all three cities, nevertheless, *tayū* were a very select few compared to the total number of courtesans. Edo's Yoshiwara in particular, had only five to seven *tayū* out of nearly 3000, making it almost impossible to gain an audience with a famous *tayū* without advance booking. In Saikaku's *Life of an Amorous Man*, Yonosuke travels a great distance to meet Takao, a *tayū* of the Miura house in Yoshiwara during the 1670s, but even he has a difficult time:

> Upon asking about meeting Takao, Yonosuke was told, 'During both September and October she has to be at the Kiriya House, in November she must be at Tsutaya, in December she is booked to appear at the Owariya. She has plans for New Years too. She has no free days before next year. How about next spring when you're a year wiser'. Yonosuke was amazed. 'Who is this guest of hers?' 'Whether his money grows on trees or found in the sea, I have no idea who it is.'
>
> Yonosuke realised that even with his 1000 gold pieces to spend he wouldn't have a chance to meet her.
> [The 620 000 *koku* Sendai daimyo, Date Tsunamasa was thought to have patronised Takao II.]

To be sure, not all *tayū* commanded such attention, but the most famous had an exalted position that money alone could not buy; such ladies had confidence and pride. Of course, many *tayū* would have been dependent upon financiers who discovered young beauties with talent, had them trained and educated, and finally orchestrated their rise to fame. At the same time, however, we must recognize that *tayū* were conscious of following in the courtly tradition of feminine 'first-class' elegance and taste among courtesans. One can only marvel at the *tayū* of the early Tokugawa period who, following in this tradition, were able somehow to overthrow the normal order of the brothel world and attain the unprecedented position of choosing their customers, instead of the other way around.

In the 1620s, Kyoto's Rokujō Misuji quarter had the so-called 'Rokujō Seven', namely: Yoshino, Tsushima, and Tosa of the Hayashi House, Mikasa of the Kashiwa, Kofuji of the Miyajima, Kazuragi of the Wakajorō and Hatsune of the Eiraku. These seven ladies are listed in the Misuji Quarter critique (*Tales of Tsuyudono*) as the stars. Each was able to pay her entire year's expenses in advance, and then have the freedom to pick and choose among her many suitors. They met only those of their choice:

> As for a guest who did not please (the *tayū*), no matter how high his standing, daimyo or otherwise, able to bribe handsomely or not, he could not meet the lady. Those known to have been refused were shamed irrevocably and fell into deep despair. (*Great Mirror of the Way of Love*)

The rate, at that time, for spending a day with one of these ladies was approximately 53 *monme* of silver (in present-day money, 110000 yen; or for one year, 400 million yen). Since these seven ladies were able to pay this in advance, their patrons must have been providing huge sums of money, even though it is they who were the chosen, not the choosers. Somehow, it seems strangely ironic to pity them, these members of the social elite. Money alone was not enough; rejection by a *tayū* branded a man as lacking in sensitivity, aristic interests, classical education or physical attributes. A sullied reputation could destroy his confidence for social intercourse in the upper class.

The next group of Kyoto star *tayū* were the 'Four Guardian Demons', active in 1641 just before the quarter was moved to Shimabara. These four were Manko and Awaji of the Man'emon House, Nokaze of the Gorō Zaemon House, and Nagajima of the Hachizaemon House, all famous for choosing customers regardless of social status. 'They chose only those they liked, following the whims of their feelings', as *The Great Mirror of the Way of Love* relates. It was the elegance, intelligence and self-confidence of these two groups of women that forced both proprietors and the public to bow to their will.

Customers wishing to obtain an audience with one of these ladies had to work hard to acquire the necessary attributes the *tayū* demanded. Merchants, who though at the bottom of the official class system had gained status through wealth, were forced to struggle further to achieve an education. It is fascinating indeed that it was these courtesans who stimulated the drive for education and aesthetic sensibility among the new bougeoisie.

Famous *tayū* of Kyoto, Osaka, and Edo

The pride of the 'Seven Gems of Rokujō' was Yoshino II (real name Matsuda Noriko), who in Saikaku's *Life of an Amorous Man* is courted by Yonosuke. Since at that point in the story Yonosuke is a true *suijin* (cultivated in the arts of love, poetry, etc.), Yoshino represents the highest ideal of this quality. Saikaku's description of her begins: 'She was a courtesan such as the world had never seen before, a *tayū* whose fame lives on forever.' Yoshino was the daughter of a *rōnin* from Higo (Kyushu) and became a *tayū* in 1619 at the age of 14, and at 26 (1631) left the quarter to become the wife of Sumiya Shōeki, the son of Hon'ami Kōeki (a member of Hon'ami Kōetsu's family) and the adopted son of Sumiya Shōyū, the head of the dyers guild in Kyoto. In 1643, she died of illness.

Her extant letters and calligraphy display her talent, and she is known to have been a master of the tea ceremony and incense, an expert player of the biwa and koto, and of the game *go*. Her talent and beauty were of wide renown, even extending overseas. When Yoshino was 22 years old in 1627, a Ming courtier Li Hsiang-shan met her in a dream, became enthralled and sent the following poem as a eulogy to her beauty:

> After hearing the name 'Yoshino' of Japan,
> I saw her fleetingly in a dream—and awoke startled.
> Longing for a glimpse of such beauty,
> I gaze eastward as the geese fly across the sea.

The following year a request came from China for her portrait, and so Yoshino's patrons had an accurate likeness painted and sent it to the Chinese merchants in Nagasaki, who mounted it on silk, and were reported to have been delighted with it. In the early seventeenth century, the famous Imperial court artist Hon'ami Kōetsu, with all his family, founded Kōetsu village in Takagamine North Kyoto, and the Buddhist priest Nikkan Shōnin (Kōetsu's spiritual master) opened the Nichiren temple Jōshōji there in 1627. Yoshino, who raised the money herself at the age of 22 while still a courtesan, endowed the temple with a gate, which still stands as a token of her faith in the priest Nikkan. Now called Yoshino or Tayū Gate, it was blown down in a storm in 1908, then restored in 1918, and remains to this day, a monument to Yoshino's piety.

Another early famous *tayū* comparable to Yoshino is Yachiyo of the Okumura House in Shimabara, who left at the age of 24 in 1658. She was a genius who mastered musical instruments such as the koto, shamisen and shakuhachi, and was an expert in *kouta* (songs), tea ceremony and various other arts. Among these accomplishments, her calligraphy was so outstanding that she is known for her 'Yachiyo' style, which became the model for courtesans. She studied poetry and the classics, frequently inviting scholars to lecture on the *Tales of Ise*, *Tale of Genji*, *Essays in Idleness* and the imperial anthologies of poetry. She was said to have loved to recite ancient poems. She also wrote *haikai* and one of her poems is in the collection *Favourite Child* (*Futokorogo*, 1660, Chapter 9).[1]

Katsura otoko	Man of the Moon
Hoho ni mo iru ya	Here in my pocket
Neya no tsuki	Moonlight in my bedroom

Yachiyo's fame also extended overseas like that of Yoshino II. In the autumn of 1655, Yachiyo's 21st year, Chinese merchants brought silk embroidered with Yachiyo's crest, the paulownia leaf, to Nagasaki, and sold it with the acclamation that she was the 'greatest courtesan in Japan—those with taste would surely buy this material at any price'. Her fame also spread to Korea, where her crest appeared as a design on tea bowls made for Japan. These two *tayū* were exceptional in their fame reaching foreign lands: sophisticated courtesans on a truly international scale.

Yachiyo's successors, however, never attained this level. Nevertheless, many ladies in the Shimabara and Shinmachi quarters did acquire considerable fame in their respective centres of *sui* culture in the latter part of the seventeenth century. One of them, well known in the theatrical world, is the *tayū* Azuma of the Fujiya House in Osaka's Shinmachi quarter, whose contract was bought out by Sakanoue Yojiemon, a wealthy village headman, for 300 gold pieces around the years 1673–75. This event gave birth to a popular song, the 'Dance of the 300 Gold Pieces', and was the source for Chikamatsu Monzaemon's later Jōruri play, *The Uprooted Pine* (*Yamazaki Yojibei nebiki no kadomatsu*), first performed at the Takemoto Theatre in 1719. Ihara Saikaku also describes Azuma in *Life of an Amorous Man* (1682), as gradually withering away and dying in 1677, due to boredom in marriage.

Another renowned *tayū* was Yūgiri of the Ogiya House, who fell sick and died at the age of 22 while still in the Shinmachi quarter. Saikaku seems to have actually met Yūgiri, and in his *Women Haiku Poets* (*Haikai nyokasen,* 1684), wrote next to her portrait:[2]

A courtesan of the Osaka Shinmachi quarter, a master (*sui*) of all the arts. She always took compassion as the source for her verse and was famed throughout the land. Once when composing a *hokku* short poem, she used her own crest, the paulownia, as a theme. The time was autumn:

Kiri no ha mo	This colourful paulownia leaf
Somewakegatashi	Difficult to dye as a crest
Sode no mon	On my kimono sleeve

Early in 1678, just after Yūgiri died, Sakata Tōjūrō, the famous Kyoto Kabuki actor and master in lover roles (*wagoto*), came to Osaka to perform at the Kaneko Rokuemon Theatre, in the play *Farewell to Yūgiri at New Year* (*Yūgiri nagori no shōgatsu*). He played opposite the star female impersonator Itō Kodayū II in the part of Yūgiri.[3] Tōjūrō, as Izaemon the effeminate lover, was a great hit, giving birth to the famous theatrical pair Yūgiri–Izaemon. The play was such a success that it was repeated several times during that year.[4] Each time, over the eighteen different performances during his lifetime, Tōjūrō added or altered elements to the Yūgiri–Izaemon love story; through Tōjūrō's acting, the Yūgiri plays became an indispensible part of the Kabuki repertoire.

It has been suggested that Chikamatsu Monzaemon was the author of this long series of Yūgiri plays. Since Chikamatsu did write many plays for Tōjūrō, it is only natural to imagine him as the author of the early plays in the 1670s and 1680s. However, the 1687 *Great Mirror of Lead-role Kabuki Actors* (*Yarō tachiyaku butai ōkagami*) says of Tōjūrō: 'He is a master of all the arts and since he writes plays too, he cannot be an illiterate.' Just like Ichikawa Danjūrō I (d. 1704) in Edo, who wrote Kabuki plays under the pen-name Sanshōya Heikō, Tōjūrō also acted in plays of his own composition. Again like Danjūrō, who wrote *haikai* in Enomoto Saimaro's school under the name Saigyū, Tōjurō wrote poetry under the name Tōtei in Saikaku's school. Further, since Tōjūrō made the role Izaemon his own hallmark, it seems reasonable to assume that Tōjūrō was the author of this series of Yūgiri plays.

Such a striking Kabuki success could hardly be overlooked by the

Jōruri world. Chikamatsu Monzaemon wrote the first one, *Memorial to Yūgiri (Yūgiri Sanzesō,* 1686), putting it into the typical plot of the *oiesōdō* (disturbance in a grand house) genre, the 'Yoshidaya' act being the most famous. The work, which became the basis for later Yūgiri plays is, however, Chikamatsu's, *Yūgiri and the Straits of Naruto (Yūgiri Awa no Naruto,* 1712). The 'Yoshidaya' act again was later rewritten for Kabuki as *Letter from the Pleasure Quarter (Kuruwa bunshō),* the version known to audiences today, first performed at the Edo Nakamura Theatre in 1808. In addition, the Yūgiri–Izaemon story made its way into the various storytelling styles of Miyazono-bushi, Tomimoto-bushi, Shinnai-bushi, Kiyomoto, Tokiwazu, etc., becoming an essential part of the repertoire of each school.

In 1678, the month after Yūgiri died, when *Farewell to Yūgiri at New Year* played in Osaka, *The Marriage of Yoshino (Yoshino miuke)* was playing in Kyoto. The model was the famous *tayū* Yoshino III of the Kikyōya (Kita Yazaemon), who had taken the name Yoshino on New Year of 1674, though she had no direct connection to Yoshino II of the Hashiya House. This Yoshino III was courted by the son of a rich Nagasaki man—the actor Arashi San'emon played the character as Ogura Genbei—who fell hopelessly into debt to pay for meeting Yoshino regularly. Yoshino took pity on his plight and pawned her clothes and accessories to clear his debt of 100 gold pieces. When the father in Nagasaki heard about this, he was so impressed with Yoshino's compassionate spirit that he sent a messenger immediately with 1000 gold pieces to buy out her contract and bring her home as bride to his son. The 1682 Kyoto source *Reflections on Love (Renbo mizukagami)* reports the incident.

The play *Marriage of Yoshino,* based on this incident, with the famous female impersonator (*onnagata*) Itō Shōdayū (d. 1688) playing the lead, was a great success and ran for six months. Itō Shōdayū is also a main character in Saikaku's *The Great Mirror of Manly Love (Nanshoku ōkagami,* 1687), where he is praised as follows: 'Especially in the play *Marriage of Yoshino,* when this *tayū* walks along the street it is as if the real Yoshino's spirit has been usurped by the wisteria (Shōdayū) which outshines the cherry (Yoshino herself).' During the last quarter of the seventeenth century, while Ichikawa Danjūrō was developing the rough *aragoto* style of Kabuki in Edo, Sakata Tōjūrō, Arashi San'emon, Uemura Kichiya and others in Kyoto and Osaka were the leaders of the soft *wagoto* style, in which *yatsushi* (a former rich man fallen into the lower classes) was the main theme. Since these dramas focused on the famous *tayū* of the time, their influence reached into the hearts and minds of the community through contemporary theatre and *ukiyo–zōshi* fiction. These courtesans were the idols of the age.

As we have seen, the pleasure quarters became the cultural centre of Edo about the time the new Yoshiwara was built after the Great Fire of Meireki in the late 1650s. Since Edo was a frontier city in the first half of the century, the public relied on Kyoto publishers even for books on Edo like *Tales of the East* (1642), published by Itaya Seibei of Nijō Karasuma. Therefore, knowledge of Yoshiwara *tayū* was confined to Edo. The first Edo *tayū* to achieve lasting fame was Katsuyama, who was employed in Yoshiwara for only three years from 1653 until 1656. She was originally a bath-house girl who was famous even before becoming a *tayū*.

Around the year 1640, more than 100 bath-houses with girl attendants (*yuna*) had arisen around Edo. These girls were lively and generous, and began to draw patrons away from the courtesans of Yoshiwara. Among these was the Kikyōya bath-house in front of the Hori Tango no Kami mansion in Kanda's Saegi area, which today is the Kanda Suta-chō and Awaji-chō of Chiyoda-ku. It was popularly known as the Tanzen Bath-house. Yoshino, a *yuna* of this establishment, became famous in the 1630s for her song and dance number 'Kata-bachi' (half plectrum), and her style of singing came to be called Tanzen-bushi. Another such girl, Katsuyama of the Kinokuni Bath-house in the same area, a disciple of Yoshino, had a generous nature and loved outlandish dress and mannerisms: she often wore a green wicker hat, with a men's formal skirt (*hakama*) and two wooden swords when performing Tanzen-bushi. This style of dress, with a jaunty manner and gait, was known at the time as *yakko-fū*. The Kabuki actor Tamon Shōzaemon (active in late 1650s and 1660s), the idol of rough samurai and city toughs (*yakko*) for his development of this Tanzen or (Rokugata) style, in fact is supposed to have got his inspiration from the courtesan Katsuyama.[5]

Since these unlicensed bath-houses, with courtesans as sophisticated as those in Yoshiwara, began to take business away from the 'legal' Yoshiwara, the government intervened. In 1653, when a brawl broke out at Tanzen Bath-house between a group of samurai and townsmen ruffians, all involved were arrested and the bath-house closed. Katsuyama had to leave, and two months later she appeared in Yoshiwara as a *tayū* of the Yamamoto Hōjun House. When she made her procession down the middle of Yoshiwara to meet her first guest, her fame drew all the grand ladies of Yoshiwara out to watch. She arranged her hair in a new style (later famous in Kabuki as the Katsuyama style), tucked up her skirts and, wearing straw thongs, strutted in the 'Katsuyama' gait (also known as *soto hachimonji*) with an outlandish, though majestic manner. The other courtesans gaped in wonder. Two years before the Meireki fire, in the spring of 1656, she announced she would retire within the year and kept her promise by leaving that autumn.[6]

Though Katsuyama was the last of 'old' Yoshiwara's famous *tayū*, Takao II popularly called 'Sendai' Takao, made her debut at the age of 15 in 'old' Yoshiwara in 1655, though it was in the 'new' Yoshiwara that she bloomed. She was, however, a fragile blossom who faded away in sickness at the tender age of 19 in 1659 (Manji 2), only the second year of the 'new' Yoshiwara. She was, therefore, called 'Manji' Takao since the Sendai daimyo, Date Tsunamasa, was known to have patronised her; she was also known as 'Sendai' Takao. Ōta Nampo and Santō Kyōzan (*On Takao* [*Takaokō*], 1849) and Katō Jakuan (*More on Takao* [*Takao tsui tsuikō*]) have recorded in great detail the histories of the eleven generations of 'Takao' courtesans of the Kyōmachi Miuraya House; among the many stars, 'Manji' Takao's fame persisted the longest.

The name came from Takao mountain on the western edge of Kyoto renowned for its autumn colours. Takao II's crest was a red and gold autumn leaf. Unlike Katsuyama, she was fragile and delicate, and excelled in the gentle arts of calligraphy, shamisen and *kouta* (short songs). We can get a sense of how much the world regretted her premature death by reading the elegiac work *Tale of Takao* (*Taka byōbu kudamono monogatari*), published soon after her death in 1660.

Partly because of the brevity of her stardom, legends soon proliferated about her. Since the Sendai daimyo Date Tsunamasa had courted Katsuyama from her days as a bath-house girl and been a regular patron of Yoshiwara, gaining a reputation of debauchery, in 1661 (the year after Takao's death), the Bakufu government ordered him to withdraw from public life (the beginning of the famous 'Date Disturbance'). Further, since Takao's death took place at nearly the same time, a legend sprouted about Tsunamasa and Takao. It was said that, no matter how ardent an admirer the daimyo was, Takao refused to give in to his wishes, and even though he bought out her contract she still remained obstinate. In desperation, he had her fingers broken one by one for ten successive days (there is evidence for this). Finally, she was said to have been taken by boat to Nakasu Mitsumata and hanged, certainly a histrionic ending to a dramatic life.

Stories circulated (in manuscript) that she had refused to accept the daimyo Tsunamasa because of her vow of love to a *rōnin*, Shimada Jūzaburō. Later the *rakugo* comic story *Hangonko*, based on this book, had Takao appear as a vengeful ghost.

Koshiba II, another famous courtesan from the same Miura House as Takao, followed her lover, the Tottori *rōnin* Hirai Gonpachi, in death, after his conviction and execution in 1679 at Suzugamori for highway robbery and murder. In 1825 a memorial to Koshiba and Gonpachi was built near the Meguro Fudō Temple (Meguro-ku, Shimo-meguro 3 chōme). In the *Jōruri* play *Memorial at Meguro* (*Meguro hiyoku-zuka*, 1779 at Edo's Bizen Theatre), a memorial is built as a trick to give the impression that the pair has died.[7] It was probably someone connected with Kabuki who built the Meguro memorial in 1825.

In succession to the early 'Six Rokujō Ladies', the star courtesans described above flourished in the cities of Kyoto, Osaka and Edo from about the mid to late seventeenth century during the golden age of the courtesan critiques (*yūjo hyōbanki*) in which the aesthetic concept of *sui* is both defined and personified.

From 'courtesan critiques' to fiction *(ukiyo-zōshi)*

From the early 1600s until the second half of the seventeenth century, guests of the licensed quarters who sought audience with *tayū* were mostly from high society, with good education and manners. In Kyoto, they were aristocrats or well-established merchants (*yoishū*); in Edo, daimyo or senior Bakufu retainers (*hatamoto*). From the 1650s and 1660s, however, *nouveau riche* townsmen gradually replaced these more sophisticated customers as patrons. To serve the needs of these less cultured folk, a new genre of literature arose, *yūjo hyōbanki* (courtesan critiques). These were written with more literary flavour than the decidedly pragmatic *saiken* genre which had simply explained the customs and manners of the quarter, and ranked courtesans in a question and answer format.

During the first half of the seventeenth century, the rising merchant class was too busy amassing wealth and knowledge to have time for the leisure or conspicuous consumption of the pleasure quarters. However, by the 1650s and 1660s, as these merchants began to amass profits, popular forms of culture such as poetry (*haikai*) and fiction (*kanazōshi*) began to flourish. Furthermore, new art forms were created, one good example being Hishikawa Moronobu's use of colour in simple monochrome woodblock prints. He and his school in Edo laid the foundations of the popular *ukiyoe* tradition in their depiction, in vivid colour, of the urban life of townsmen. In painting as well, this mid-century period was a golden age for the portrayal of women and their kimono, the so-called *kambun kosode*, when the most elaborate robes were created with woven designs, gold-leaf and gold thread, as well as spotted, applique and painted designs. These became so extravagant that the government issued sumptuary legislation in 1683, ending the reign of *kambun kosode* and giving birth to simpler *yūzen* dyed type.

It was also during this surge of townsmen culture that Kabuki matured into a true theatrical form. After women had been banned from the stage in 1629 due to public disturbances, they were replaced by young boys (*wakashū*), whose performance too was banned in 1652 for the same reason. Two years later, on the condition that men actors shave their seductive forelocks and put on realistic plays with dialogue and acting (*monomane kyōgen-zukushi*) instead of the song and dance revues of the past, 'Men's Kabuki (*yarō kabuki*) was born. The licensed quarters furnished much of the material for this new Kabuki, which was based on the life of courtesans.

Though no texts survive, these early pieces appear to have been simple skits with little plot. *The Actors' Analects* (*Yakusha rongo*, ca. 1690s), however, gives a general outline of the early type. The play opens with an announcement that the 'courtesan encounter' (*tayū-kai*) is about to begin, after which the wealthy guest saunters down the bridge (*hashi-gakari*) to the main stage, strikes a pose, and announces himself to the audience. Next, from the small door at stage left, a clown-like proprietor emerges and greets the guest. He then looks over at the bridge saying, 'The *tayū* will now appear'. The courtesan enters, greets the guest, and laughs when taking his hand. They strike a pose after which the proprieter suggests some saké and fish, and asks the *tayū* to dance. An orchestra appears and the scene concludes with the *tayū's* dance—a very simple plot. As Kabuki was forced to become more theatrical, it found in the 1650s and 1660s that the subject of the hitherto secret world of high society, where wealthy men court *tayū* in the pleasure quarters, met with great acclaim among popular audiences. A new age of Kabuki had begun.

At the same time 'courtesan critiques' began to appear in rapid succession: in 1655 two works set in Shimabara, *A Collection of Peaches* (*Tōgenshū*) and *Tales of Naniwa* (*Naniwa monogatari*), appeared; the following year *Sleeping Tales* (*Nemonogatari*) (on Shimabara), *Tall Grasses* (*Masarigusa*) (on Shinmachi) and *Tales of Miyako* (*Miyako monogatari*) (on Shimabara) were published. 1660 saw the issue of *Mirror of Yoshiwara* (*Yoshiwara kagami*) and *Tale of Takao* (*Taka byōbu kuda monogatari*), both set in Edo's Yoshiwara. *A Collection of Peaches* and *Tall Grasses* are little more than appraisals of courtesans' looks and talents, with selected Chinese and Japanese comic poems (*kyōshi* and *kyōka*). *Tales of Naniwa* and the others, however, as is evident from their titles as 'tales', are more literary in intention. In *Tales of Naniwa*, a young man becomes fascinated by the world of the pleasure quarters after seeing a Kabuki drama in Kyoto on the theme of courting *tayū*. He then goes to visit an expert on the subject who answers his questions and explains the art of pleasure, as well as the merits of the various ladies of Shimabara. In *Sleeping Tales* the pattern is for a customer to be initiated by a *tayū* into the ways of this high-class world of pleasure.

Leaving aside the guidebook *Tales of the East* published in the 1620s, the first true 'courtesan critique' on Edo's Yoshiwara was the *Mirror of Yoshiwara* published by Urogataya. It shows a map of the 'new' Yoshiwara followed by the text in a question and answer format, in which 25 different *tayū* and their customers discuss the ways of love and pleasure, presenting the reader with a veritable 'study of the art of *sui*'. However, it must be stated that the essence of this 'education' is an exact replica of the Shimabara *Sleeping Tales* published five years earlier. This plagiarism was inevitable, since Edo was at that time simply a colony of Kyoto–Osaka culture, and as yet lacking writers able to create a distinctive Edo style of the art of pleasure. Nevertheless, the publication of such guidebooks and critiques brought the *tayū* vividly into the hearts and minds of the populace who had no other way of knowing their life. Through both Kabuki and fiction, the average young man, vicariously at least, was able to participate in and taste the delights of this unattainable world; *tayū* soon became the idols of the masses.

Accordingly, during the 1690s, these works begin to approach true fiction of the genre *ukiyo-zōshi*, then in its earliest stages. The literary level of the 'courtesan critiques' continued to rise, culminating in the following works: the three-part *Kindling, Charred Timber, Charcoal* (*Takitsuke, moekui, keshizumi*, 1677), the 1680 *Key to Naniwa* (*Naniwadora*) and the 1681 *Souvenirs of Nagasaki* (*Nagasaki miyage*), which can all be considered literature in the genre of *kanazōshi* or *ukiyo-zōshi*. A clear example of this trend is the work *Key to Naniwa*, which vividly brings to life the *tayū* and *tenjin* of the Osaka Shinmachi quarter who, through realistic lively 'quarter' language, describe their way of life and aesthetics. Readers of the time considered it literature, for the work was republished in 1694 as an *ukiyo-zōshi* with only a change of title, *Amorous Jaunt Among Poppy Flowers* (*Kōshoku keshiga no ko*).

Though the 'courtesan critiques' of the 1670s had become truly literary, it took Saikaku, in his *Life of an Amorous Man* (1682) and its sequel (1684), to open up the constraints of this genre. 'Courtesan critiques' were bounded by facts, real dates, places, people and happenings known to their readers. They could not invent time and place to create a fictional novel. Saikaku broke through this barrier and brought the 'floating world' into the domain of fantasy.

With the publication of Saikaku's novels, the stars of traditional 'courtesan critiques' real *tayū* and *tenjin*, were absorbed into the sphere of literature. Subsequently, the 'courtesan critique', which had spawned this new genre of fiction, soon lost its literary *raison d'être*, and returned to its original role as a practical guidebook to the pleasure quarters. The 1688 *Guide to the Pleasure Quarters of the Land* (*Shokoku irozato annai*) was the first example of this reversion. On the other hand, the 'pleasure quarter' genre of fiction developed by Saikaku continued for decades in the books published by the Hachimonjiya, the first being the *Courtesans and Erotic Shamisens* (*Keisei iro jamisen*, 1701), which began a sub-genre of fiction with courtesans as the main characters. This trend exactly coincides with the flourishing of Kabuki courtesan (*keisei*) plays during the 1680s and 1690s, in which the actor Sakata Tōjūrō was prominent.

Eighteenth century afterglow

The golden age of 'high' courtesan culture, when the standards of the *tayū* were at their peak and when the pleasure quarters were the true focus of urban culture, lasted from the mid-1600s until the turn of the century. This parallels the 40-year boom in the economy from 1660 to around 1700, when many famous and enduring *zaibatsu* commercial empires such as Kōnoike, Sumitomo and Mitsui were founded. This golden age saw its first tarnish, however, when the Bakufu sought in 1695 to redress years of fiscal mismanagement through a series of currency devaluations, as well as more stringent and harsher controls over 'wealthy' townsmen. These actions soon damped down the open extravagance of the merchant class and moderated their 'work hard, play hard' lifestyle. The most obvious symbols of this 'new' age were the downfall of the two most opulent houses, Osaka's Yodoya and Edo's Kinokuniya, whose wealth had given the pleasure quarters much of their lustre.

Yodoya was the greatest Osaka merchant family, with a lineage going back to the days of official patronage under Hideyoshi in the late sixteenth century. In particular, the second generation Koan (d. 1643) was a city elder who held a monopoly for silk-thread transport and was the major rice broker for many daimyo. He was so powerful that other rice merchants collected around his store in Ōgawa-machi, eventually developing the area into the famous Kitahama rice market. This market, which had moved to Dōjima in 1688, was by 1697 beginning to suffer the effects of a recession, and in 1705 the fifth generation Yodoya head, Yodoya Sanrōemon (known as Tatsugorō) was punished by confiscation and banishment because his extravagance exceeded the proper limits of a townsman's station.

At the time, this fifth generation Yodoya was but a lad, barely out of adolescence, enjoying the dreamlike world of the Shinmachi quarter, removed from the cares of reality; he was carried to and fro in a daimyo-style palanquin, dressed in daimyo's clothes, and smoked a silver pipe, for all of which he had special permission. Even before the scandal became public, he had come under official scrutiny. Seeking to marry his love, the *tayū* Azuma of the Ibaragiya House in Shinmachi, he arranged to buy out her contract for 2000 gold pieces. His plan, however, did not go smoothly, as he was unable to raise the money. The affair became public when a clerk in the Yodoya shop forged a promissary note, using his master's official seal, and borrowed the sum of 2000 gold pieces from the Tennōjiya exchange house, then failed to pay it back. Behind the scenes in this incident, however, were the huge debts owed to Yodoya by various daimyo, amounting to more than 20000 silver pieces (*kanme*) and a note signed by Tokugawa Ieyasu acknowledging the Bakufu's debt of 80000 gold pieces (*ryō*).[8] It seems clear that the Bakufu used the forgery incident as a pretext to rid the ruling class of an embarrassing obligation.

Since the buying out of a Shinmachi *tayū*'s contract was the reason for the fall of the most prestigious Osaka business house, even before the final verdict was handed down on the first day of 1705, Kabuki plays were staged in Kyoto and Osaka with the Yodoya scandal as their theme. Such plays included:

- *Courtesans and Golden Yodo Carp* (*Keisei kogane no yodogoi*), New Year in Kyoto at Mandayū-za;
- *A Courtesan and Strings of Lotus* (*Keisei hachisu no ito*) New Year in Kyoto, at Kameya-za;
- *The Monju Unveiling* (*Monju no kaichō*) (a variant title for *Keisei hachisu no ito*), second month in Osaka at Iwai-za.

Further, in the same year two novels on the Yodoya affair appeared: *Residence with the Great Quince Gate* (*Karanashi daimon yashiki*) and *The Millionaire's Bag of Treats* (*Chōja kigenbukuro*).

The repercussions of this incident shook the top class of Kyoto–Osaka merchants, who realised all too clearly the restraints on wealth under the strict Tokugawa system. The work *Records at Random* (*Sōmanroku*) states their feelings succinctly: 'Consider loaned money irrecoverable. If you make up the principal in interest you have been repaid, and any further interest is pure profit.' Well aware of the limits to their prosperity under such an absolutist system, Osaka's foremost citizens, such as Kōnoike Matashirō, Dōmyōjiya Kichizaemon and Funabashi Shirozaemon invited the Chu Hsi scholar Miyake Sekian to form a school in Azuchi-machi called Tashōdō (later the famous Kaitokudō) in 1713, eight years after the incident. The leaders of Osaka society took pains to adjust themselves to the feudal system; they became conservative in order to maintain their position. Thereafter, it became impossible for people in real life or fiction, such as Saikaku's character in *Life of an Amorous Man* and his other stories, even to consider risking their lives for the elusive goal of *sui* aesthetics; Saikaku's heroes were relegated to the archive of history.

In Edo, it was the self-made timber merchant Kinokuniya Bunzaemon whose extravagance brought reprisals that sent shock waves throughout the townsmen's quarter of the city. The famous comic actor Nishuban Kichibei (d. 1765) wrote: 'To be sure, China and Korea have extravagant playboys, but no one can surpass the notorious Kinokuniya Bunzaemon.' Using his penname 'Senzan', Bunzaemon gathered about him artists such as haiku poet Kikaku, calligrapher Sasaki Bunzan, Buddhist sculptor Mimbe, sculptor Yokotani Sōmin and painter Hanabusa Itchō. Many contemporary works describe his extravagance in the pursuit of pleasure with the famous spirited *tayū*, Kichō of the Miuraya. Four years after the Yodoya incident of 1709 (following the death of the fifth Shogun Tsunayoshi) Bunzaemon's business, due to political scandals, was closed down and the master evicted. Bunzaemon fell after his patrons, the minister Yanagizawa Yoshiyasu and the magistrate Hagiwara Shigehide, lost favour upon the accession of the sixth Shogun, Ienobu. Bunzaemon, unable to make ends meet, closed shop, shaved his head, and from 1714 lived in retirement near the Fukagawa Hachiman Shrine.

A disciple of the famous haiku poet Kikaku, Bunzaemon left the following verse on a neglected courtesan:

Nushi wa tare	Who's its owner
Izutsu wa sabite	The well-curb has rotted
Kiri no hana	Covered with pawlonia flowers

Though he does seem to have had some sense of aesthetics, the manner of his pleasure jaunts, as reported in various works, was—like that of his business rival Naraya Mozaemon—wild and far from the ideal of *sui*. Bunzaemon's single most extravagant gesture was to spend 1000 gold pieces to reserve all of Yoshiwara for one night. He was also famous for using coins instead of beans at the spring ceremony for driving out demons and bringing in good fortune. Two comic *senryū* describe his habits: 'Before closing the door, he closed the Great (Yoshiwara) Gate.' and 'He sent demons away with coins, not beans.' To say that his style was rather crass and 'commercial' is perhaps an understatement.

From the 1710s, when Bunzaemon was in retirement, Edo began to emerge from the shadow of Kyoto–Osaka culture and bask in its wealth and population of 1 000 000 (half of these military retainers and their servants), more than that of the other two cities combined. The symbols of this new prosperity were the Bakufu's official merchants (*fudasashi*), who in 1724 got permission to form a guild 109 strong. Furthermore, Yoshimune, who had become the eighth shogun in 1716, encouraged scholarship, helping Edo to become a centre of learning. During the 1720s and 1730s Edo began to mature as an independent economic and cultural entity.

The 1720 *Complete Mirror of Yoshiwara* (*Yoshiwara marukagami*) lists the number of courtesans at more than 3000 and describes the style of the top ladies—Takao and Usugumo of the Shirōemon Miuraya; Otowa, Shiraito, and Hatsugiku of the Yamaguchi House, and the Six Beauties of Jinzaemon's Miuraya—as different from the grand scale of 1680s *tayū*, more relaxed with a distinctly Yoshiwara flavour. Yoshiwara had finally succeeded in producing its own culture independent of Kyoto–Osaka.

Katō-bushi, an important Edo Jōruri musical narrative genre, developed in the early eighteenth century and had a strong base in Yoshiwara. Its founder was Masumi Katō (d. 1725), a fishmonger's son and a disciple of the famous chanter Edo Handayū. In 1717 he started his own school under the name of Edo Handayū Katō and gained popularity among intellectuals and the upper classes through private performances. The second generation Katō was one Kajō Kawatake, child of a Yoshiwara House. His disciple, Katō III, was the master of a courtesan tea house. The great Katō-bushi performer Masumi Ranshū I (the Yoshiwara brothel owner Tsurutsutaya Shōjirō), a pupil with Masumi Katō in Handayū's school, was the patron who made it possible for Masumi Katō to form his own school of singers. Ranshū II was also a Yoshiwara brothel owner.

The writer who supplied these early Katō-bushi singers with texts was one Chikufujin, the haiku poet Kanjū in the Kishi Senshū school, whose real name was Tenmaya Nizaemon, a Yoshiwara brothel owner. In 1726 the *tayū* Tamagiku of the Manjiya House, a devoted fan of Katō-bushi, fell sick and died at the age of 25. At the *obon* festival that autumn, all the Yoshiwara houses agreed to display a simple box-lantern in commemoration, but from 1727 a more fancy lantern was displayed and the famous Tamagiku lantern festival was born. On the third anniversary of her death in 1728, Masumi Ranshū performed the elegiac *Water Rhythms of a Courtesan* (*Keisei mizu chōshi*) written by Chikufujin (Kanjū). Subject, composer and performer were all from Yoshiwara. The 1720s saw many Yoshiwara people active in the creation and promotion of popular arts; the quarter truly served as the centre of popular culture. Of course, this was the time when the giant city of Edo began to free itself economically and culturally from Kyoto–Osaka control, ushering in the so-called eighteenth century 'eastward movement' of popular culture.

During the mid-eighteenth century when Yoshiwara was quietly enjoying its golden age, we unfortunately have no good records to tell us about Kyoto's Shimabara or Osaka's Shinmachi. However, we do have one prime relic from Shimabara to give us a glimpse of the last days of its glory. Though there were many *ageya* houses where guests were entertained by the high class *tayū* or *tenjin*, all but one of these have succumbed to the ravages of fire. The only remnant of that luxurious world is the Sumiya of Shimabara which dates back to the seventeenth century. A map of Shimabara in the 1678 *Great Mirror of the Way of Love* (*Shikidō ōkagami*) includes it. The 1681 courtesan critique *Mirror of Shujaka* (*Shujaka showake kagami*) notes that the Sumiya had a great room that could serve a banquet of 50 to 100 guests. The Sumiya of today, designated an Important Cultural Property is, however, a structure rebuilt in the eighteenth century. The second floor rooms contain an array of wall and screen paintings by famous artists of the second half of the eighteenth century; as shown in Table 1.1.

Table 1.1 Sumiya paintings

Room	Artist	Date
Green bamboo	Yamada Gazan	1765
Flowers	Yamada Gazan	1765
Horses	Maruyama Ōkyo	1760s
Plum	Yosa Buson	1760–1770s
Blue shells	Iwakoma	1760–1770s
Cypress fence	Yosa Buson	1780
Peacock	Emura Shun	1780s

The 1757 guide to Shimabara, *1000 Houses at a Glance* (*Hitome senken*) indicates that many of Shimabara's buildings had been repaired or rebuilt at that time, so we can sense that the time when the above paintings were done (1760–1780s) was a prosperous one, and that it served as a centre for literati culture.

Donshi, the editor of *Hitome senken*, spent some time in gaol for his extravagant ways. He was the nephew of Tasuke, the son of Kōsai, proprietor of the Shinmachi Ibaragiya House. Tasuke wrote haiku poetry under the name Dongei, moved to Shimabara and bought the Kikyōya House. His nephew Tonshi succeeded him in this business. The *Random Jottings of an Old Man* (*Okinagusa*, 1776) records that this house 'flourished with about 200 people living under its roof'.

This Donshi, along with other proprietors of important Shimabara Houses, Yoshimojiya Gain, Sumiya's Tokuno (seventh generation), and Tachibanaya's Fūsen, were members of the poet Tan Taigi's school. Donshi was a particularly influential patron who built a residence for Taigi next to his own home, calling it 'The Nightless Castle' and had his *tayū* learn poetry. Taigi's close friend Yosa Buson also is known to have frequented Shimabara; his paintings at Sumiya certainly attest to the relationship. Furthermore, on the third anniversary of Taigi's death, Donshi invited Taigi II (Goun), Buson and Kitō for a haiku memorial.

In this way, Shimabara was one of the salons for Kyoto's literati culture which flourished in the 1750s to 1770s, much as Yoshiwara in earlier times was the base for the development of Edo's Katō-bushi music. However, this prosperity lasted only a few years and by the end of the century Shimabara had lost its lustre. Takizawa Bakin records a visit to Kyoto in 1802:

> The Shimabara quarter has greatly deteriorated. The walls are crumbling and the old establishments are in disrepair. The courtesans now are inferior to those in Gion. Kyoto people no longer go to Shimabara, complaining of the distance. Therefore, even visitors to the city now tend to be taken to Gion. (A Traveler's Record [*Kiryo manroku*, 1802])

Due to its convenient position as well as its more relaxed and less expensive setting, Gion came to usurp Shimabara's customers.

Yoshiwara's final days

During the 1750s and 1760s, when Shimabara was having its last gleam of glory, Yoshiwara's prosperity of the 1720s to 1740s had become a distant dream. The six *tayū* of the quarter were reduced to one, Hanashiba of the Tamaya House, and only one proper *ageya* (a house where *tayū* met guests) remained, the Owariya of Seijūrō. This decline also meant the disappearance of the second-level *kōshi* courtesans (the same as *tenjin* in Kyoto–Osaka). Therefore, by the late 1760s the traditional elaborate custom of meeting high-class courtesans at an *ageya* had disappeared, giving way to the intermediary *hikite chaya* through which guests would be escorted to large reception houses. The 'replacement' for *tayū* were *yobidashi* (literally 'callgirls') who met their customers through *chaya* (tea houses) without any other formalities; the *kōshi* were now the *chūsan* (three quarters of one gold piece). Though these new classes took the place of the top-level courtesans they were in fact middle-level courtesans (*sancha-jorō*), who had been raised in status to fill the gaps left by the decline of *tayū*. Santō Kyōden writes in *Yoshiwara Toothpicks* (*Yoshiwara yōji*, 1788): 'The guests of *yobidashi* and *chūsan* are samurai accountants, ignorant travellers, rich merchants, and retired daimyo.' These samurai accountants were the representatives of the various fiefs responsible for managing the Edo warehouses. They used Yoshiwara to entertain merchant clients or for other 'official' duties. The standard of entertainment had plummeted from the extravagance of Genroku days or the finesse of the 1720s to 1740s; Yoshiwara had succumbed to popular tastes.

However, the customers who kept up some level of standard for a short span were the *fudasashi* (official merchants), employed by the Bakufu officials in Edo. The scale of pleasure-quarter play of the Osaka townsmen who dealt with the wealthiest daimyo of the entire country naturally differed from that of the *fudasashi* in Asakusa, entertaining the *hatamoto* and other officials of the Tokugawa government whose income amounted to one-tenth or one-hundredth of that of a daimyo. Nevertheless, the centre of popular culture shifted eastwards from Kyoto–Osaka during the second half of the eighteenth century with an effusion of unique Edo literature: *kyōka* (crazy poems), *senryū* (comic poems), *sharebon* (comic fiction) and *kibyōshi* (satirical fiction). Possession of a *fudasashi* 'monopoly right' (*kabu*) was worth nearly 500 *ryō* gold pieces. A number of these brokers who had grown wealthy on the debts of *hatamoto* came to be known as the 'Eighteen Great Connoisseurs' (*jūhachi daitsū*) for their extravagant life style centred in Yoshiwara. Sanshōya Nisōji (Gion Minsai, lyric writer for Nagauta and Kiyomoto music, d. 1856), a grandson of Gion Minri, one of the famous 'Eighteen', wrote in detail about their antics in *Eighteen Great Connoisseurs* (*Jūhachi daitsū*, 1846) also known as the *Tale of the Kuramae Fools* (*Okuramae baka monogatori*). However, they were not simply boorish new rich, lavishing money on wild jaunts. In 1733, four *fudasashi* published the haiku work *Four Views* (*Shijikan*). They were followers of Inazu Gikū (Keiu) of the Kikaku school, and resisted the popular trends in Edo haiku toward satirical or frivolous *senryū*-like verse. The title, *Shijikan* became the name of the Kuramae school, the prominent line of Edo haiku. The most famous Edo haiku poet of the period 1790s to 1810s, Natsume Seibi (the fifth-generation *fudasashi*, Izutsuya Hachiroemon) was of this lineage.

The first of the great 'Eighteen' was Yamatoya Tarōji (haiku name,

Bungyo) who died in the last years of the eighteenth century. He was a pupil of Katō V and a famous Katō-bushi singer in his own right under the name Masumi Bunshi. Of Bungyo, Rinsai says:

> All the 'great *tsū*' in Edo were followers of Bungyo and sought out his training in social graces and customs; his home was sometimes called a training ground for the pleasure quarter. Each follower was given the character 'bun' from his name, allowing them into the company of 'great *tsū*'.

The term 'great *tsū*' (*daitsū*) began to be used around 1770, at first as a slang word among men of refined taste. Use of the term expanded, and by 1777 it had become common throughout Edo, according to the *sharebon*, *One Glance Over the Riverbank* (*Hitome tsutsumi*, 1788). In 1778, a year after the *daitsū* fad had boomed in popularity, the *sharebon Eighteen Great Connoisseurs and 100 Pillows*, subtitled *Guide to the Pleasure Quarters* (*Jūhachi daitsū momo temakura*) was published, with Bungyo as the model hero.

The real-life models for the golden age of Edo pleasure-quarter literature in the 1770s were recorded in the *Eighteen Great Connoisseurs of Kuramae*, but their aesthetic sensibilities cannot be compared with the *sui* of Genroku times; the *tsū* of *sharebon* is definitely on the level of the petty merchant. Nevertheless, though Yoshiwara had suffered irreparable damage to its prestige through the lowering of its standards in the 1750s and 1760s, it remained the focus of Edo's particular aesthetic *tsū*, and was able to continue its role as a cultural centre because of the financial and cultural backing of the *fudasashi* of Kuramae.

The relatively liberal Tanuma period (1760s–1780s) was followed, however, by the age of Matsudaira Sadanobu who, under the eleventh Shogun Ienari, implemented the Kansei Reforms in 1789. One of these reforms was the cancellation of the debts of *hatamoto* who had fallen into poverty; at one blow the *fudasashi* lost more than 1 187 800 *ryō* of gold. The famous 'Eighteen', also staggered by this, were forced to retire from Yoshiwara and to live a self-disciplined, restrained life. The *Eighteen Great Connoisseurs* states:

> Though there is much to write about the *fudasahi* of the earlier An'ei–Tenmei era (1770s–1780s), there is nothing to record about Kansei–Kyōwa (1783–1803). Today the Kuramae *fudasahi* are but average merchants and, furthermore, their style has altered: 'no wit, no ideas, not even a fool among them'.

With the retirement of the great 'Eighteen', Yoshiwara, as Shimabara had earlier, found itself slipping even further into oblivion. The

1803 preface to Tegara Okamochi's collection of essays, *A Later Tale of Times Past* (*Ato wa mukashi no monogatari*), notes: 'I have heard that these days only two *yobidashi* are to be found in Yoshiwara.' Further, Shikitei Samba, in the 1811 preface to his *Miscellaneous Notes* (*Shikitei zakki*) records:

> Yoshiwara has now fallen on hard times. Recently, for the first time in ages, I looked in a guidebook and noticed that there are only two *yobidashi*: Takigawa of the Ogiya House and Karauta of Chōjiya. Ogiya has no Hanaogi; Matsuya, no Segawa. Tamaya has no *sancha*; all are the lowly *umecha* . . . It seems to me that the courtesans are fewer and the number of famous ladies halved.

Samba's words vividly depict the wasted state of Yoshiwara twenty years after the Kansei Reforms. The *sancha* mentioned by Shikitei were the *tsukemawashi* of the 1770s, and the lower *umecha* were the *zashiki-mochi* or *heya-mochi* of that time. Yoshiwara, proud of its high status, had declined dramatically after the *fudasashi* were forced to withdraw. With Yoshiwara's downfall, the more convenient, more relaxed and cheaper 'semi-licensed' (*oka-basho*) pleasure quarters began to thrive. In Kyoto, Shimabara's precedence had been usurped by Gion; similarly, in Edo the geisha of Fukagawa came to hold pride of place over Yoshiwara. In the literary world, the transition meant the demise of *sharebon* and the rise of romance (*ninjōbon*), which had geisha as the main characters.

To summarise, the role of the Kyoto, Osaka and Edo pleasure quarters in urban culture changed greatly during the Tokugawa period. Initially, in the 1650s, each quarter began to serve the role as the centre of culture. Around 1700, which was the turning point, this function began to decline in the face of more strict government control over merchant life. Then, in the mid-eighteenth century, the quarters of all three cities began to decline more rapidly, receiving the final blow of the Kansei Reforms which ended their role as cultural centres. This rise and fall mirrors exactly the changes in Tokugawa urban society. The city culture of Genroku was generated by elite townsmen, a culture of pleasure. The early eighteenth century, however, saw the rise of middle-class urban culture, and the gradual spread of wealth led finally to a popular culture like that of today. Along with these changes the quarters lost their function as centres of sophisticated culture with a high level of aesthetics and manners, and became nothing more than marketplaces for sex.

(*Translated by C. Andrew Gerstle*)

Notes

1 Though the particular section is missing in the extant text *Higenshū* (Crude proverbs, 1662) (Jikūken Ansei, ed.), Fujimoto Kizan records in the *Shikidō ōkagami* that one of Yachiyo's poems is included, together with one of his own. The author Fujimoto Kizan, under the name Seiyō, also has one poem in the collection *Futokorogo* with Yachiyo.
2 Saikaku also describes her in some detail in Chapter 6 in Part 2 of *Life of an Amorous Man.*
3 *Yakusha ōkagami*, [Great mirror of actors], 1692
4 In 1679 he played in *Yūgiri isshūki* (First memorial to Yūgiri). The next year he again played in *Yūgiri sannenki* (Third-year memorial to Yūgiri); in 1684, he performed in *Yūgiri shichinenki* (Seventh year memorial to Yūgiri); next in 1692 was *Yūgiri jūsannenki* (The thirteenth-year memorial to Yūgiri).
5 *Ihon dōbō goen* [Variant *Dōbō Goen*], 1720
6 *Shikidō ōkagami, Ihon dōbō goen*
7 This was later adapted by Sakurada Jisuke I as the Kabuki *Banzui Chōbei seishin manaita* (1803 at the Edo Nakamura Theatre) and by Tsuruya Namboku as the Kabuki play *Ukiyo zuka hiyoku no inazuma* (1823 at the Edo Ichimura Theatre) as well as others, giving some credence to the Koshiba–Gonpachi legend.
8 *Setsuyō kikan* [Records of Osaka], 'Record of the Yodoya confiscation'.

References

Professor Teruoka, in Japanese traditional style, has not given the exact editions of the works he cited, some of which are original texts. Since many of the works, however, are likely to be obscure even to Japanese scholars, I have supplied the following list of sources not available in English translation, noting a modern print edition where it exists. Entries are arranged in alphabetical order by title, with the characters given for the title. This essay was first published in *Engekigaku* (Theatre studies), No. 25, 1984.

Azuma monogatari あづま物語 (Tales of the East, 1642). *Kanazōshi shūsei* (Collection of *kanazōshi*) Vol. 1, Asakura Haruhiko (ed.), Tokyo: Tōkyōdō, 1980

Banzui chōbei shōjin manaita 幡随長兵衛精進俎板 (Kabuki play, 1803) by Sakurada Jisuke. *Meisaku kabuki zenshū* (Complete collection of famous Kabuki plays) Vol. 15, Toita Yasuji et al. (eds), Tokyo: Sōgen Shinsha, 1969

Chōja kigen bukuro 長者機嫌袋 (The millionaire's bag of treats, 1705). *Chinpon zenshū* (Collection of rare texts) *(Teikoku Bunko)*, Tokyo: Hakubunkan, 1895

Dōbō goen 洞房語園 (Writings from the bedroom, 1783) *Nihon zuihitsu taisei* (Collection of Japanese essays), 3rd Series, Vol. 1, Tokyo: Nihon Zuihitsu Taisei Kankōkai, 1929

Futokorogo 懐子 (Favourite child, 1660), original woodblock or reproductions, no modern print edition

Haikai nyokasen（古近）俳諧女歌仙 by Ihara Saikaku. *Teihon Saikaku zenshū* (Complete works of Saikaku) Vol. 11, No. 2, Ebara Taizō et al. (eds), Tokyo: Chūō Kōron Sha, 1972

Hangonkō 反魂香 (*rakugo*). *Koten rakugo taikei* (Great collection of classical *rakugo*) Vol. 4, Ekuni Shigeru, (ed.), Tokyo: San'ichi Shobō, 1970

Higenshū 鄙諺集 (Crude proverbs, 1661), no modern print editions

Hitome senken 一目千軒 (1000 houses at a glance, 1757). *Kinsei bungei sōsho* (Collection of Edo-period writings) Vol. 10, Tokyo: Kokusho Kankō Kai, 1911

Hitome tsutsumi 一目土堤 (One glance over the riverbank, 1788). *Sharebon taisei* (Great collection of *sharebon*) Vol. 14, Tokyo: Chūō Kōron Sha, 1981

Ihon dōbō goen 異本洞房語園 (Variant *Dōbō goen*, 1720). *Nihon zuihitsu taisei* (Collection of Japanese essays) 3rd Series, Vol. 1, Tokyo: Nihon Zuihitsu Taisei Kankōkai, 1929

Jūhachi daitsū 十八大通 (Eighteen great *tsū*, 1846). *Nihon zuihitsu taisei* (Collection of Japanese essays) 2nd Series, Vol. 6, Tokyo: Nihon Zuihitsu Taisei Kankōkai, 1928

Jūhachi daitsū momo temakura 十八大通百手枕 (Eighteen great *tsū* and 100 pillows, 1778) (also known as *Keiseikai shinansho* [Guide to the pleasure quarter]). *Sharebon taisei* (Great collection of *sharebon*) Vol. 7, Tokyo: Chūō Kōron Sha, 1980

Karanashi daimon yashiki 棠大門屋敷 (*ukiyo-zōshi*, 1705), *Chinpon zenshū* (Collection of rare texts) (*Teikoku Bunko*), Tokyo: Hakubunkan, 1895

Keisei hachisu no ito けいせい蓮の糸 (A courtesan and strings of lotus, 1705), not extant

Keisei iro jamisen 傾城色三味線 Courtesans and erotic shamisens, 1701). *Ukiyo-zōshi (Nihon meicho zenshū* [Complete collection of famous works of Japanese literature]) Vol. 9, Tokyo: Nihon Meicho Zenshū Kankōkai, 1928

Keisei kogane no yodogoi けいせい金淀鯉 (Courtesans and golden Yodo carp, 1705), not exant

Keisei mizu chōshi 傾情水調子 (Courtesans and water rhythms, 1728) (Katōbushi). *Nihon kayō shūsei* (Collection of Japanese songs) Vol. 11, Takano Tatsuyuki (ed.), Tokyo: Tokyōdō, 1942

Keisei shutendōji 傾城酒呑童子 (Courtesans and demons, 1710) by Chikamatsu Monzaemon. *Chikamatsu zenshū* (Complete works of Chikamatsu) Vol. 11, Fujii Otoo (ed.), Osaka: Asahi Shimbunsha, 1928

Kiryo manroku 羇旅漫録 (A traveler's records, 1802) by Takizawa Bakin. *Nihon zuihitsu taisei* (Collection of Japanese essays) 1st Series, Vol. 1, Tokyo: Nihon Zuihitsu Taisei Kankōkai, 1927

Kōshoku ichidai otoko 好色一代男 (Life of an amorous man, 1681) by Ihara Saikaku. *Teihon Saikaku zenshū* (The complete works of Saikaku) Vol. 1, Ebara Taizō, et al. (eds), Tokyo: Chūō Kōronsha, 1951

Kōshoku keshiganoko 好色罌粟鹿 (Amorous jaunts among poppy flowers, 1694); alternate title of *Naniwa-dora*

Kōshoku nidai otoko 好色二代男 (Life of an amorous man II, 1684) by Ihara Saikaku; alternate title for *Shoen ōkagami*

Kuruwa bunshō 廓文章 (Letter from the pleasure quarter, 1808). *Meisaku kabuki zenshū* (Complete collection of famous Kabuki plays) Vol. 7, Toita Yasuji et al. (eds), Tokyo: Tokyo Sōgen Shinsha, 1969

Masari-gusa 満散利久佐 (Tall grasses, 1656). *Yūjo hyōbanki shū* (Collection of courtesan critiques) (*Tenri toshokan zenbon sōsho*). Noma Kōshin (ed.), Tokyo: Yagi Shoten, 1973

Meguro hiyoku-zuka 驪山比翼塚 (Memorial at Meguro, 1779) by Hiraga Gennai. *Fūrai Sanjin kessaku shū* (Masterpieces of Fūrai Sanjin) (*Teikoku Bunko*), Tokyo: Hakubunkan, 1894

Miyako monogatari 美夜古物語 (Tales of Miyako, 1656). *Kinsei shoki yūjo hyōbanki shū* (Collection of early Edo-period courtesan critiques) (*Kinsei bungei shiryō* [Sources on Edo-period arts] Vol. 9, Tokyo: Koten Bunko, 1954

Monju no kaichō 文珠の開張 (The Monju unveiling, 1705); alternate title of *Keisei kogane no yodogoi*

Nagasaki miyage 長崎土産 (Souvenir of Nagasaki, 1681). *Kisho fukuseikai sōsho* (Collection of reprints of important texts) 3rd Series, Tokyo: Yoneyamadō, 1940

Naniwa-dora 難波鉦 (Key to Naniwa, 1680). *Kana-zōshi (Kinsei bungei shiryō* [Sources on Edo-period arts]) Vol. 5, Tokyo: Koten Bunko, 1957

Naniwa monogatari 難波物語 (Tales of Naniwa). *Kanazōshi shū* (Collection of *kanazōshi*) Vol. 1, (*Nihon koten zensho*), Noda Sumio (ed.), Osaka: Asahi Shimbun Sha, 1948

Nanshoku ōkagami 男色大鑑 (Great mirror of manly love) by Ihara Saikaku. *Teihon Saikaku zenshū* (Complete works of Saikaku) Vol. 4, Ebara Taizō et al. (eds), Tokyo: Chūō Kōron Sha, 1964

Nemonogatari ね物語 (Tales in bed, 1656). *Yūjo hyōbanki shū* (Collection of courtesan critiques) (*Tenri toshokan zenbon sōsho*). Noma Kōshin et al. (eds), Tokyo: Yagi Shoten, 1973

Nochi wa mukashi no monogatari 後は昔物語 (A later tale of times past, 1803) by Tegara Okamochi. *Nihon zuihitsu taisei* (Collection of Japanese essays) 3rd Series, Vol. 6, Tokyo: Nihon Zuihitsu Taisei Kankōkai, 1929

Ōezu 大画図 (Great map of Yoshiwara, 1689). Reprint in *Yoshiwara saiken ezu yonshū*. Supplement to *Yūjo hyōbanki shū* (Collection of courtesan critiques) (*Tenri toshokan zenhon sōsho*), Noma Kōshin et al. (eds), Tokyo: Yagi Shoten, 1973

Okina-gusa 翁草 (Random jottings of an old man, 1770s–1780s). *Nihon zuihitsu taisei* (Collection of Japanese essays) 3rd Series, Vols. 11–13, Tokyo: Nihon Zuihitsu Taisei Kankōkai, 1927–1931

Okuramae baka monogatari 大蔵前馬鹿物語 (Tale of the Kuramae fools, 1846); alternate title for *Jūhachi daitsū*

Renbo mizukagami 恋慕水鏡 (Reflections on love, 1682). *Edo jidai bungei shiryō* (Sources on Edo-period arts) Vol. 4, Tokyo: Kokusho Kankō Kai, 1916

Setsuyō kikan 摂陽奇観 (The wonders of Setsuyō, 1833), *Naniwa sōsho* (Collection of writings on Naniwa) Vols. 1–6, Funakoshi Seiichirō et al. (eds), Osaka: Naniwa Sōsho Kankō Kai, 1929

Shijikan 四時観 (Four views, 1733). *Kyōhō haikai shū* (Kyōhō-period haiku) (*Koten haibungaku taikei*) Vol. 11. Suzuki Katsutada and Shiraishi Teizō (eds), Tokyo: Shūeisha, 1970

Shikidō ōkagami 色道大鏡 (Great mirror of way of love, 1678), Noma Kōshin (ed.), Kyoto: Yūzan Bunko, 1961

Shikitei zakki 式亭雑記 (Miscellaneous notes, 1810–1811) by Shikitei Sanba. *Zoku enseki jisshu (Enseki jisshu*—continued) (*Zoku teikoku bunko*), Tokyo: Kokusho Kankō Kai, 1908

Shoen ōkagami 諸艶大鑑 (Great mirror of love, 1684) by Ihara Saikaku. *Teihon Saikaku zenshū* (Complete works of Saikaku) Vol. 1, Ebara Taizō et al. (eds), Tokyo: Chūō Kōron Sha, 1951

Shokoku irozato annai 諸国色里案内 (A guide to the pleasure quarters of the land, 1688). *Nihon shomin bunka shiryō shūsei* (Collection of sources for Japanese popular culture) Vol. 9, Geinōshi Kenkyūkai (ed.), Tokyo: San'ichi Shobō, 1974

Shujaka showake kagami 朱雀諸分鑑 (Mirror of Shujaka, 1681). *Kisho fukuseikai sōsho* (Collection of reprints of important texts), Tokyo: Yoneyamadō, 1918–1940

Sōmanroku 窓漫録 (Records at random), manuscript

Takabyōbu kuda monogatari 高屏風くだ物語 (Tale of Takao, 1660). Sasaki Kotarō (ed.), reprinted 1915. Also facsimile in *Yūjo hyōbanki shū* (Collection of courtesan critiques) (*Tenri toshokan zenbon sōsho series*, No. 11), Noma Kōshin et al. (eds), Tokyo: Yagi Shoten 1973

Takaokō 高尾考 (On Takao, 1849) by Ōta Nampo and Santō Kyōzan. *Enseki jisshu zoku-ensekijisshu 2* (Collection of Edo-period sources) (*Zoku teikoku bunko*), Tokyo: Kokusho Kankō Kai, 1807

Takao tsui tsui kō 高尾追々考 (More on Takao) by Katō Jakuan. *Sohaku jisshu* (Collection of Edo-period Sources) Vol. 1 (*Zoku teikoku bunko*), Tokyo: Kokusho Kankō Kai, 1899

Takitsuke moekui keshizumi たきつけ・もえくひ・けしずみ (Kindling, charred timber, charcoal, 1677). *Kinsei shikidō ron* (Tokugawa-period theories of love) (*Nihon shisō taikei*) Vol. 6, Ienaga Saburō et al. (eds), Tokyo: Iwanami Shoten, 1976

Tōgenshū 桃源集 (A collection of peaches, 1655). *Yūjo hyōbanki shū* (Collection of courtesan critiques) (*Tenri toshokan zenbon sōsho* No. 11), Noma Kōshin et al. (eds), Tokyo: Yagi Shoten, 1973

Tsuyudono monogatari 露殿物語 (The tale of Tsuyudono, 1620). *Kanazōshi shū Ukiyo-zōshi shū* (Collection of *kanazōshi* and *ukiyo-zōshi*) (*Nihon koten bungaku zenshū*) Vol. 37, Jimbō Kazuya et al. (eds), Tokyo: Shōgakkan, 1971

Ukiyozuka hiyoku no inazuma 浮世柄比翼稲妻 (Kabuki play, 1823) by Tsuruya Namboku. *Tsuruya Namboku zenshū* (Complete works of Tsuruya Namboku) Vol. 9, Gunji Masakatsu et al. (eds), Tokyo: San'ichi Shobō, 1974

Yakusha ōkagami 役者大鑑 (Great mirror of actors, 1692). *Kabuki hyōbanki shūsei* (Collection of Kabuki critiques) Vol. 1, Tokyo: Iwanami Shoten, 1972

Yakusha rongo 役者論語 (The actors' analects). *Kabuki jūhachiban shū (Nihon koten bungaku taikei)* Vol. 98, Gunji Masakatsu (ed.), Tokyo, Iwanami Shoten, 1776; translations: *The Actors' Analects*, by Dunn, Charles and Torigoe Bunzō, New York: Columbia University Press, 1969

Yarō tachiyaku butai ōkagami 野良立役舞台大鏡 (Great mirror of lead-role Kabuki actors, 1687). *Kabuki hyōbanki shūsei* (Collection of Kabuki critiques) Vol. 1, Tokyo: Iwanami Shoten, 1972

Yodoya kessho mokuroku 淀屋闕所目録 (Records of the confiscation of Yodoya). *Setsuyō kikan* (Wonders of Setsuyō) (*Naniwa sōsho*, Vol. 3), Funakashi Seiichirō et al. (eds), Osaka: Naniwa Sōsho Kankō Kai, 1927

Yoshino miuke 吉野身受 (The marriage of Yoshino, 1678), not extant

Yoshiwara kagami 吉原鑑 (Mirror of Yoshiwara, 1660). *Edo-jidai bungei shiryō* (Sources on Edo-period arts) 4, Tokyo: Kokusho Kankō Kai, 1916

Yoshiwara marukagami 吉原丸鑑 (Round or complete mirror of Yoshiwara, 1720). *Tokugawa bungei ruijū* (Collection of sources on Tokugawa arts) Vol. 12, Tokyo: Kokusho Kankō Kai, 1914

Yoshiwara yōji 吉原楊枝 (Yoshiwara toothpicks, 1788) by Santō Kyōden. *Sharebon taisei* (Great collection of *sharebon*) Vol. 7, Tokyo: Chūō Kōron Sha, 1981

Yūgiri Awa no Naruto 夕霧阿波鳴渡 (Yūgiri and the Straits of Naruto, 1712) by Chikamatsu Monzaemon. *Chikamatsu zenshū* (Complete works of Chikamatsu) Vol. 9, Fujii Otoo (ed.), Osaka: Asahi Shimbun Sha, 1927

Yūgiri isshūki 夕霧一周忌 (First memorial to Yūgiri, 1679), not extant

Yūgiri jūsannenki 夕霧十三年忌 (Thirteenth memorial to Yūgiri, 1692), not extant

Yūgiri nagori no shōgatsu 夕霧名残の正月 (Farewell to Yūgiri at New Year, 1678), not extant

Yūgiri sannenki 夕霧三年忌 (Third memorial to Yūgiri, 1680), not extant

Yūgiri sanzesō 夕霧三世相 (Memorial to Yūgiri, 1686) by Chikamatsu Monzaemon. *Chikamatsu zenshū* (Complete works of Chikamatsu) Vol. 2, Fujii Otoo (ed.), Osaka: Asahi Shimbunsha, 1925

Yūgiri shichinenki 夕霧七年忌 (Seventh memorial to Yūgiri, 1784) by Chikamatsu Monzaemon. *Chikamatsu kabuki kyōgenshū* (Collection of Chikamatsu Kabuki plays) Vol. 1, Takano Tatsuyuki (ed.), Tokyo: Rokugōkan, 1927

2

Flowers of Edo : Kabuki and its patrons

C. Andrew Gerstle

Kabuki today at the Tokyo National Theatre usually consists of plays conceived and performed during the eighteenth and nineteenth centuries, yet the audience experience is radically different from that of the period before 1868. Patrons of Edo Kabuki in 1770 would not have felt comfortable having their theatre so close to the seat of government—in view of the Diet and Imperial Palace and next to the Supreme Court—nor would they have enjoyed the quiet, almost solemn atmosphere or the ban on eating and drinking during a performance. In short, they would be bored to tears amid the posh furnishings of the exalted National Theatre. They would, perhaps, feel a bit more comfortable at the Kabukiza or might have at the former Enbujō theatre, but if they wanted to get closer to Edo-period Kabuki, they would have to leave Tokyo altogether and travel to the Naka-za in Osaka's Dōtombori or the Minami-za in Kyoto during the *kao-mise* (face-showing of top stars) performance in December, but they would still be bored by the stiffness of the audience and performance. They would not be part of the show. It would not be a festival.[1]

For Edoites of the eighteenth century—commoner or samurai—Kabuki was one of the centres of social and cultural life. It was something in which they participated vigorously throughout the year, as the Kabuki calendar was arranged in bi-monthly programs following the rhythms of city life. Each program began around the festival dates of New Year, Dolls (third month), Boys (fifth), Obon (seventh) and Autumn (ninth), with the special *kao-mise* performance in the eleventh month. A comic *senryū* poem attests to the heights of its smashing popularity. 'A big hit/Finally/Corpses all carted away.'[2] There is no doubt that Edo was a lively and creative place in which to

33

be; most likely the largest city in the world, it had a range of entertainment facilities rivalling any city. Kabuki at the centre of this urban culture, to a certain extent, embraced all levels of society, from the outcastes (*hinin*), who were allowed to enter free, to grand daimyo, who entered through doors other than the small *nezumi* (rat) door at the front, namely the direct passages from adjoining teahouses. Because actors' names were used to advertise products, their fame extended into nearly every Edo home on kimono patterns, hair styles, candy, cakes—such products were fashionable with famous actors' sobriquets attached to them.

Further, through actor prints and touring companies, Kabuki's influence penetrated far into rural areas. Yet patronage of the theatre was not confined to the masses. Most Edo writers also were fascinated by this distinctive world of fantasy, and many actors conversely took part in literary groups as amateur poets. Ichikawa Danjūrō V (1741–1806), with the pen name Hakuen, is a famous actor well known for his literary activities and relations with writers of this period. Popular demand for information on theatre life was insatiable. Playbills, critiques and woodblock actor prints, as well as a continuous array of books on, or set in, the theatrical world flourished nearly all through the eighteenth and nineteenth centuries, increasing as time progressed. For better or worse (depending on one's moral perspective), the theatre touched all corners of Edo life.

Of course, not everyone in Edo society fully appreciated the breadth or depths to which Kabuki's radiance permeated. For the top conservative echelon of the Bakufu, Kabuki was an unpleasant evil, tolerated but pushed as far away from the centres of city life as possible. The Bakufu's attitude toward Kabuki is generally well known because of the research of historians. In English, there is the work of Donald Shively in such articles as 'Bakufu versus Kabuki' (1955), 'The Social Environment of Tokugawa Kabuki' (1978) and 'Tokugawa Plays on Forbidden Topics' (1982). Especially in the period before 1720, the Bakufu was continually banning or restricting all aspects of Kabuki. 'The official attitude was that actors were a social group lower than merchants, and only a little above the pariah class.'[3] This attitude remained official policy because actors were continually, throughout the Tokugawa period, restricted in where they could live, and legally administered as beggars. They were considered male prostitutes and accordingly the theatre district was put near the Yoshiwara pleasure quarter, far from the centre of Edo. However, this does not mean that men of education or position did not patronise actors. In fact, samurai interest in Kabuki, particularly from the mid-eighteenth century until the Kansei Reforms in the 1790s, seems to have been more widespread than is usually claimed. Though we imagine samurai (especially the young) in their large wicker hats steathily making their way to the Yoshiwara pleasure quarter, the general view is that samurai and intellectuals had little love for Kabuki. Gunji Masakatsu[4] emphasises, however, that the distinction, first created in the Meiji period, between the brothel and theatrical worlds did not exist in the Tokugawa period. Commoners—as well as the Bakufu—viewed these two spheres of entertainment as two sides of the same coin. The following *senryū* from the Kansei (1790s) period jokingly puts them in perspective: 'Yoshiwara / Kabuki / The back and front of dice.'[5] For city-dwellers these two areas were the worlds of pleasure and fun, a forbidden sphere outside restrictive society, often termed *akusho* (evil places) or *chikushō* (Buddhist realm of beasts), while the popular term was 'Paradise'.[6]

These contradictory attitudes toward Kabuki—one of moral and social disdain, and the other of fascination and adulation—are an intriguing phenomenon. At least some actors seem to have been clearly aware of their official station. The source *Chūko kejōsetsu* (On theatre of the past, 1805) records that Ichikawa Danjūrō II (1689–1758) was visited by a famous samisen player and had him eat from a separate fire, showing explicitly that Danjūrō considered himself to be of the outcaste class.[7] However, this humble attitude of Edo actors did not continue into the latter half of the eighteenth century, when records tell of actors visiting daimyo residences. Nor did this humility extend to the samurai class, because the same Danjūrō II was the creator of many of the most famous *aragoto* (rough style) pieces which display an open defiance toward samurai. (*Plate 6*: Danjūrō II) No matter what the official Bakufu attitude towards actors was, their popularity was enormous and continued to grow throughout the Tokugawa period. During the latter half of the eighteenth century this fascination for the world of Edo Kabuki fully matures, encompassing all levels of society. The tension between official disdain and popular adoration was always felt more acutely by Edo actors, who lived under close samurai scrutiny, than by their counterparts in Kyoto or Osaka. This may help to explain the distinctive Edo *aragoto* tradition with its more bombastic and rebellious style. Playwrights were conscious of the sharp distinction in styles. The author of the 1801 *Sakusha shihō kezairoku* (Treasury of rules for playwrights) compares Kabuki in the three cities: the *kokoro* (heart) of Kyoto Kabuki is a 'beautiful woman'; of Osaka, a 'dandy'; and of Edo, a 'samurai'.[8] *Aragoto*, the essence of Edo Kabuki as described by Danjūrō I, is recorded in the important book *Kokon yakusha rongo sakigake* (Advanced actors' analects from the past and present, 1772):

When invited to a daimyo's residence, after saké was served, I was asked to show them *aragoto*. Therefore, to the chanting of the Nō play *Kagekiyo*, I stripped to my underclothes and violently smashed the *shōji* and *fusuma* (sliding doors) with my feet. Whereupon, the patrons asked what are you doing? When I replied that this is *aragoto*, the daimyo was delighted and rewarded me well. Even in front of daimyo you must never be afraid, or it won't be *aragoto*.[9]

The essence of *aragoto* is defiance toward the samurai. The actor must consider his audience to be samurai. Though most today imagine such defiance as symbolic or abstract, I shall show that in fact, during the eighteenth century, samurai were more intimately involved in Kabuki life than previously thought. (*Plate 7*: Danjūrō I in *aragoto* pose, by Kiyomasu)

Edo Kabuki fans regarded the actors as god-like hero figures, and Ichikawa Danjūrō—whoever had the name—was the King of this world; he was 'the flower of Edo' (*Edo no hana*). During January 1982, in an interview with Ichikawa Ebizō (1946–), whose father was Danjūrō XI and who has since become Danjūrō XII, I asked him to elaborate on his ideas of the past and present 'Danjūrō' image. One reason for asking this question is that, on viewing a Danjūrō-type piece in the Edo Kabuki repertoire for the first time, a spectator may be totally baffled by the ritual-like formality, lack of action and the grandiose exaggerations of the hero-role character. In the famous and annually performed play *Shibaraku* (Wait a minute!) almost nothing happens. The stage is filled with an array of red-bodied thugs, evil-looking villains, conniving priests, innocent victims, and beautiful princesses. (*Plate 8*: Danjūrō as Gongorō, by Kiyomasu) The background to the story is a complicated power struggle for control of a family treasure, but in the scene performed nothing happens except for the grand entrance of Gongorō in an oversized outfit with a gigantic sword, who yells *shibaraku* (wait a minute) from off stage to halt the villains' actions and then enters along the *hanamichi*. He stops midway and announces his name and lineage, along with an assortment of hyperbole and humorous references to contemporary happenings. This kind of soliloquy is called a *tsurane* and is the most famous in traditional Edo Kabuki. The play on first view may seem absolutely bizarre. During the Edo period, however, this was (and can be today) a magic moment in the theatre. The contemporary Danjūrō's view (and sources support it) is that 'Danjūrō' was considered a deity for the Edo *chōnin* (townsman), a god whose fierce look—like that of the guardian god Fudō Myōō at a temple—could exorcise evil and cure sickness.[10] (*Plate 9*: Danjūrō as Fudō Myōō) Danjūrō was a super-hero above the samurai, even above the Shogun himself: 'In all the world / There's Danjūrō / And a spring morn' (In this world [Edo] only Danjūrō matters—not the Shogun).[11] Evidence from Danjūrō's letters to temples and shrines shows that he considered his performance to be inspired by the powers of this god: 'My fame as the founder of Kabuki is not due to human effort'.[12] Gunji Masakatsu takes a step further and suggests that Danjūrō's *aragoto* performances then were 'not just theatrics, but prayers'.[13] Various references indicate that the myth of the Danjūrō relationship with Fudō was significant in the eighteenth century. The 1774 *Yakusha zensho* (All about actors) states:

> Danjūrō I prayed to the Fudō at Narita temple and was blessed with a son, who later became Danjūrō II. Because of the circumstances of his birth Danjūrō II had, from his childhood days, deep faith in Fudō Myōō. Eventually he excelled and became a famous actor. The sacred mirror he presented to the temple is said to be still there . . . During his lifetime he performed the Fudō role many times, always with great success. No other actor could charm audiences as he did in moments of non-acting. It was surely the power of Fudō Myōō. His eyes looked exactly like Fudō, frightening; the pupils would remain fixed for an extraordinarily long time. He was certainly inspired by the spirit of the god.[14]

The earlier *Kabuki jishi* (Origins of Kabuki, 1762) records a similar story. Danjūrō II was having a difficult time keeping his eyelids from blinking during the Fudō Myōō stare. He went to the Narita temple and pledged to pray continuously for seventeen days. After completing his pledge, 'How strange. His eyes had exactly the fierce look of a Fudō, and could stay fixed in a stare. He surely was possessed by the spirit.'[15] In a play like *Shibaraku* or *Fudō*, the audience went to see their favorite actor as super-man, the guardian of Edo's citizens.

The third element central to the myth of *aragoto* acting, along with defiance toward the samurai class and religious devotion, is the play-boy image. Danjūrō, as an outlaw hero, swaggers boldly with flair and brashness, perhaps comparable to the 'rebels' of modern film or rock music. Like them, Danjūrō was the rugged ladies man, the sex-idol of Edo. A short, fictional work gives us an insight into the popular legend. The 1782 *kibyōshi* (illustrated satirical fiction) *Ichikawa sanshōen* (Ichikawa Danjūrō) refers to an oracle at the Narita Fudō temple, proclaiming a miracle drug 'Ichikawa sanshōen'— namely Danjūrō. 'Listen folks, drink this potion three times, and pass through the Yoshiwara gate; no courtesan will ever turn away from you again.'[16] In Edo, one's reputation among courtesans was the touchstone for male sexual prowess. Edoites saw Danjūrō (or other actors) in the popular play *Sukeroku* as a virile, sexual powerhouse—

loved by all the courtesans of the Yoshiwara pleasure quarter. In the entrance soliloquy, the actor gives a confident, egotistical, humorous self-introduction, that brashly glorifies his role as the saviour of the Edo townsmen—who sat in daily life beneath the sword of approximately 500 000 resident samurai. (*Plate 13*: Danjūrō as Sukeroku) Edoites took pride in the actor Danjūrō, their number one 'Edokko'. Sukeroku is an especially intriguing role, because though really Soga Gorō, a samurai of the twelfth century, he is on the surface the townsmen's townsman—standing up to a samurai. However, as the contemporary Danjūrō remarks, for most today that magic is gone. There are no longer official distinctions between tycoons and outcastes.

As for the *onnagata* (female impersonators), famous actors were greatly influential in ladies' fashion—in coiffure, kimono design, walking style and a general sense of 'femininity', extending from commoner homes through samurai residences all the way to the Shogun's castle. Segawa Kikunojō II (1741–1773), also known as Rokō, was a particularly popular eighteenth-century *onnagata*, and the name Rokō came to be used as a brand-name for various products. (*Plate 10*: Kikunojō II) Another *senryū* poem expresses Kikunojō's popularity and the wealth it brought him. 'One glance / A thousand gold pieces / Kikunojō on the *hanamichi*.'[17] Rokō's fame extended even to the nether world. In Hiraga Gennai's *Nenashigusa* (Floating weeds, 1763),[18] Emma, Lord of the underworld, becomes infatuated with the actor after seeing a print and demands that his subjects bring Rokō in the flesh.[19] His name adorned incense, hair oil, tea, hair ornaments, etc.; an incident in Shikitei Samba's *Ukiyoburo* (Bath in a floating world, 1809), where a young girl persuades her mother to colour her kimono with *rokōcha* dye, suggests the extent of actor adulation.[20] Most famous Kabuki actor names of the period adorned products, and adoring fans were loyal to their particular actor's wares. Another *senryū* attests to the competition: 'Face powder too / Chrysanthemum (Kikugorō) vs. Peony (Danjūrō) / Patrons argue.'[21] Of course, Bakufu officialdom constantly frowned at such fawning over actors by Edo citizens. Even courtesans, who had been the models for the development of the *onnagata* style, with the basic role being the *keisei* (courtesan) in the formative period during the seventeenth century, were in the eighteenth century rather imitators of Kabuki actors. They looked to males acting as women for the ultimate in the arts of femininity. It is still a strong tradition, in Kyoto at least, that geisha are expected to attend the December *kao-mise* Kabuki.

For townsmen, and samurai as well, the theatre district, with its restaurants and tea-houses, provided a venue, like Yoshiwara, of complete freedom from the strictures of an officially moralistic Confucian society. The content of much eighteenth-century Edo Kabuki, particularly the *jūhachi-ban* (eighteen favourites) is super-human, most of the characters—Sukeroku, Kagekiyo, Gongorō, etc.—being brash outlaw-like heroes who stand in defiance of the samurai class. Theatre was a fantasy world and delicious, often ridiculous fun— surely, to some extent, because of the official disfavour it continually received.[22] Perhaps people today would call it escapist art; an Edoite would surely not have disagreed. To what extent was the Edo preference for this type of drama (including later gangster-hero plays) influenced by an atmosphere in which 'outcaste' Kabuki actors played for a mostly commoner audience in a samurai-dominated city? Certainly it was an unusual setting.

It is still generally thought today that Kabuki performances were directed at and patronised by the commoner population of Edo, while the samurai class kept their distance from the plebeian art. Nō drama was supposed to have been their theatre. Numerous references—particularly in the second half of the eighteenth century—clearly indicate, however, that among low-level samurai retainers through *hatamoto* Bakufu officials to some powerful daimyo, these outcaste Kabuki performers had devoted fans.

Several works of fiction from the late eighteenth century make jest of the daimyo craze for Kabuki. One published in 1784 is *Kyōgenzuki yabo daimyō*, literally, *The Boorish Daimyo in Love with Kabuki*, by Kishida Tohō.[23] The character Umanosuke, or Horseface, is a young, uncouth daimyo whose retainers introduce him to Kabuki and courtesans for aesthetic training. Horseface is an impossible fool who follows all suggestions to the letter and has Kabuki performed at his residence. After this exposure, he becomes so theatrical that he imagines his servant committing adultery with a salesman and accusses them in grand Kabuki language. His retainers, worried that his histrionics may get out of hand, introduce him to the women of the pleasure quarter. They invite a group to his residence and Horseface has them put on a Soga Kabuki play with himself in a leading role: courtesans and actors, a daimyo's dream! This fictional work is a hearty satire aimed at the highest of the samurai class—especially robust considering that the author was a lowly townsman picture-framer.

We know, however, that satire on daimyo's love for Kabuki was not simply idle fantasy because of records from diaries and essays of the time. One Bakufu official, Moriyama Takamori (1738–1815), records various current happenings, and in *Shizu no oda maki* (Humble mutterings, 1802) scornfully discusses eighteenth-century samurai love for imitating Kabuki actors' speech and manners, and for putting on Kabuki skits. Theatrical singing, *bungo-bushi* and *gidayū* became popular during this time among samurai. He notes:[24]

> The samisen became extremely popular during the 1740–60s. Eldest sons of good samurai families and even other sons all took lessons; from morn till night samisen sounds were always to be heard. Eventually they began to perform other Kabuki music and full dramas, etc., and followed this depravity to the extent of performing amateur Kabuki plays in residences. High *hatamoto* officials mimicking riverbed beggars (actors), aping female impersonators and stage heroes![25]

However, he adds, 'But with the Kansei reforms in the 1790s, all this ceased and society returned to normal.'

In an earlier work, *Tōdai Edo hyakabutsu* (A hundred strange things in Edo, 1758), Baba Bunkō, also a Bakufu official, discusses unusual characters in society.[26] He mentions that the Matsue daimyo, Matsudaira Munenobu (1729–1781) built a stage in his Edo residence for Kabuki and invited merchants to see productions. He invited the actor Segawa Kikunojō to perform and later, when he met Mizoguchi Naoatsu (1715–1780), the Shibata daimyo, he was thanked by Mizoguchi for being kind to his Kikunojō—as if Kikunojō was a member of Mizoguchi's family. Mizoguchi thereafter acquired the nickname of 'Foster-father'. In *Nenashigusa*, Gennai expands this theme in satirical fiction, poking fun at samurai love for Kikunojō and other actors. Lord Emma can be seen as representating a daimyo or even, dare he say it, the shogun. Consistent references in a variety of sources support an hypothesis that such activities were anything but uncommon. Ōta Nanpo (1749–1823), a Bakufu official, poet, critic and fiction writer, records in *Hannichi kanwa* (Idle chatter)[27] an incident in 1776 of a senior samurai official arranging seats on behalf of his daimyo's wife for a *Sukeroku* performance at the Ichimura theatre. However, upon arrival he discovers a mix-up: no seats are available. At that point, as an apology, the samurai commits *seppuku* in the theatre tea-house. This all sounds rather fantastic, and Nanpo admits his doubts on the truth of the affair. True or not, we can be sure that Kabuki was not completely alien to the warrior class in Edo.

Our most authoritative source on this matter is a diary by the 150 000 *koku* (measure of rice) daimyo, Yanagizawa Nobutoki (grandson of Yanagizawa Yoshiyasu), called *Enyū nikki* (A banquet diary), compiled over the years of 1773–85 (and continued thereafter as *Shōkaku nikki*).[28] This source, printed for the first time in 1977, confirms the fictional and other accounts of samurai interest in Kabuki theatre. Nobutoki was such an avid fan that he kept a separate record of all performances attended. He describes in detail day-long excursions (with entourage) to the theatre district and of collecting playbills and other materials from the theatrical world. His diary covers the years after retiring from active duty, but it is clear his interest did not suddenly emerge at the age of 50.

He was active in *haikai* circles and other arts but was an extraordinarily devoted admirer of popular theatre. He patronised directly one actor only, Nakamura Nakazō, but had indirect relations with other actors. His devotion to Kabuki was fantastic, his commitment perhaps unparalleled. He appears to have hired ladies-in-waiting according to their acting and dancing talents, and eventually created a small Kabuki troupe within his household.[29] Directed by Nobutoki and assisted by Nakazō, the women's troupe performed once or twice a year in a play written by the daimyo himself. He would take an old Jōruri play, rewrite it into Kabuki, arrange cast and props, prepare playbills, and finally write his *hyōbanki* (critique) after the performance. For these shows he had a stage—complete with *hanamichi*—built within his residence. Certainly, he was a fascinating daimyo who preferred the popular theatre of Kabuki and Jōruri over the austere Nō, and as we have seen, was most likely not the only daimyo with such proclivities. The Kansei Reforms of the 1790s did, however, suppress this kind of open flirtation with the demi-monde; daimyo were forced to pursue their theatrical pleasures more discreetly. Nevertheless, Kabuki was far more central to the life of all levels of Edo society than most historians prefer to admit.

Another sub-stratum of Edo society for which Kabuki was essential comprised the *gesaku* (popular fiction) writers and poets. For Utei Emba, Ōta Nanpo, Hiraga Gennai, Santō Kyōden and Shikitei Samba—to name but a few of the many samurai and commoner authors—Kabuki was an important venue, particularly for the communal arts of *haikai* and *kyōka* (crazy poem) in which all the artists participated. Kabuki was not just a meeting place or common ground for them; actors often were poets who entered the writers' *bundan* (coterie) under poetic names. One actor, Ichikawa Danjūrō V (1741–1806), was a favorite among these writers and published *kyōka* with them under the name Hakuen. References exist from the writers themselves that Hakuen was friends with Nanpo, Emba, Kyōden and others.[30] Hino Tatsuo[31] has suggested that the *kyōka* world of fantasy was, for these writers, an imaginary escape or utopia away from the restrictive society, and that Hakuen stood as the pillar of this coterie. The fictional 'Danjūrō' image was central to their fantasy world.

Along with this social contact with actors, fiction writers continually drew on the theatre for source material and inspiration to such an extent that a contemporary scholar of Edo fiction, Mizuno Minoru,[32] bewails the inescapable grip the theatrical world had on Edo fiction. *Gesaku* writers borrowed content and styles from Kabuki and Jōruri books, and certain writers—Kyōden, and in particular Shikitei Samba—seem to have always kept their eyes on the theatres. Samba wrote guide books on Kabuki and used the audience of Kabuki as fictional settings for his works, which give us today a magnificent picture of past Kabuki audiences. His *Kejō suigen maku no soto* (Theatre on the other side of the curtain, 1806) shows the audience to be lively and riotous at times—even causing performances to be halted briefly until calm is restored. Popular fiction was part of the theatrical world. An awareness of this fact helps us to understand the context of Edo fiction which has not been well received in the twentieth century in Japan or otherwise. It might be useful to consider an approach to Edo fiction as vehicles of performance in which acting is central to the reading experience.

For the Edokko commonfolk, popular theatre was a source of both festive entertainment and endless amateur activities. Shikitei Samba's *Kakusha hyōbanki* (A Critique of Audiences, 1811)[33] humorously delineates all types of lively fans—from patrons through connoisseurs, actor worshippers, young ladies, loud-mouthed ruffians, boorish samurai and country folk to tough old ladies. One of the most fascinating types is the actor mimic, who apes stage dress and actions all the time—even outside the theatre. These characters literally live an actors' life; art and life are reversed. Others specialise in mimicking monologues and spontaneously begin reciting during performances—without care for those around. This imitation of Kabuki dialogue actually developed into a formal art and practice texts are extant from the period for this *kowairo* hobby. Kabuki fans today, as well, love to imitate the histrionic style of declamation, a style that certainly begs mimicry.

Other amateur arts emerging from the theatre were *chaban* (skit), *zashiki-kyōgen* (home Kabuki), dance and *gidayū* (puppet theatre) chanting. The first two were not formalised but were nevertheless very popular in Edo. *Chaban* was the art of performing a Kabuki-style skit when serving tea or something to a guest. In competitions, a theme would be given and the person had to improvise a skit. There are references to *chabanshi* or semi-professional teachers, and numerous works of fiction contain episodes of *chaban* games.[34] *Zashiki-kyōgen* was the more elaborate art of putting on Kabuki plays in private residences. Evidence for the extent of the popularity of amateur productions is found in the 1774 book *Zashiki-kyōgen haya gatten* (The basic book of home Kabuki), which explains the whole procedure and includes references to speciality shops in Edo for stage props and make-up. Kabuki-style dance became increasingly popular during the eighteenth century and professional schools developed that still exist today. *Gidayū* chanting also was a popular hobby for Edoites as well as Osaka city folk. Numerous records and fictional works attest to the popularity—particularly among women.[35] In fact, women *gidayū* performers became such a craze that official edicts were issued frequently against public performances—but to no apparent avail. Edo *gidayū* puppet theatre flourished particularly from the 1770s, when Hiraga Gennai and others wrote new plays for Edo theatres, giving further impetus to amateur devotees.[36] Most theatrical singing styles (*tokiwazu, shinnai-bushi, nagauta*, etc.) also matured and flourished from the mid-eighteenth century onwards.

The fondness for things theatrical among the merchant class in Edo extended from the lowest clerk to the richest brokers. In the records of crimes of clerks in the huge Shirokiya department store, two reasons for theft stand out: the young gents' wish, first of all, to buy an expensive courtesan, and secondly, to lavish a fortune on a day of theatre.[37] With both women and theatre, all desires were satisfied. Of course these young chaps were trying to imitate the famous eighteen grand-*tsū* (connoisseur) wealthy merchants, who made an art of spending the money they had amassed as rice brokers and financiers for *hatamoto* (bannermen) samurai.[38] By the mid-eighteenth century, nearly all *hatamoto* were in debt to these *fudasashi* (official merchants and brokers) and were only saved by the cancellation of debts that came with the 1790s Kansei Reforms. All of these grand-*tsū* were Kabuki fans and usually patrons of particular actors. Some even had their own stages for private performances. The Kansei Reforms, however, put an end to this overt extravagance. These imitators of Kabuki had succeeded at last in their attempts to emulate theatre life; Matsudaira Sadanobu, the architect of the Reforms, was convinced: he called these wealthy men 'Kabuki actors'.[39]

Depending on your viewpoint, theatre was either a source of depravity which corrupted the moral fibre of Confucian society, or a source of life, imagination, fun and creativity—an escape from that same Confucian society. This tension, created by living directly under continuous official disfavour, certainly contributed to the rebellious tone of Edo Kabuki. Told that popular theatre was frivolous and immoral, Edo actors and playwrights seem to have agreed (tongue in cheek) with gusto, producing marvellous, outlandish bombast with a vigor rarely matched in world theatre. What did it mean for actors in the mid-to-late eighteenth century to find themselves the darlings of daimyo and intellectual society, as well as idols in the popular mind? It must have been a strange mixture to be idolised, taken seriously as artists, and at the same time officially remain prostitutes of pleasure, wealthy but restricted to the outcaste ghetto. Contact with sophisticated patrons surely affected their self-esteem as artists. This atmosphere, in which theatre thrived under such contradictory attitudes, must have affected the particular development of Edo Kabuki, which is so different from that in Kyoto or Osaka. Kabuki was by and for the commoners of Edo, but unlike in Kyoto and Osaka, actors could not ignore the samurai presence both as police and as patrons. They always had something before their eyes to react against, producing an irreverent flavour particular to Edo popular culture. Further, due to the fluctuations in the enforcement of Bakufu policy throughout this most crucial eighteenth century when it matured (relaxed Genroku 1690s to 1710s, strict Kyōhō Reforms 1720s to 1740s, relaxed Tanuma period 1750s to 1780s, strict Kansei Reforms 1790s), Edo Kabuki could hardly be anything but a bit 'twisted' in its attitude toward the samurai class and its morality. Even with the overwhelming eighteenth-century influence of Osaka Jōruri and Kabuki, Edo Kabuki, at its core, kept to its 'swaggering outlaw' image with its amoral stance. The role of the samurai class in Edo Kabuki's development should not be forgotten. In Danjūrō's words, *aragoto* is performed for daimyo; samurai were never out of sight for Edo actors. Though modern Kabuki, clothed in artistic respectability, must suffer its fate of becoming representative of 'national' culture, we mustn't forget its defiant past. *Aragoto* thrived on the tension implicit in the class structure of Edo society. Let me conclude with a comment by that great observer of Edo life, Shikitei Samba, on the ambiguity and equivocality of Edo Kabuki's position vis-à-vis its enemies and patrons:

> Theatre-lovers think theatre-haters fools.
> Theatre-haters think theatre-lovers fools.
> Theatre-lovers who think theatre is about morality are fools.
> Theatre-haters who think theatre has no morality are fools.
> Such fools know not that all morality is in theatre.
> Such fools know not that all theatre is in morality.
>
> Fools, fools, if you truly know morality and attend theatre,
> you'll realise theatre is morality,
> Ah! Theatre, thou art morality!

Samba adds, however, that:

> This, too, is written by a fool,
> the chief priest of the Temple of Fun.[40]

Note: A version of this article was published in *Asian Theatre Journal* Vol. 4, No. 1, Spring 1987.

Notes

Abbreviations used in text and notes:
KGR   *Kinsei geidō ron*
NZT   *Nihon zuihitsu taisei*
NSBSS   *Nihon shomin bunka shiryō shūsei*

1 Gunji Masakatsu (*Kabuki: yōshiki to denshō*) uses the term *kyōen* (banquet) to describe Kabuki theatre. Shikitei Samba, in *Kejō suigen maku no soto*, [1973] 1806, p. 468 has a character say, 'If you don't like Ichikawa Danjūrō's rough-style acting, Toraya *yōkan* sweets, and Katōbushi singing, you're not a true Edokko.' See Jacob Raz *Audience and Actors*, Leiden: E. J. Brill, 1983 and Barbara Thornbury *Sukeroku's Double Indentity*, Ann Arbor: University of Michigan, 1982, respectively, for descriptions of the liveliness of audiences and the year-long schedule of programs.

2 Quoted in Gunji's important little book *Kabuki to Yoshiwara*, Tokyo: Awaji Shobo, 1956, p. 160. See Nishihara Ryūu *Senryū Edo kabuki*, Tokyo: Shun'yōdō for (*senryū*) poems on Kabuki.

3 Shively, Donald, 'Bakufu versus Kabuki' *Harvard Journal of Asiatic Studies*, Vol. 18 (Dec.) 1955. Also reprinted in Hall and Jansen (eds) *Studies in the Institutional History of Early Modern Japan*, Princeton: Princeton University Press, 1968.

4 Gunji Masakatsu *Kabuki to Yoshiwara* (Kabuki and Yoshiwara) Tokyo: Awaji Shobo, 1956, p. 10

5 Gunji Masakatsu *Kabuki to Yoshiwara*, p. 10

6 One reference to the pleasure quarter as the Western Paradise (*saihō gokuraku*) is in Ki no Kaion's play *Wankyū sue no Matsuyama* (1708).

7 Quoted in Gunji *Kabuki to Yoshiwara*, p. 69. Original text is in *Enseki jisshu*.

8 *Kinsei geidō ron* (*KGR*) 1972, p. 511

9 *KGR*, 1972, p. 480

10 See Gunji (*Kabuki: Yōshiki to denshō*), chapter on *aragoto* style, and *Kabuki jūhachiban shū* (1965). See Watanabe *Shōkō Fudō Myōō*, Tokyo: Asahi Shimbunsha, 1975, pp. 103–14 for information on the Narita Fudō. A verse by Kikaku 'Here inside / With Danjūrō / Demons driven outside' (quoted in *Yakusha zensho* [1973] 1774, p. 218) expresses the popular image of Danjūrō as the protector.

11 Gunji Masakatsu *Kabuki to Yoshiwara*, p. 65

12 *KGR*, 1972, p. 690

13 ibid.

14 *Nihon shomin bunka shiryō shūsei* (*NSBSS*), Vol. 6, 1973, p. 122

15 ibid., p. 124

16 Hino Tatsuo *Edojin to yūtopia* (Edoites and utopia) Tokyo: Asahi Shimbunsa, 1977, p. 57; Mori Senzō *Kibyōshi kaidai* (Guide to *kibyōshi*) Tokyo: Chūō Kōronsha, 1972, p. 283

17 Gunji Masakatsu *Kabuki to Yoshiwara*, p. 66

18 [1961], 1763, pp. 46–8

19 In this work Gennai was parodying certain daimyos' fascination for actors.

20 Shikitei Samba, *Ukiyoburo* (Bath in a floating world), Tokyo: Iwanami

shoten, [1973], 1811, p. 187; there are numerous references to Rokō fashion in fiction of the time. See *Yakusha zensho* ([1973] 1774, pp. 229–30) for a list of some products with actor names.

21 Gunji Masakatsu *Kabuki to Yoshiwara*, p. 81

22 Eight of the eighteen plays are in *Kabuki jūhachiban shū*. There are translations of *Sukeroku* and *Narukami* in James Brandon *Kabuki: Five Classic Plays*, Cambridge, Ma.: Harvard, 1975

23 *Nenashigusa* (1763) by Hiraga Gennai has already been mentioned as a satire on daimyo love for Kabuki. Satirical *kibyōshi* fiction has many examples of absurd characters imitating Kabuki; Santō Kyōden's *Edo umare uwaki no kabayaki* (1785) is a famous example; the fellow is a rich, young merchant.

24 Moriyama Takamori *Shizu no odamaki*, p. 658

25 Moriyama was a supporter of Sadanobu's reforms. In another work, *Ama no yakimo no ki* in *Nihon zuihitsu taisei*, 2nd series, Vol. 11, Tokyo: Nihon Zuihitso Taisei Kankōkai, [1929] 1798, p. 706, Moriyama relates Sadanobu's attitude to the Kabuki-like behaviour and debauchery of samurai. An earlier Confucian scholar, Inoue Kinga (1732–84) notes in his *Byōkan chōgo*, Tokyo: Hakubunkan, [1891] 1763, p. 28 that young samurai 'enjoy dressing up like commoners and going to Jōruri theatres'.

26 Baba Bunkō *Tōdai Edo hyakabutsu*, p. 402

27 [1927], p. 491

28 Printed in NSBSS, Vol. 13, 1977. *Shōkaku nikki* was published in 1981; the text is a photocopy of the manuscript.

29 Koike Shōtarō 'Daimyō nikki ga egaku aru Edo joyū', *Rekishi to jimbutsu* Vol. 10, No. 11, pp. 214–18

30 Hamada Giichirō *Shokusanjin*, Tokyo: Seigodō, 1942, pp. 70–73 cites examples from Ōta Nampo's writing of his frequent contact with Ichikawa Danjūrō V. For Danjūrō II's relations with poets see Ichikawa Danjūrō *Oi no tanoshimi shō* in *Kinsei geidō ron*, Tokyo: Iwanami Shoten, [1972] 1734–1747

31 *Edojin to yūtopia*, pp. 63–4

32 *Edo shōsetsu ronsō*, Tokyo: Chūō Kōronsha, 1974, p. 59; cf. Suwa Haruo *Edo: sono geinō to bungaku* Tokyo: Mainichi Shimbunsha, 1976, pp. 187–93

33 Text is in NSBSS, Vol. 6, 1973. See Raz, *Audience and Actors*, for a summary of its contents.

34 Shikitei Samba's *Chaban kyōgen hayagatten*, Tokyo: Kokusho Kankōkai, [1915] 1824 gives one all the basics of this amateur art.

35 Saiza Sanjin *Jōruri keiko buri* [1980] 1777 in *Sharebon taisei*, Vol. 7, Tokyo: Chūō Kōronsha, gives us a picture of *gidayū* lessons in Edo given by a woman teacher. The book attests to the popularity of Jōruri puppet theatre in Edo which increased in the last 30 years of the eighteenth century.

36 Wakatsuki Yasuji *Ningyō jōrurishi no kenkyū*, Tokyo: Sakurai Shoten, 1943 outlines this development. See also Stanleigh Jones 'Miracle at Yaguchi Ferry: A Japanese Puppet Play and its Metamorphosis to Kabuki' in *Harvard Journal of Asiatic Studies*, Vol. xxxviii, June 1978.

37 Hayashi Reiko in 'Edo tana no seikatsu' (*Edo chōnin no kenkyū*, Vol. 2, Tokyo: Yoshikawa Kōbunkan, 1972, pp. 125–8) quotes from *Meikan roku*, the Shirokiya store record of crimes by employees, to show the popularity of *gidayū* lessons and Kabuki.
38 There are numerous sources for the eighteen grand-*tsū (daitsū)*, including *kibyōshi* and *sharebon* as well as non-fictional accounts. Their antics were extremely marketable products for book publishers. *Okuramae baka monogatari*, (or *Jūhachi daitsū*), [1928] 1846, by the popular dramatist and former *fudasashi* Mimasuya Nisōji (1784–1856), gives a history of these characters.
39 Kitahara Susumu 'Fudasashi to daitsūjin' in *Edo sanbyakunen* Vol. 2, Tokyo: Kodansha, 1975
40 Shikitei *Shibai kinmo zui*, p. 478. He is perhaps echoing Hiraga Gennai's *Nenashigusa*, p. 61: 'If you watch Kabuki with a moral heart, then it becomes teachings or admonitions . . .' He is also parodying a common style of exposition found in Buddhist sutras.

References

Abbreviations used in text and notes:
KGR *Kinsei geidō ron*
NZT *Nihon zuihitsu taisei*
NSBSS *Nihon shomin bunka shiryō shūsei*
Adachi Yoshio *Edo senryū to shomin monshō fūzoku* (Edo *senryū* and popular customs) Tokyo: Tōyōkan Shuppansha, 1973
Baba Bunkō *Tōdai Edo hyakkabutsu* (A hundred strange things in Edo), in *Nihon zuihitsu taisei* (Collection of Japanese essays) 2nd series, vol. 1, Tokyo: Nihon Zuihitsu Taisei Kankōkai, [1928] 1758
Brandon, James *Kabuki: Five Classic Plays* Cambridge, Ma.: Harvard, 1975
Chūko kejōsetsu (On theatre of the past) in *Enseki jisshu* (Enseki collection) Tokyo: Kokusho Kankōkai, [1907] 1805
Edo chōnin no kenkyū (Study of Edo townsmen) (4 vols) Nishiyama Matsunosuke, (ed.). Tokyo: Yoshikawa Kōbunkan, 1972
Edo sambyaku nen (Three hundred years of Edo) (3 vols) Nishiyama Matsunosuke et al. (eds) Tokyo: Kōdansha, 1975
Ema Tsutomu 'Kabukimono to fukusō no ryūkō' (Kabuki actors and fashion) in *Ema Tsutomu chosakushū* (Collected works of Ema Tsutomu) Vol. 3, Tokyo: Chūō Kōronsha, [1976] 1921
Gunji Masakatsu *Kabuki to Yoshiwara* (Kabuki and Yoshiwara) Tokyo: Awaji Shobō,1956
—— *Kabuki: yōshiki to denshō* (Kabuki: style and tradition) Tokyo: Kōdansha, 1969
—— *Jishibai to minzoku* (Country theatre and folk culture) Tokyo: Kōmeisha, 1971
Haifū yanagi daru (Collection of comic poems) (2 vols) in *Kinsei bungei sōsho, senryū* (Collection of literature—*senryū*). Tokyo: Kokusho Kankōkai, [1911] 1765

Hamada Giichirō *Shokusanjin* (Ōta Nanpo) Tokyo: Seigodō, 1942

Hattori Yukio *Kabuki no kōzō* (Structure of Kabuki) Tokyo: Chūō Kōron-sha, 1970

—— *Edo kabuki ron* (Study of Edo Kabuki) Tokyo: Hōsei Daigaku Shuppankyoku, 1980

Hayashi Reiko 'Edo tana no seikatsu' in *Edo chōnin no kenkyū* Tokyo: Yoshikawa Kōbunkan, 1972

Hino Tatsuo *Edojin to yūtopia* (Edoites and utopia) Tokyo: Asahi Shimbunsha, 1977

Hiraga Gennai *Nenashigusa* (Floating weeds) in *Fūraisanjinshū* (Collection of works of Fūraisanjin) (Nihon koten bungaku taikei series [Collection of classical Japanese literature], Vol. 55) Tokyo: Iwanami Shoten, [1961] 1763

—— *Inaka shibai* (Country theatre) in *Sharebon taisei* (Collection of sharebon) Vol. 13 Tokyo: Chūō Kōronsha, [1981] 1789?

Hōseidō Kisanji *Ukan sandai zue* (Edo's three theatres: illustrated) Hattori Yukio (ed.) Tokyo: Kokuritsu Gekijō, [1971] 1791

Ichikawa Danjūrō *Oi no tanoshimi shō* (The joys of old age) in *Kinsei geidō ron* (Collection of Edo-period art treatises) Tokyo: Iwanami Shoten, [1973] 1734–1747

Inoue Kinga *Byōkan chōgo* (A long tale told while sick) in *Onchi sōsho* (Collection of essays) Tokyo: Hakubunkan, [1891] 1763

Jones, Stanleigh 'Miracle at Yaguchi Ferry: A Japanese Puppet Play and its Metamorphosis to Kabuki' *Harvard Journal of Asiatic Studies* xxxviii : 1 June 1978

Kabuki hyōbanki shūsei (Collection of Kabuki critiques) (11 vols) Tokyo: Iwanami Shoten, 1972

Kabuki jishi (Origins of Kabuki) in *Nihon shomin bunka shiryō shūsei* (Collection of sources on Japanese popular culture) Vol. 6, Tokyo: San'ichi Shobō, [1973] 1762

Kabuki jūhachiban shū (Collection of 18 Kabuki favorites). Gunji Masakatsu (ed.) (Nihon koten bungaku taikei series [Collection of classical Japanese literature] No. 98) Tokyo: Iwanami Shoten, 1965

Kabuki nempyō (Chronology of Kabuki) (8 vols) Ihara Toshirō (ed.) Tokyo: Iwanami Shoten, 1956

Kinsei fūzoku jiten (Dictionary of Tokugawa-period customs) Ema Tsutomu et al. (eds) Tokyo: Jinbutsu Ōraisha, 1967

Kinsei geidō ron (Collection of Edo-period art treatises) Nishiyama Matsunosuke (ed.) Tokyo: Iwanami Shoten, 1972

Kishida Tohō *Kyōgen-zuki yabo daimyō* (The boorish daimyo in love with Kabuki) in *Kibyōshi nijūshū* (Collection of twenty *kibyōshi*) Tokyo: Nihon Meicho Zenshū Kankōkai, [1926] 1784

Kitahara Susumu 'Fudasashi to daitsūjin' (Fudasashi and great-*tsū*) in *Edo sambyakunen* (Three hundred years of Edo) Vol. 2 Tokyo: Kōdansha, 1975

Koikawa Harumachi *Sanpuku tsui murasaki Soga* (The Soga brothers and Edo Kabuki) in *Kibyōshi hyakushū* (One hundred *kibyōshi*) Tokyo: Hakubunkan, [1901] 1778

Koike Shōtarō 'Daimyō nikki ga egaku aru Edo joyū' (An Edo actress as portrayed in a daimyo's diary) *Rekishi to jimbutsu* (History and individuals) Vol. 10, No. 11, pp. 214–18, 1980

Kokon yakusha rongo sakigake (Advanced actors' analects from the past and present) in *Kinsei geidō ron* (Collection of Edo-period art treatises) Nishiyama Matsunosuke (ed.) Tokyo: Iwanami Shoten, [1972] 1772

Mimasuya Nisōji *Okuramae baka monagatari* (Tale of Kuramae fools) in *Nihon zuihitsu taisei* (Collection of Japanese essays) 2nd series, Vol. 6, Tokyo: Nihon Zuihitsu Taisei Kankōkai, [1928] 1846

Minami Kazuo *Edokko no sekai* (World of Edoites) Tokyo: Kōdansha, 1980

Mizuno Minoru *Edo shōsetsu ronsō* (Essays on Edo fiction) Tokyo: Chūō Kōronsha, 1974

Mori Senzō *Kibyōshi kaidai* (Guide to *kibyōshi*) Tokyo: Chūō Kōronsha, 1972

Moriyama Takamori *Ama no yakimo ki* (Tale of fishermen burning seaweed) in *Nihon zuihitsu taisei* (Collection of Japanese essays) 2nd series, Vol. 11, Tokyo: Nihon Zuihitsu Taisei Kankōkai, [1929] 1798

—— *Shizu no odamaki* (Humble mutterings) in *Nihon zuihitsu taisei* (Collection of Japanese essays) 3rd series, Vol. 2, Tokyo: Nihon Zuihitsu Taisei Kankōkai, [1929] 1802

Nihon shomin bunka shiryō shūsei (Collection of sources on Japanese popular culture) Vol. 6, *Kabuki*, Tokyo: San'ichi Shobō, 1973

Nishihara Ryūu *Senryū Edo kabuki* (Edo Kabuki and *senryū*) Tokyo: Shun'yōdō, 1925

Ōta Nampo *Hannichi kanwa* (Idle chatter) in *Nihon zuihitsu taisei* (Collection of Japanese essays) first series, Vol. 4, Tokyo: Nihon Zuihitsu Taisei Kankōkai, [1927]

Raz, Jacob 'The Audience Evaluated: Shikitei Samba's *Kyakusha hyōbanki*', *Monumenta Nipponica* Vol. 35 (Summer), 1980

—— *Audience and Actors* Leiden: E. J. Brill, 1983

Saiza Sanjin *Jōruri keiko buri* (Jōruri lessons) in *Sharebon taisei* (Collection of *sharebon)* Vol. 7, Tokyo: Chūō Kōronsha, [1980] 1777

Sakusha shihō kezairoku (Treasury of rules for playwrights) in *Kinsei geidō ron* (Collection of Edo-period art treatises) Nishiyama Matsunosuke (ed.) Tokyo: Iwanami Shoten, [1972] 1801

Santō Kyōden *Edo umare uwaki no kabayaki* (Broiled eel, Edo born dandy) in *Kibyōshi sharebon shū* (Collection of *kibyōshi* and *sharebon*) (Nihon koten bungaku taikei series [Collection of classical Japanese literature], Vol. 59) Tokyo: Iwanami Shoten, [1958] 1785

Santō Kyōzañ *Kumo no ito maki* (The spider's web) in *Nihon zuihitsu taisei* (Collection of Japanese essays) 2nd series, Vol. 4, Tokyo: Nihon Zuihitsu Taisei Kankōkai, [1928] 1806

Seji kenmon roku (Record of current happenings) in *Nihon shomin seikatsu shiryō shūsei* (Collection of sources on Japanese life) Vol. 8, Tokyo: San'ichi Shobō, [1969] 1816

Shikitei Samba *Shibai kinmo zui* (Illustrated guide to the theatre) Tokyo: Kokuritsu Gekijō, [1969] 1803

—— *Kejō suigen maku no soto* (Theatre on the other side of the curtain) in

Nihon shomin bunka shiryō shūsei (Collection of sources on Japanese popular culture) Vol. 6, Tokyo: San'ichi Shobō, [1973] 1806
—— *Ukiyoburo* (Bath in a floating world) (Nihon koten bungaku taikei series [Collection of classical Japanese literature] No. 63) Tokyo: Iwanami Shoten, [1957] 1809
—— *Kakusha hyōbanki* (A critique of audiences) in *Nihon shomin bunka shiryō shūsei* (Collection of sources on Japanese popular culture) Vol. 6, Tokyo: San'ichi Shobō, [1973] 1811
—— *Kyōgen inaka ayatsuri* (Country puppet theatre) in *Kibyōshi hyakushū* (One hundred *kibyōshi*) Tokyo: Hakubunkan, [1901] 1811
—— *Shiroto kyōgen monkirigata* (Amateur theatre types) in *Kibyōshi hyakushū* (One hundred *kibyōshi*) Tokyo: Hakubunkan, [1901] 1814
—— *Chaban kyōgen hayagatten* (All about *chaban* skits) in *Zatsugei sōsho* (Sources on miscellaneous arts) Tokyo: Kokusho Kankōkai, [1915] 1824
Shively, Donald 'Bakufu versus Kabuki', *Harvard Journal of Asiatic Studies*, Vol. 18 (Dec.) 1955; also reprinted in Hall and Jansen (eds) *Studies in the Institutional History of Early Modern Japan*, Princeton: Princeton University Press 1968
—— 'The Social Environment of Tokugawa Kabuki' in Brandon, Malm and Shively *Studies in Kabuki* Honolulu: University of Hawaii, 1978
—— 'Tokugawa Plays on Forbidden Topics' in *Chūshingura: Studies in Kabuki and the Puppet Theatre* J. R. Brandon (ed.) Honolulu: University of Hawaii Press, 1982
Shōkadō Hajō *Shibai nenjū gyōji* (The theatre year calendar) in *Kyōgen sakusha shiryōshū* 1 (Sources on Kabuki playwrights) Tokyo: Kokuritsu Gekijō, [1974] 1771
Suwa Haruo *Edo: sono geinō to bungaku* (Edo: its theatre and literature) Tokyo: Mainichi Shimbunsha, 1976
—— *Edokko no bigaku* (Aesthetics of *edokko*) Tokyo: Nihon Shoseki, 1980
Terakadō Seiken *Edo hanjōki* (Splendors of Edo) (3 vols) Tokyo: Tōyō Bunko, [1974] 1832
Thornbury, Barbara *Sukeroku's Double Identity: A Study in Kabuki Dramatic Structure* (Michigan Papers in Japanese Studies, No. 6) Ann Arbor: University of Michigan, 1982
Wakatsuki Yasuji *Ningyō jōrurishi no kenkyū* (A history of Jōruri puppet theatre) Tokyo: Sakurai Shoten, 1943
Watanabe Shōkō *Fudō Myōō* Tokyo: Asahi Shimbunsha, 1975
Yakusha zensho (All about actors) in *Nihon shomin bunka shiryō shūsei* (Collection of sources on Japanese popular culture) Vol. 6 Tokyo: San'ichi Shobō, [1973] 1774
Yanagizawa Nobutoki *Enyū nikki* (A banquet diary) in *Nihon shomin bunka shiryō shūsei* (A collection of sources on Japanese popular culture) Vol. 13 Tokyo: San'ichi Shobō, 1977
—— *Shōkaku nikki* (Shōkaku diary) (7 vols) Tokyo: Yumani Shobō, 1981
Zashiki-kyōgen hayagatten (The basic book of home Kabuki) *Zatsugei sōsho* (Sources on miscellaneous arts) Tokyo: Kokusho Kankōkai, [1915] 1774
Zuihitsu jiten (Guide to Japanese essays) (5 vols) Shibata Shōkyoku, et al. (eds) Tokyo: Tōkyōdō, 1960

3

Edo Jōruri

Torigoe Bunzō

Edo Jōruri is of three kinds: Old Jōruri, popular at the beginning of the Tokugawa era; *gidayū-bushi* (Bunraku), composed by Edo playwrights after 1772; and Jōruri in the Bungo-bushi tradition, comprised primarily of Kabuki stage music. All three will be described in this chapter, but first let us consider the history of the term.

The origins of Jōruri

Edo-period works on Jōruri all record the name of the writer Ono Ozū. The following account of the origin of Jōruri is summarised from *Naniwa miyage* (Souvenir of Naniwa).[1]

In the service of the wife of Toyotomi Hideyoshi there was a highly talented lady-in-waiting whose name was Ono Ozū. She wrote *Jōruri hime monogatari* in response to her mistress's suggestion that she should emulate women of the past like Sei Shōnagon and Murasaki Shikibu who had attained undying fame through their literary achievements.

The work may be described as a love story of the young heroine, Princess Jōruri and the youthful Minamoto no Yoshitsune (Japan's most popular historical figure).

The 'Tale of Princess Jōruri' was disseminated by the *biwa-hōshi*, wandering monks who chanted *The Tales of the Heike* (*heikyoku*), to the accompaniment of the lute, and the story seems to have achieved great popularity in a short time. With its rise in popularity the rather long title, *Jōruri hime monogatari* was shortened to simply *Jōruri* and it became associated with the spread of a new style of singing to

Figure 3.1   An historical outline of Japanese music

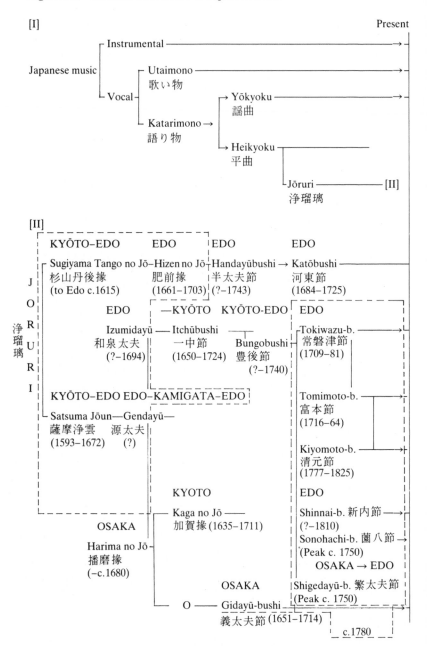

musical accompaniment which differed somewhat from the older conventional *heikyoku*.

After this, even when new works differing in content were performed, all came to be categorised as 'Jōruri'. As time went by, the content of Jōruri became rich and varied. With the introduction of the shamisen there was considerable development of the musical element, but there was never any deviation from its original character as the telling of a story (*katarimono*). In this respect it can be clearly differentiated from songs (*utaimono*), the main purpose of which was to convey a melody. In Japanese music, vocal pieces are more highly developed than instrumental works, and within the broad genre of vocal music *katarimono* (chanted narrative) is more highly developed than *utaimono* (melodic songs). In this respect Japanese music seems to have developed along different lines from its European counterparts.

After 1750 it became clear that the derivation given in *Naniwa miyage* was incorrect. Ryūtei Tanehiko (1783–1842), the novelist and scholar, discovered a reference to Jōruri dated 1531 in the diary of the *renga* poet Sōchō (1447–1532). So long before Ono Ozū could possibly have described it, there was already a type of *katarimono* known as Jōruri. Moreover, it was sufficiently widely known to be referred to simply as Jōruri and not as *Jōruri hime monogatari*. The dates of Ozū's birth and death are not certain. One view has it that she was 68 years old in 1616 and another claims she died in 1631 at the age of 64. At any rate, she was born after Sōchō's death.

Suffice it to say that Jōruri was clearly popular at the beginning of the Edo period. Two major reasons for this were probably the introduction of the shamisen from the Ryūkyūs and its use for Jōruri accompaniment, and the fact that Jōruri came to be a stage art affiliated with the puppet theatre. The history of puppets themselves can be traced back to before the eighth century, but even by the early 1600s the puppet theatre was a far cry from the Bunraku we know today. The puppets were rather small and their movements clumsy, so there is no doubt that it was primarily the chanting of the Jōruri which made the form so popular.

Old Jōruri

Among the works representative of the early 1600s are those known as Kinpira Jōruri. Jōruri first began to become popular as stage music to shamisen accompaniment in Kyoto, but when the Tokugawa family made Edo the centre of government in 1603 its population increased rapidly. It took more than twenty years for it to develop into a city with sophisticated entertainment facilities, including a theatre for puppet performances. Naturally the first performances were given by entertainers who had made the journey from Kyoto, but as the local pupils of masters who had settled in Edo increased, local Jōruri began to differ from that of Kyoto, with a content more befitting the temperament of the newly emerged city dominated by the warrior class. The Jōruri which became popular in Edo at the beginning of the Tokugawa era became known as Edo Jōruri. Before examining it more closely, however, it is necessary to say a little about Kinpira Jōruri.

The much-loved figure of Kintarō is prominent among the dolls displayed at the boys' festival, celebrated on May 5 in the desire that boys should grow up to be healthy and strong. Kintarō was so strong that as a child he amused himself by wrestling with bears or riding them around like horses. This legendary youth grew up to be known as Sakata Kintoki who, as one of the most trusted generals of Mina-moto Raikō, distinguished himself in countless deeds of military valour. Kintoki's son was Kinpira, portrayed as an even more heroic warrior than his father. A very popular Edo Jōruri play dealt with how a revolt against the Minamoto family had been put down through the military prowess of Kinpira. Jōruri with Kinpira in the role of hero are known as Kinpira Jōruri. A famous chanter, Izumi-dayū, specialised in this type of Jōruri. He was reputed to have been an extremely powerful man who brandished an iron bar two feet long as he chanted. On one occasion, the story goes, when he was flailing around with this iron bar during a performance, he staved in the head of one of the puppets.

Kinpira Jōruri, celebrating the prosperity of the Minamoto family, was at the same time an invocation for the prosperity of the Tokuga-wa house, which traced its descent from the Minamoto. Those en-couraged to settle in Edo by the policies of the Tokugawa Shogunate naturally desired the peace and prosperity of the city. Consequently, Kinpira Jōruri became very popular there.

Edo Jōruri is a general term for the style performed at the begin-ning of the Tokugawa era—a Jōruri portraying the exploits of super-men, so dear to the hearts of Edoites, of which Kinpira Jōruri is a prime example.

Gidayū-bushi (Bunraku) 1772–88

The outstandingly talented Jōruri chanter Takemoto Gidayū was born in Osaka and received his training in Kyoto. He opened a permanent puppet theatre in Osaka in 1684. Most scholars agree that this year marks the transition between 'old' and 'new' Jōruri. All Jōruri performed since the appearance of the *gidayū-bushi* of Takemoto Gidayū is known as *Tōryū* (New) Jōruri, while the various forms previously performed by numerous chanters are collectively known as Old Jōruri. In the Old Jōruri period, probably because the appeal of the music had priority over that of the narrative content, the various styles of Jōruri came to be known by the names of individuals, so that the Jōruri performed by *tayū* (chanter) *A* was known as *A-bushi*, that of *tayū B* as *B-bushi* and so on. However, after Gidayū, although his disciples took various names of their own, they came to be known merely as chanter A or chanter B of *gidayū-bushi*.

The puppet theatre, which continues even today to be practised as traditional theatre, generally known as Bunraku, has developed around the Jōruri of the *gidayū-bushi*. Incidentally, the name Takemoto Gidayū was used only by the founder (1651–1714) and his pupil Takemoto Gidayū (1691–1744),[2] after which it fell out of use because nobody had sufficient ability to carry on this illustrious name. Even so, in roughly 250 years of Jōruri, most chanters noted for their superb performances have added their names to the roll of honour of *gidayū-bushi*.

From its start in Osaka, *gidayū-bushi* spread into Kyoto and Edo, monopolising the musical side of the puppet theatre. Or to put it another way, the mainstream of puppet theatre switched to *gidayū-bushi* Jōruri.

The three great cities of the Tokugawa era—Kyoto, Edo and Osaka—all had flourishing entertainment districts, in which Jōruri had to compete with Kabuki. Even Chikamatsu Monzaemon, as quoted in *Naniwa miyage*, describes 'how to compete with the talents of live actors, particularly those of the Kabuki stage', giving us an idea of the prodigious efforts made by Jōruri playwrights, *tayū* and puppeteers to compete with the flamboyant spectacle and brilliant actors of the Kabuki theatre. In time these efforts paid off and the Jōruri puppet theatre came to enjoy a period of prosperity which led one commentator to remark, 'the puppet theatre has gradually become so popular that Kabuki seems hardly to exist'. This comes from an entry for 1747 in *Jōruri-fu*, a guidebook published in Osaka around 1801. Some historians of drama claim that only Japan had a puppet theatre more popular than performances by live actors, and which became the dominant theatrical form throughout the nation. *Jōruri-fu* only describes the situation in Osaka, but can be taken to illustrate an important episode in the history of performing arts in Japan.

This extraordinary popularity of puppet (*ningyō*) Jōruri was at its peak for several years around 1747. Some years later, entries in this same *Jōruri-fu* often record 'poorly attended' (*fuiri*) or 'extremely poor attendance' (*hanahada fuiri*); the form had started on a downhill slope towards decline. Finally the Takemoto-za, established by Takemoto as a specialist theatre for the performance of puppet plays to Jōruri narration, closed in 1767. It was no longer profitable to run throughout the whole year with puppet plays alone. Even so, the puppet theatre did not perish entirely. It continued with performers going from one theatre to another in various parts of Osaka. Frequent tours were also made to the provinces. Puppet theatre thus spread throughout the country and its audience broadened. Especially in Edo, there was a great increase in performances by *tayū* from the Takemoto-za, who had hitherto rarely visited the city.

In the Meiwa period (1764–1771), Edo was in name and reality the capital of Japan. Some 160 years after the establishment of the Tokugawa Bakufu, Edo was the centre of both government and culture. Its popular culture came to extend over the whole country, unlike the culture of the imperial court which had for so long been confined to Kyoto. The happy-go-lucky 'Edokko', born and bred in the city, became renowned, and indeed it is said that this term was first used during these years.

Until the demise of the Takemoto-za in 1767, the Jōruri of Osaka was often performed in Edo. This is not to say that Edo had no *gidayū-jōruri* of its own, but the vast majority of works had their first performances in Osaka. Inevitably, these works bore the mark of Kamigata (Kyoto–Osaka) culture. It is not until the 1770s that Osaka-style Jōruri was frequently written by Edo writers and first performed in that city. The impetus for this was provided by Jiroemon, head of the southern branch of the Mitsui family. His business interests required him to spend alternate years at the main shop in Kyoto and the branch shop in Edo. When resident in Edo, he provided financial support to encourage local writers to write Jōruri for first performances in Edo. Mitsui Jiroemon was himself such a lover of Jōruri that he wrote some pieces under the pen name of Ki no Jōtarō. Among those he encouraged were Fukuuchi Kigai (the noted intellectual, better known as Fūrai Sanjin or Hiraga Gennai) and Utei Enba, originally a master carpenter by trade, a close friend of the Kabuki actor Danjūrō V and author of *Kabuki nendaiki* (1811). More than a dozen others wrote under his patronage. In contrast to the earlier Osaka Jōruri, these authors set their pieces in Edo, either within the walls of the castle—for example, *Kagamiyama kokyō no nishikie* (1782)—or in its environs as in *Shinrei yaguchi no watashi* (1770), and they used Edo language: Utei Enba, in writing *Go Taiheiki shiroishi-banashi* (1780), the story of two sisters from Shiroishi in Okushū province (present-day Miyagi prefecture) who meet by chance in the Yoshiwara district of Edo, is reputed to have gone all the way to the Shiroishi area to hear the local dialect. Characters from the Tōhoku area had often appeared in Jōruri plays, but hitherto they had been made to speak in the Osaka dialect. The use of the Tōhoku dialect was a distinctive feature of Edo Jōruri. This reflects the different spheres of cultural and regional influence exerted by Edo and Osaka. While many of those who moved to Edo were from the Tōhoku area, virtually no northerners were employed in the Kamigata area. The death of Mitsui Jirōemon in 1799 deprived the Jōruri writers of their patron, and literary activity slowed. As a result in Edo, as in Osaka, older Jōruri plays were revived. This was the first step towards Jōruri becoming a classical art form. In some 30 years up to 1799, about 50 Jōruri plays are known to have been scripted by Edo playwrights. These are known as Edo Jōruri.

Edo Jōruri, as it is now styled, coincided with a strong trend towards rewriting Kabuki plays as Jōruri pieces: as mentioned above, Kabuki and Jōruri remained in hot competition throughout the Edo period. Although both theatrical forms had a strong following, they differed greatly in character. Put simply, Kabuki was for the eyes, Jōruri for the ears. However, they exerted a mutual influence on each other. As usually happens, the form which currently enjoyed more popularity had the greater sway. In the period of peak popularity around 1747, Jōruri plays were performed as Kabuki. Once it ceased to be vibrant contemporary theatre and became part of the classical tradition, Jōruri's influence waned. Although Edo Jōruri may seem nothing more than a fleeting blossom, it becomes very significant indeed if we also consider Kabuki. Edo Jōruri could no longer resist the temptation to adapt Kabuki plots and was finally overwhelmed by the flamboyant spectacle of the Kabuki theatre.

Edo Jōruri as Kabuki stage music

The third use of the term Edo Jōruri refers to the music of the Kabuki theatre. By 1700, when Takemoto Gidayū's style heralded the era of 'new' Jōruri and became the musical accompaniment for the puppet theatre, *handayū-bushi* was the form popular in Edo. It was performed in Edo puppet plays and in the Kabuki theatre, which also staged a variety of musical performances. It was popular, too, as *zashiki-jōruri*, private performances in the houses of the well-to-do, in which the prime interest was the voice of the chanter and the shamisen accompaniment. Katō-bushi is descended from this school. On the other hand, in Kyoto there was Miyako Itchū, who performed Jōruri known as *itchū-bushi*. Being a form of vocal music, Jōruri did not necessarily have to be performed in a theatre to attract an audience or win devotees. Among Itchū's pupils was one Bungo no Jō who chanted Jōruri called *bungo-bushi*, a form which became immensely popular in Edo. This was no doubt largely due to the Edo liking for *zashiki-jōruri* of the *katō-bushi* type. Departing from the accepted convention that only the daughters of merchants practised music, even women of samurai families were attracted to *bungo-bushi* and many became ardent students of the art.

Moreover, as most Jōruri chanted to *bungo-bushi* dealt with love affairs and double suicides, it seems that while rehearsing *bungo-bushi* many of its adherents were overcome by similar emotions leading, we are told, to frequent cases of imitation. Consequently *bungo-bushi* was banned and Bungo no Jō was driven out of Edo. His pupils continued, altering the content of their Jōruri slightly and by claiming adherence to new schools such as the *tokiwazu-bushi* and *shinnai-bushi*. *Tokiwazu-bushi*, in particular, came to enjoy even greater popularity when it advanced into the theatre as musical accompaniment for Kabuki dance. Some chanters even broke away from the *tokiwazu-bushi* style to establish separate schools of their own, such as the *tomimoto-bushi* or the *kiyomoto-bushi*.

The various forms which originated and flourished in Edo in the 1700s are known as Edo Jōruri in the third sense of the term. Sometimes Edo Jōruri is taken to include *miyazono-bushi* (or *sonohachi-bushi*) and *shigedayū-bushi* which, although originating in Kyoto, are in the *itchūbushi–bungobushi* tradition. These forms fall outside our strict definition of Edo Jōruri, but resemble these examples of the genre in being basically *zashiki-jōruri* or *uta-jōruri* (also known as 'hors d'oeuvres jōruri' or *sakana-jōruri*, as they provided entertainment at drinking parties). Edo Jōruri in the sense of Jōruri created in Edo, particulary *tokiwazu-bushi*, *tomimoto-bushi* and *kiyomoto-bushi*, known collectively as the *bungo sanryū* (three schools of Bungo) became theatre music for Kabuki actors and hence was quite different from the other forms of Edo Jōruri. Composed as Kabuki dance music, it frequently dealt with affairs of the heart. The *bungo jōruri* tradition had from the outset concentrated on love and double suicide, so it was inevitable that the text and music would become romantic or sentimental.

We have seen how the term Edo Jōruri may be interpreted in three ways. In the first stage, Edo Jōruri dealt with paragons of courage and manly vigour, whereas in the third stage the situation underwent a complete reversal to become the romantic depiction of tender dramas of the heart. Between these two, lies the *gidayū-bushi*, the second stage of Edo Jōruri. Although this form at first concentrated on tragic suffering in human life, it developed at a time when the romantic 'Edo Jōruri' was popular and was inevitably influenced to some extend by the sentimentality of this genre.

Changes in the popularity of the various types of Jōruri give a clear indication of how tastes changed in Edo from its early days as a samurai city, as more power progressively came into the hands of the townsman class.

(Translated by H. B. D. Clarke)

Notes

1 Written by Hozumi Koretsura. Published 1738. *Naniwa Miyage* ([Souvenir of Naniwa], ed. Ueda Kazutoshi, Tokyo: Yūhōkan, 1904). At the beginning of this work mention is made of the aesthetic theory that 'truth and falsehood are thinly separated' put forward by Japan's foremost playwright Chikamatsu Monzaemon.

2 After the first Gidayū took the name Chikugo no Jō, there is a plaque bearing the name Segare Gidayū (Gidayū the son), but I have decided not to include this in the lineage of Gidayū. See *Gidayū nenpyō—Kinsei hen*, Vol. 1, p. 21.

PART II

EDO LANGUAGE

4

The development of Edo language

H. B. D. Clarke

Eighteenth-century Edo language exhibits the extraordinary variety we find in many other aspects of culture and society. Its story is one of contrasts and minute diversification—contrasts between Kansai (Kyoto/Osaka) and Edo, spoken and written language, and between writing in the native style (*wabun*) and writing in Chinese (*kanbun*), coupled with a greater degree of diversification according to region, social class, occupation and sex than is to be found in any other period in Japan's history.

It was not until about 150 years after Tokugawa Ieyasu had established his castle in a small village in Toshima-gun, Musashi province, that a separate Edo language emerged. From about the mid-eighteenth century there is an enormous growth in literature and popular writing in the Edo dialect. The Edo *sharebon* (books of the pleasure quarter), began to appear in the Hōreki period (1751–63). These were followed in the Meiwa (1764–71) and An'ei (1772–80) periods by *senryū* (humorous verse in the *haikai* format) and *kibyōshi* ('yellow covers'), the literary comic-book which was a unique Edo contribution to Tokugawa literature. These are in turn followed by the *yomihon* (story books), *kokkeibon* (comic fiction) and *kusazōshi* (illustrated popular novels) of the Bunka–Bunsei periods (1804–29) and the *ninjōbon* (love stories) which appear from around the 1820s. In addition there was a rich profusion of Kabuki and popular songs such as Edo *nagauta*, all containing Edo colloquial language.

The 1750s, then, mark the emergence of the language of Edo as a literary and political medium, for the first time beginning to rival the language of the Kansai area as a *lingua franca* for the entire country. This period heralds the birth of a separate Edo consciousness and a confidence in the worth of the Edo idiom. The fact that it took 150 years to achieve this position was due mainly to the immigrant nature of the Edo metropolis. From the time Tokugawa Ieyasu established himself in the castle until 1700, Edo's population reached one million. Tokugawa family retainers from Mikawa, Owari and Suruga congregated in Edo in large numbers and these were followed by merchants, mainly from the cities of Kyoto, Osaka, Fushimi and Sakai. Other inhabitants of the castle town included some from villages along the Tōkaidō and a small number of craftsmen from the north, but the vast majority of immigrants were from Kantō area provinces adjacent to Edo like Musashi, Sagami, Shimōsa and Kazusa. With the adoption of the *sankin kōtai* (alternate attendance) system in 1636, daimyo from all over the country came to Edo with large retinues of retainers and servants, setting up permanent quarters and bringing with them a diversity of regional dialects. It is probably safe to assume that in this early period a great variety of dialects were used in Edo, with the Mikawa, Owari and Suruga dialects being well represented among the samurai, the Kansai dialect being used by the merchants, and the Kantō dialect being dominant among the artisans, labourers and peasants. The influence of the Kansai and Kantō persists until after the Meiji Restoration, but little trace of the dialects of Mikawa, Owari and Suruga can be discerned in the language of eighteenth-century Edo. The Suruga dialect, in particular, shares many features with Kantō; perhaps elements, such as *-ro* imperatives (*miro* 'look!') and *-nai* negatives (*minai* '(I) don't look') which the two dialects had in common, were least likely to be influenced by Kansai speech. Conversely, the tenacity of negative forms like *-nu*, *-nanda* and *-neba*, existing in the Edo dialect alongside the usual Kantō forms, may perhaps be explained, as is pointed out below, by the widespread distribution of these forms in central Japan. This is particularly true of the pitch accent. Intonation and contrastive pitch contours are extremely resistant to outside influence and this is one area in which the Kansai dialect has exercised no influence on Edo speech. Owari, Mikawa, Suruga and Edo have *HAshi* 'chopsticks' and *haSHI* 'bridge' contrasting with Kansai *haSHI* 'chopsticks' and *HAshi* 'bridge'. It seems likely that the samurai had quickly abandoned their local dialects. In their efforts to acquire a veneer of culture and sophistication they tried to imitate the language of the court aristocracy of Kyoto, but never managed to lose the pitch patterns of their native dialects. In the 1600s Kansai language must have been used in Edo as a *lingua franca* in communication between speakers of widely differing regional dialects.

Although there is little source material for the formative stages of the Edo dialect itself, we have a good description of the characteristic features of the Kantō dialects from the Portuguese missionary–interpreter João Rodriguez, whose grammar *Arte da Lingoa de Iapam* came off the Jesuit press in Nagasaki from 1604–08. It is clear from Rodriguez that by the end of the 1550s the Kantō dialects were already beginning to influence the language of Kyoto and that the Japanese language was undergoing major changes in phonology and grammar. Rodriguez's account of Japanese is particularly important because it is written in a romanised transcription, based not on the historical *kana* spelling, but on the contemporary pronunciation.

Rodriguez states that the Kantō dialects had a word-initial 'h-' in contrast to 'f-' in Kyoto and that the contrast between voiced fricatives and affricates, the so-called 'four-kana distinction' between *zu*, *zi* and *dzu*, *dji* (as in *midzu* 'water', *suzu* 'bell' and *fujisan* 'Mt. Fuji', *fudji no hana* 'wisteria blossom') had been lost. By 1700 these changes had also reached the Kansai area. He mentions the Kantō preference for geminate consonants, particularly in the past-tense forms like *satta* 'left' and *waratta* 'laughed'; the negative suffix *-nai*, the *-ro* imperative and the clause-final particle *kara*, all of which continue to set the eastern dialects apart from those of western Japan. So by 1600 it seems that the eastern characteristics were already established in virtually the same form as in the dialect of Edo townsmen portrayed in early nineteenth century comic *kokkeibon* such as Shikitei Sanba's *Ukiyoburo* (Bath-house of the floating world) and *Ukiyodoko* (Barber in a floating world). In fact, it may safely be said that Edo speech had come to be an amalgamation of Kantō and Kansai elements, the former strong in the speech of the townsman class, and the latter being most evident among the samurai.

While not yet strictly part of the Edo dialect proper, certain expressions from the Kantō dialect began to be used for special effect in Edo Kabuki after 1625. This was the language known as *yakko kotoba* or *roppō kotoba*, which was originally a slang used by ruffian gangs, made up mainly of *rōnin* and other unemployed youth who congregated in the downtown area of Edo (*machi-yakko*) or in the Yamanote (*hatamoto-yakko* or *Yamanote-yakko*). The *machi-yakko* and the *hatamoto-yakko* language combined the vulgarity of the eastern dialects and the irreverence towards authority and Confucian morality with a fresh vitality and flamboyance that appealed to theatre-goers. Actors assuming the dress and manners of *machi-yakko* and *hatamoto-yakko* began to appear in the 1620s and remained until the end of the century. The *aragoto* (rough-style acting) and the *akutai* (abusive language) so successfully employed by the Ichikawa Danjūrō family owed much to the brash clipped language of Kantō and it is probably this use of the Edo dialect by bravado actors in Kabuki that accounts for the view universally held in Japan that the

Edo dialect is crisp, strong and masculine and the Kyoto dialect is languid, soft and feminine. Some characteristics of *yakko-kotoba* were the dropping of syllables, for example, *nada* (for *namida* 'tear'), the introduction of pre-nasalised consonants as in. . .*konda* for . . .*koto da* 'it is a fact that. . .', the use of the emphatic prefix *but*-from *butsu* 'to hit', as in *bukkobosu* (for *kobosu* 'to spill, tip out') and *bukkakeru* (for *kakeru* 'to put on, to hang') and the typically Kantō suffix indicating conjecture or intention -*bee* as in *ikubee* 'let's go'. In the Kanbun period (1661–72), certain courtesans in Yoshiwara began to imitate *yakko-kotoba* and their speech was known as *Yoshiwara kotoba*. This style of language was also used in the *yakko haikai* which was popular around 1650.

In the seventeenth century, however, when the Kantō idiom found its way into drama and fiction, it aimed for special effect: to surprise or shock the audience with vulgar, expressive language. Most popular writing and much of the drama of seventeenth-century Edo still followed the Kansai models of language. The spoken language of the lower classes was probably pure Kantō dialect, but without the connotations of modernity, sophistication and *savoir-faire* that the Edo dialect was to assume by 1800.

It is with the *sharebon* and *kibyōshi* of the 1750s, 1760s and 1770s that the Edo language *per se* becomes a major element in popular fiction. Since colloquial writing was in its infancy, much remains of the traditional plots and language of the Kyoto-Osaka area. One of the first *sharebon* to use Edo dialect is *Isorokuchō* (1757). It uses the eastern copula *da*, but still retains most features of Kansai in phonology and grammar. *Kakuchū kitan* (Strange tales of the pleasure quarter, 1769) has the copula *da*, the imperative suffix -*ro* (as in Edo *shiro* contrasting with Kansai *seyo* 'do!'), the negative -*nai* and the conjectural suffix -*yoo*, geminate consonants in past-tense forms like *katta* 'bought' contrasting with Kansai *koota*, adverbial forms of adjectives in -*ku* (as in *yoku* compared with Kansai *yoo*), but retains some Kansai influence in past tense forms like *yuuta* 'said' and *waroota* 'laughed'. How far such retention reflects the contemporary spoken language of Edo and how far it is a product of literary convention is hard to say.

In *Yūshi hōgen* (The playboy's dialect) of 1770, the Edo features become even more prominent. There was, however, a degree of overlap in the use of Edo and Kansai forms and in some cases both forms were acceptable until well into the nineteenth century. For example, in the speech of the *tōrimono*, or self-styled connoisseur, both the negative suffixes -*nu* and -*nai* are used. The past-tense negative form is -*nanda*, for example, *ora ikananda* 'I didn't go'. In fact, the use of the Kansai forms -*nu*/-*nanda* and -*neba* where the Kantō dialect has -*nai*, -*nakatta* and -*nakereba* was common in Edo until this century. This phenomenon of two negative suffixes being used side by side may have something to do with the fact that in the Chūbu area (Mikawa, Owari and Tōtomi), the -*nu*/-*nanda* forms are the most widely used negatives. The Chūbu dialects are close to the eastern dialects in phonology, but to the western in grammar. Another example of this free variation between Kansai and Kantō dialect forms in the *Yūshi hōgen* is with the copula forms *ja* and *da*, as in the dialogue between the self-styled expert and the callow youth who is being introduced to the delights of the pleasure quarter:

Youth: *Hon ni okashi na nioi de gozarimasu.* (What a very odd smell.)

Expert: *Korya shibito o yaku nioi da.* (That's dead bodies being burnt.)

Ja ga dote de kageba, shibito no nioi mo ee mono ja nai ka. (But here on the bank overlooking Yoshiwara even the smell of dead bodies is wonderful, isn't it!)

There are other inconsistencies, such as the variation between *yutta* and *yuuta* 'said' and there are some old expressions such as *ni yotte* used to express reason, as in *yoi hiyori ja ni yotte* ('since the weather is fine') occurring alongside the more typically Edo form *da kara* as in *anmari shitta tokoro ga takusan da kara* ('it's because I know so many places'). The adverbial forms of adjectives often take the Kansai form where the -*k*- of the suffix is dropped and the resulting vowel sequence shifts to a long vowel, for example, *yoku* becomes *yoo* as in *yoo o-ide nasaremashita* ('I'm glad you were able to come').

The author of *Yūshi hōgen*, who writes under the name of Inakarō-jin Tadanojiji, was, some say, the Osaka bookseller Tanbaya Rihei, but the fluctuation between Kansai and Kantō forms in this *sharebon* is the same as can be found in most of the others.

While the rough masculine language of the *machi-yakko* and *hatamoto-yakko* played an important part in the formation of the Edo vernacular, women's speech has exercised an even greater influence, the results of which can still be seen in the standard language today. The role played by mothers in the language acquisition of children makes it likely that linguistic innovations by women will find their way into men's language. Two groups of women at opposite ends of the social scale were particularly influential: women serving at court or in the households of the aristocracy and highest military families, whose speech was called *nyōbō-kotoba*; and women of the pleasure quarter, whose language was termed either *kuruwa-kotoba* or *yūri-kotoba*.

Nyōbō-kotoba developed in the 1400s as a kind of jargon used to avoid direct mention of certain words connected mainly with food and clothing. This can probably be associated with a general taboo against pollution derived from bodily functions.

The *Ama no mokuzu* (The fisherfolk's scraps of seaweed, 1420) lists about 120 words. Most are euphemisms with the polite prefix *o-* or combinations of the first syllable of a word and *-moji*, 'letter' or 'character'; for example, *sushi* becomes *sumoji*, the letter 's'. These words gradually came to be taken as elegant alternatives for words in general use, and *nyōbō-kotoba* spread into the speech of women serving in samurai households and to upper-class merchant women. *Onna chōhōki* (The women's treasure trove, 1696) recommends that women use *nyōbō-kotoba* as an indication of softness and femininity.

By 1700 many new terms had been coined, bringing the number of *nyōbō-kotoba* to about 500. Many of these are listed in *Onna chōhōki* and some remain in the language today. The tendency to add the prefix *o-* became stronger towards the end of the Edo period, for example, *hiyashi* 'cold water' became *o-hiya(shi)* and *kachin* 'rice cakes' became *o-kachin*. Other *nyōbō-kotoba* used in the 1700s were: *o-ashi* 'money'; *o-shitaji* 'soy sauce'; *oishii* 'tasty', 'delicious'; *o-hiroi* 'walking', 'on foot'; *o-yoru* 'to sleep'; *muzukaru* 'to sulk', 'to be peeved', 'to fret'; *sumoji* 'sushi' (raw fish on vinegared rice), *kamoji* 'hair'; *o-nasu* 'eggplant'; *o-den* 'boiled fish cakes and vegetables'; *o-naka* 'stomach', 'belly' and *himojii* 'hungry'.

The *kuruwa-kotoba* language of the brothel quarter is said to have originated in Shimabara, Kyoto around the 1670s and to have spread from there to Shinmachi in Osaka and finally to Yoshiwara and Fukagawa in Edo. The language probably developed as a result of occupational solidarity among the women from different regional backgrounds who were compelled to spend from ten to perhaps twenty years in an extremely confined environment. In return for the high prices they were obliged to pay, patrons expected to be entertained by women skilled in artistic accomplishments, displaying a high degree of education and cultivation. The *tsūjin* (connoisseur) who frequented the pleasure district would hardly be impressed by a bewildering array of boorish regional accents. It is clear from *sharebon* like *Yūshi hōgen* that customers too could use *kuruwa-kotoba* when talking to the courtesans in the pleasure quarters and it is claimed that one function of this language was to conceal the social origins of the customers.

In the introduction of the *Ryūkō kagen* (Dialect of the pleasure quarters, 1791) mention is made of the fact that the language varied slightly from one brothel to another. 'At Chōjiya they say "*ozansu*" and at Matsubaya it is "*osu*". At Ōgiya it is "*watakushi*" (I) and at Tamaya they say "*omaesama*" (you).'

A typical feature of this *kuruwa-kotoba* is the suffix *-insu*, which is a contracted form of the polite ending *-masu*, for example:

Nanika shirenu koto bakkari osshinsu kara aitsu ga shinikuu gozarinsu.
(I can't understand a word he is saying, so that fellow is really difficult to handle.)

The honorific verb *nasaimasu* 'to do' becomes *nansu, nanshi* or *nanse*. The *gozansu* style which became general among Edo merchants towards the end of the eighteenth century appears to be derived from the language of the pleasure quarter. The standard first person pronoun *watakushi* is also believed to have originated in the brothel district along with the associated forms of *wachiki* and *watchi*. *Bakarashii* 'stupid', 'ridiculous' was a vogue word in Yoshiwara towards the end of the 1770s. The first-person pronoun *oira*, which is said to be the origin of the word *oiran* 'courtesan', was also used about this time in the pleasure quarters.

In addition to this *kuruwa-kotoba* proper, women of the brothels used a variety of secret jargons for their own amusement and to keep their conversation from the ears of patrons. A particularly interesting example, known as *karakoto*, a kind of mock Chinese in which each syllable is followed by another beginning with *k-*, is recorded in the *kibyōshi* story, *Kinkin sensei no eiga no yume* (Mr Moneybags' dream of prosperity, 1775).

Ikimakani ikekuko kakura makochike nakoto ikikkete kukon kena.
(which with the superfluous syllables removed becomes, *Ima ni iku kara machi na to itte kunna.* 'Will you tell him to wait and I'll be there soon.')

Sharebon provide us with particulary rich material for the study of the language of the women of the brothel district and their *chōnin* patrons. Even so, they still retain a good deal of Kansai influence and are too restricted in scope to present an overall picture of Edo language. Although they are an Edo innovation, *kibyōshi* too use traditional Kyoto language in the narrative, restricting the use of Edo dialect to the dialogues.

Good source material for the language of Edo at the end of the eighteenth century is provided by the *kokkeibon* (comic fiction) which begin to appear from around 1800. Shikitei Sanba, in particular, in his *Ukiyoburo* (Bathhouse of the floating world, 1809) records in minute detail the speech of the various social, occupational and regional groups who come to the bathhouse. He breaks away from the traditional kana spelling to record speech phonetically and even devised a diacritical mark, the *shiroki nigori* to indicate the contrast between the stop and nasal pronunciation of the voiced velar, that is, the distinction between [g] and [ng]. The *shiroki nigori* are used to indicate the stop pronunciation of non-Edo dialects. The raised circle, *maru*, is used with syllables beginning with s- to indicate syllables with an initial affricate such as *tsa*, *tso*, which are not catered for in the traditional orthography. Words like *otottsan* 'father' were commen in *chōnin* speech. The labial fricative which in Edo had, from the beginning of the seventeenth century, been lost before all vowels but 'u', is indicated in the speech of northern dialect speakers with the kana syllables *fuha* (*fuwa*), *fuho* and so on, as in this example:

> *Fambun ga yama no yomo de fambun ga unagikko daa.* (It's half yam and half eel.)

A celebrated exchange in which a Kansai woman comments on the language of an Edo woman she meets at the bathhouse appears in Chapter 5.

Townsman speech as it appears in *Ukiyoburo*, however, is the language of the lowest stratum. Among the townsmen there were upper, middle and lower subdivisions, each exhibiting slight differences in language. The Kantō suffix -*bee* came to be regarded as vulgar even by the *chōnin* and is found mainly in the speech of artisans and *otokodate*, self-appointed defenders of the common people. Furthermore, a person would often change his speech to suit the conversational situation. In *Ukiyoburo,* for example, the same character may shift from *omee* and *minee* to *omae* and *minai* according to the status of the person addressed. In *Yūshi hōgen* a certain woman uses *omaesan*, *anata* and *nushi*, all second-person pronouns, when addressing the same customer.

Shikitei Sanba's keen observation, ear for detail and precision in notation make him seem as much a sociolinguist as a novelist. An abiding fascination with language can also be found at all levels of Edo society. Philology and kana orthography were basic to the scholarship of the National Learning scholars (*kokugakusha*), such as Motoori Norinaga and Kamo no Mabuchi. Dialects were regarded as a rich source of vocabulary for *haikai* and as the repositories for old words vital for textual analysis.

From 1700 this interest in dialects gave rise to the publication of numerous dialect manuals written by samurai and scholar dilettantes. Unlike earlier works such as Yasuhara Teishitsu's *Katakoto* (Babble, 1650), which compared regional dialects with the Kyoto language, those of the eighteenth and nineteenth centuries compared them with Edo, whose superiority was constantly acclaimed. These dialect manuals aimed to give instruction in the Edo language to provincials so they could master it and make themselves understood in the Shogun's capital.

The popular interest in dialect is also successfully exploited in works of fiction such as Jippensha Ikku's *Tōkaidō dōchū hizakurige* (Shank's mare along the Tōkaidō, 1802–09). The Edo townsmen no doubt derived great satisfaction in seeing their own language favourably contrasted with rude provincial dialects or pompous samurai speech. Donald Keene captures the feeling nicely in this description of Yaji and Kita, the principal characters of *Hizakurige*:

> Both are completely uninterested in considerations of honour or reputation, lust after every woman they see, enjoy nothing more than a fight, and are yet not without a crude charm. They speak the rough language of the Edo man and show immense contempt for what they consider the effeminate speech of everybody else. (Keene, p. 413)

The Edo dialect took on the useful role of a national language as it spread throughout the country, carried by the retinues of local daimyo returning home after a period of duty in Edo.

Such interest in language extended even beyond Japanese. In the *Wakan sanzui zue* (Illustrated encyclopaedia of Japan and China, 1713), 70 Korean words, sixteen Ryukyuan words and 54 Ezo (Ainu) words are rendered in kana.

Many foreign loanwords which had found their way into the Japanese language during the sixteenth century were lost after the proscription of Christianity in the early 1600s. But some Portuguese words not directly connected with religion remained—for example: *konpeitō* (from *confeitos* 'confectionary') a type of candy; *tabako* (*tabaco*) 'tobacco'; *pan* (*pāo*) 'bread'; *kappa* (*capa*) 'a cape'; *jiban* or *juban* (*gibāo* 'doublet') 'an under kimono'; *botan* (*botäo*) 'button'; *kanakin* (*canquim*) 'finely woven cotton cloth'; *sarasa* (*saraça'printed cotton fabric';* *birōdo* (*veludo*) *'velvet';* *rasha* (*raxa*) 'wollen cloth'; *karuta* (*carta*) 'cards'; *kasutera* (*päo* de Castella) 'a kind of sponge cake'; *meriyasu* (Portuguese *meias* or Spanish *medias* 'stockings') 'knitted goods', 'knitted fabric'.

When the Bakufu began to encourage foreign studies after the 1720s, loanwords from Dutch began to enter the language. These were principally concerned with Western technology, for example, *buriki* (*blik*) 'tin plate'; *gomu* (*gom*) 'rubber'; *ponpu* (*pomp*) 'pump'; *garasu* (*glas*) 'glass'; *gasu* (*gas*) 'gas'; *arukooru* (*alcohol*) 'alcohol'; *kantera* (*kandelaar*) 'lantern'; *ereki* (*electriciteit*) 'electricity'; *mesu* (*mes*) 'scalpel'; *zukku* (*doek*) 'canvas'.

Gradually, as the language of Edo came more and more to take on the role of a national language, many Kantō dialect features were discarded. The suffix *-bee* was one of the first to go and the long vowel *-ee* replacing vowel sequences *-ai* and *-oi* failed to establish itself in the standard language.

Some features of Kantō vocabulary, such as *okkanai* 'frightening', *zunai* 'huge' and *dekai* 'big', were used less after 1850. The same was true of the typically Edo system of abuse characterised by the verb-suffix *-yagaru* 'to have the cheek to. . .' as in *ikyagaru* 'to have the cheek to go', *iiyagaru* 'to have the cheek to say'; the nominal suffix *-me* as in *yarōme* 'rascal'; *bakame* 'fool' and certain disparaging verbs like *kutabaru* 'to drop dead'. These were not absorbed into the standard language, though they they are still very much alive among the *shitamachi* speakers of downtown Tokyo and are frequently employed for histrionic or authentic effect in the numerous period dramas so popular on television.

References

Asou Isoji, annotations *Tōkaidōchū hizakurige* (Shank's mare along the Tōkaidō) *Nihon koten bungaku taikei* Vol. 62, Tokyo: Iwanami Shoten, 1961

Doi Tadao (ed.) *Nihongo no rekishi* (History of the Japanese language) rev. edn., Tokyo: Shibundō, 1960

Keene, Donald *World within Walls—Japanese Literature of the Pre-Modern Era* London: Secker and Warburg, 1976

Matsumura Akira *Edogo, Tōkyō no kenkyū* (Studies on Edo language and Tokyo language) Tokyo: Tōkyōdō, 1960

Mizuno Minoru, annotations *Kibyōshi, sharebon-shū* (Collection of *kibyōshi* and *sharebon*) *Nihon koten bungaku taikei* Vol. 59, Tokyo: Iwanami Shoten, 1961

Nakamura Michio *Tōkyōgo no seikaku* (The character of the Tokyo idiom) Tokyo: Kawada Shobo, 1948

—— annotations *Ukiyoburo* (Bathhouse of the floating world) *Nihon koten bungaku taikei* Vol. 63, Tokyo: Iwanami Shoten, 1961

Sugimoto Tsutomu "Nihongo no rekishi" (History of the Japanese language) in *Iwanami kōza Nihongo* Vol. 2 *Gengo seikatsu* Tokyo: Iwanami Shoten, 1977

Yasuhara Teishitsu, *Katakoto* (Babble) *Nihon Koten Zenshū* 4th series, Vol. 1, To.:yo: Gendai Shichōsha, (1926) 1987 Reprint

Yuzawa Kōkichirō *Edo kotoba no kenkyū* (Studies on Edo language) Tokyo: Meiji Shoin, 1951

5

Edo and Tokyo dialects

Hiroko C. Quackenbush

The regional and social dialects of Japan show considerable diversity of pronunciation. Sound changes and inter-dialect borrowing, often going back many centuries, plus changing socio-linguistic factors, have led to complicated relationships among dialects both between and within areas. The purpose of this essay is to examine some dialect differences which existed in Edo from the late 1700s to the early 1800s, and to relate them to linguistic patterns in Tokyo today. By an examination of two sound changes of an opposite nature, some insight may emerge into the ways in which both linguistic and social factors contribute to the development of a standard language.

As a starting point, one can use Shikitei Samba's two famous fictional works, *Ukiyoburo* (Bath in a floating world, 1809) and *Kyōgen inaka ayatsuri* (Country puppet theatre, 1811). Extracts have been chosen from these because Shikitei's works are generally recognised as the best guide to the speech of the period.

Edo and Tokyo

Describing the speech of Edo people, Shikitei Samba in *Kyōgen inaka ayatsuri*, makes a distinction between what he calls Hon-Edo ('Proper' Edo) and Edo-Namari ('Corrupt' or 'Common' Edo). Hon-Edo was the type of language used by samurai, and also by well-educated merchants, while Edo-Namari was confined mainly to the lower class ordinary townsmen.[1] A specimen of Edo-Namari is quoted below. The Hon-Edo dialect was free from Edo-Namari features and more

closely resembled the Kyoto dialect, at least with respect to the phonological aspects analysed in this chapter.

Present-day Tokyo dialects have important similarities with those
of eighteenth-century Edo. Most linguists agree that there are two major dialects in Tokyo today—Yamanote and Shitamachi.[2] The Yamanote dialect is usually recognised as the basis for Standard Japanese,
while the Shitamachi dialect is purely regional and as such is used in
informal situations only, and by a decreasing number of native speakers. The majority of Japanese speak two dialects, in that they have a
command of the local approximation to Standard Japanese, as well as
that of their native region. This is just as true of Shitamachi dialect
speakers, most of whom are also competent in Standard Japanese.

The parallel between the speech of Edo and Tokyo can be seen in
both types of dialects and their respective speakers. Standard
Japanese, which is almost synonymous with Yamanote speech, can
be compared with Hon-Edo, while the Shitamachi dialect corresponds to Edo-Namari.

Edo and Kyoto

An oft-quoted passage from *Ukiyoburo,* in which a Kyoto woman
ridicules the speech of an Edo counterpart, clearly illustrates some
outstanding features of the *Edo-Namari* dialect. The broad phonetic
transcription and the translation are mine. I have underlined the
Edo-Namari features in the Japanese text.

(*E* = Yama, an Edo woman; *K* = Kami, a Kyoto woman)

E . . . *Edokko no arigatasa ni wa, umare ochi kara shinu made,*
umareta tochi o issun mo hanare_nee_yo ai. O_mee_gata no yoo ni kyoo
de umarete oosaka ni sumattari, samazama ni magotsuki-mawatte
mo, ageku no hate wa arigatai oedo da _kara_, kyoo made kurashite
iru jaa _nee_ ka na. Sore da _kara_ om_mee_gata no koto o kamigata-
zeeroku to yuu wa na.
We, Edo-ites are lucky; from the time we are born until the time
we die we don't move out of Edo. But you people who were born
in Kyoto often live in Osaka and move around quite a bit. And
then you end up living in Edo, like you have been until today.
That's why we call you 'Kamigata-zeeroku' (useless Westerners).

K *_Zeeroku_ to wa nan no kotcha e.*
What do you mean by zeeroku?

E *Sairoku to.*
I said *sairoku.*

K   *Sairoku to wa nan no kotcha e.*
    What's *sairoku*?

E   *Shirezu wa ii wa na.*
    Ah! Ignorance is bliss!!

K   *He-he, kwantoo-bei ga, sairoku o <u>zee</u>roku to, ketai na kotoba-tsuki*
    ja naa, oryogwai mo, oryo<u>gee</u>, kwannon-sama mo, <u>ka</u>nnon-sama.
    Nan no kotcharo na. Soo da <u>kara</u> koo da <u>kara</u> to, ano maa, <u>kara</u> to
    wa nan ja e . . .
    Ha ha, you Kwantoo-bei (crass Easterners)!! You say 'zeeroku'
    for *sairoku*! What a strange language! You say 'oryogee' for
    oryogwai, 'kannon' for *kwannon*. How strange! You say so and so
    kara. What on earth does *kara* mean? . . .

E   *Son nara ioo ka e. Edo-kotoba no <u>kara</u> o warai naharu ga, hyaku-*
    ninis<u>shi</u> no uta ni nan to aru e.
    Let me tell you then. You laugh at *kara*, but what do you find in
    the One Hundred Poems?

K   *Sore sore, moo hyakuninis<u>shi</u> ja. Are wa shi ja nai.*
    Hyakuninis<u>shu</u> ja wai na. Mada maa <u>sha</u>kuninisshi to iwai de tano-
    moshii na.
    There you go again, saying *hyakuninisshi*!
    It should be *shu* not *shi*. There's some hope left for you though,
    because at least you don't say *shakuninisshi*!

E   *Soryaa, watashi ga iizoko<u>nee</u> ni mo shiro sa.*
    Forgive my slip of the tongue.

K   *Zoko<u>nee</u>, ja nai. Iisokonai ja. Eroo kiki-zurai na. Shibai nado*
    miru ni, ima ga <u>see</u>go da, <u>ka</u>nnen nan tara yuu tari, <u>dee</u>gan-jooju
    katajike<u>nee</u> nan no ka no to yuute, man<u>zee</u> no, <u>see</u>zoo no to, gippa
    na otoko ga yuute ja ga . . .
    'Zokonee?' You mean *sokonai*, don't you? It's so difficult to
    understand you. In the Kabuki plays, too, the actor says. Now it's
    your 'seego' (*saigo* 'one's end'), so 'kannen' (*kwannen* 'you might
    as well give up'). Or he would say 'katajikenee' (*katajikenai*
    'thanks for') 'deegan-jooju' (*daigwan joonu* 'the success'). And he
    would say 'manzee' (*manzai* 'manzai comic dancers'), and
    'seezoo' (*saizoo* 'saizoo comic dancers')!

The text shows a striking abundance of the vowel sequence /ee/ in
the Edo dialect as the equivalent of both /ai/ and /ae/ in the Kyoto
dialect, as summarised in Table 5.1.
    Another Edo feature which is ridiculed by the Kyoto woman is the
use of the sounds /ka/ and /ga/ for /kwa/ and gwa/ (see Table 5.2).

Table 5.1   Comparison between Edo and Kyoto dialects: ee/ai/ae

Edo	Kyoto	English
nee	*nai*	adjectival negative
zeeroku	*sairoku*	a swear word
oryogee	*oryogwai*	rude
iizokonee	*iisokonai*	mistake in speech
seego	*saigo*	the last time
manzee	*manzai*	manzai comic dancer
seezoo	*saizoo*	saizoo comic dancer
omee	*omae*	you

Table 5.2   Comparison between Edo and Kyoto dialects: ka/ga/kwa/gwa

Edo	Kyoto	English
oryogee	*oryogwai*	rude
Kannon	*Kwannon*	Goddess of Mercy
deegan	*daigwan*	a great desire

The Edo pronunciation of /shi/ and /sha/ for Kyoto /shu/ and /hya/ respectively is also mentioned, as in *hyakuninisshi* (Edo) and *hyaku-ninisshu* (Kyoto) (The Hundred Poems) or *shakuninisshi* (Edo) and *hyakuninisshu* (Kyoto) (The Hundred Poems).

Particles and inflectional differences can be seen in such examples as: *kara* (Edo) and *sakai* (Kyoto) (because); and *hanarenee(nai)* (Edo) and *hanaren* (Kyoto) (do not leave—verbal negative).

Edo and Kyoto features in present-day Japanese

Some items of each dialect have been incorporated into the Standard Japanese of today, while others remain as dialectal features of certain regions only. Table 5.3 summarises their status today. Capital letters indicate forms or pronunciations which have become standard.

The pronunciation /ee/ still remains in the Shitamachi dialect. /Kwa/ has disappeared even from the Kyoto dialect, and is now found main-ly in Kyushu and Shikoku. /Shi/ occurs in the Shitamachi dialect in words such as *teeshi* instead of the Standard *teeshu* 'husband', and *shijitsu* for *shujutsu* 'operation'. Confusion of /hi/ and /shi/, and /hya/ and /sha/ is a well-known feature of the Shitamachi dialect in which, for example, *hyaku* 'one hundred' is pronounced *shaku*, and *hito* 'person' becomes *shito*. The particle *sakai* and the verbal negative 'n'

Table 5.3   Edo and Kyoto features in Standard Japanese

Edo	Kyoto
ee	AE
ee	AI
KA, GA	kwa, gwa
shi	SHU
sha	HYA
KARA	sakai
NAI, nee	n

are still widely used in Kyoto and other western dialects. The verbal negative 'n' is actually one of the hallmarks of the western dialects today.

Why, then, have some features of the Edo-Namari dialect of the eighteenth century been retained and some replaced in the process of the evolution of Standard Japanese? In order to answer this question, let us examine in some detail the fate of the most notable dialectal differences, /ai/ vs /ee/, and /kwa/ vs /ka/. /Ai/ was the pronunciation of Kyoto as well as Hon-Edo, and was a preferred pronunciation over /ee/ in any formal situation. Similarly, /kwa/ was regarded as more prestigious than /ka/. However, though /ai/ remains today in Standard Japanese, /kwa/ has been replaced by /ka/, which was regarded as sub-standard during the Edo period.

/Ai/ vs /Ee/

Historically, the relationship between these two vowel sequences is that of a sound change in which /ai/ became /ee/. This sound change can be regarded as a case of assimilation, that is, /a/ a low vowel and /i/ a high vowel, having an opposite degree of tongue height, influenced each other. The result was a single long mid-vowel.

This can also be seen as part of a wider pattern of sound change which had been in operation for several centuries. For example, those vowel sequences in which the second vowel is /u/ underwent changes before 1650 in most parts of Japan, including both Kyoto and Edo. For example, *mausu* 'to say' came to be pronounced *moosu*, and *omou* 'to think', *omoo*.

After 1750, a time when the sound change /ai > ee/ was spreading in Edo, a similar change was also taking place in other vowel sequences, namely /ei/, /oi/ and /ui/, as well as /ae/, /ie/, /oe/ and /ue/, though to a lesser degree in these latter cases. Examples include:

kirei>*kiree* 'pretty'; *futoi*>*futee* 'big'; *kaeru*>*keeru* 'to return'; *oshieru*>*oseeru* 'to teach'.

Table 5.4 summarises these sound changes. Stage 1 sound changes were completed both in Kyoto and Edo long before 1700. Stage 2 sound changes were in process from 1600 to 1850 in the regional dialect of Edo, but not in Kyoto.

Table 5.4   Sound changes

Stage 1	Stage 2	
au>oo	ai>ee	ae>ee
eu>joo	ei>ee	ie>ee
iu>juu	oi>ee	oe>ee
ou>oo	ui>ii	ue>ee

Although the sound change is represented above simply as ai>ee, it actually resulted in a variety of pronunciations. For present day pronunciations of adjectives ending in /ai/, such as *akai* 'red', and *kurai* 'dark', the *Linguistic Atlas of Japan* (1966) lists the following phonetic transcriptions [je:, jɛ:, ɪe, ei, eɪ, e:, eɛ, eæ, e∂, ɛi, ɛɪ, ɛe, ɛ:, ɛæ, ɛ∂, æɛ, æ:, æ∂]. At any rate, all these pronunciations can be seen to involve some degree of assimilation between the two vowels involved.

There is a parallel situation in Australian English today where the Standard /ei/ sound in words such as 'tame' and 'day' is pronounced [æɪ, æ:, ∂ɪ, ɛɪ, ʌɪ] and so on, depending on individual speakers and the particular occasion.

Looking at the map in Figure 5.1 opposite, we can see that, in terms of geographical spread, the /ai>ee/ sound change now extends to most parts of Japan, including the Kanto area in which Tokyo is situated.

This means, therefore, that the Yamanote dialect of Tokyo, which uses /ai/ rather than /ee/, is a linguistic island surrounded by other regional dialects where /ee/ is the norm. It shows that the /ai/ of the Hon-Edo ('Proper Edo') dialect was resistant to any influences from immediately surrounding dialects, including Edo-Namari ('Corrupt Edo').

The question then arises: why did the sound change ai>ee not spread to the speech of the samurai class and the educated merchants of Edo? First of all, the endurance of the original /ai/ pronunciation may be a result of the prestige attached to it. For example, it is interesting to note that, as far as can be judged from the available evidence, the speech patterns of the ruling Tokugawa family and their

1 Beautiful Woman, 17th Century, private collection

2 Pleasure Quarter Scene, 17th Century, private collection

3 Courtesan Takao (*tayū*), 17th Century, private collection

4 Bathhouse Girl (*yuna*), 17th Century, MOA Art Museum, Important Cultural Property

5 Courtesan Yachiyo, 17th Century, private collection

6 Ichikawa Danjūrō II as Gorō in *Ya no ne*, Ichikawa Danjūrō family collection

7 Ichikawa Danjūrō I as Soga Gorō uprooting a bamboo, 1697,
Tokyo National Museum

8 Ichikawa Danjūrō II as Gongorō in *Shibaraku*, (Torii Kiyomasu), Ricar Museum

9 Ichikawa Danjūrō IX as Fudō Myōō, Narita Shinshōji Temple

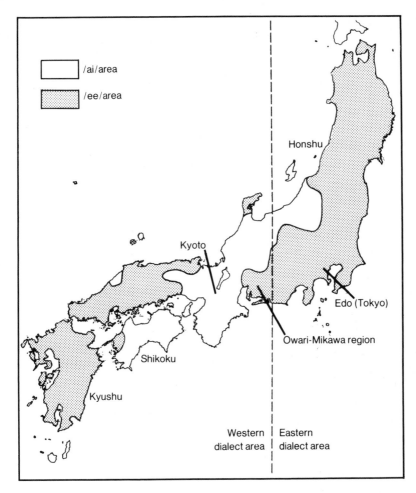

Figure 5.1   The /ai/ > ee/ sound change — geographical spread

attendant samurai, when in Edo, do not appear to have exhibited the /ee/ pronunciation typical in their home region of Owari-Mikawa. At such times, their speech conformed to the more prestigous Kyoto-type pronunciation. At any rate, /ai/, along with other non-assimilated vowel sequences, was definitely a prestige feature. The samurai said *akai* 'red', *kaeru* 'to return' and, *kuroi* 'black' while the lower-class townsmen said /akee/ /kuree/ just as the Shitamachi dialect speaker does today.

Although it seems that prestige value was primarily responsible for the continued use of /ai/, there are several other important factors which should be considered as additional causes. The first was clarity. Since the Edo population comprised speakers of many different dialects, there must have been a need for a considerable degree of clarity in speech in order to achieve efficient communication.

Phonetically the three basic and most highly differentiated vowels are /a/, /i/ and /u/. The /ai/ sequence exhibits the maximally contrastive combination of the most open, sonorant vowel /a/ followed by the closed, palatal vowel /i/. Stampe[3] claims that in the hyperarticulated, or careful, speech style the vowels in this sequence, having the 'incompatible properties' of sonority and palatality, would tend to polarise and dissimilate, in the absence of any other influences. This clearly represents an opposite tendency to hypoarticulated, or casual, speech in which assimilation takes place.

The various pronunciations of the combination of vowels in the words 'I am' in English support this hypothesis. Depending on the style, speed or emphasis of articulation, pronunciation may range from /aɪæm/ to /aɪəm/, /aɪm/ or even just /əm/.

The need for clarity of speech in this cosmopolitan city was reinforced by another factor leading to the maintenance of the pronunciation /ai/—the avoidance of homonym clash or confusion. There are many cases where two or more separate words would have become indistinguishable as the result of a merger of sounds, as they indeed did in Edo-Namari. In this dialect, because other vowel sequences—most notably /ae/, /oi/ and /ui/—had also undergone sound change, many homonyms had resulted. For example *kuroi* 'black' and *kurai* 'dark' would both have been pronounced /kuree/. By not adopting the sound changes, these words remained phonologically distinct in the Hon-Edo dialect.

It is also possible that the writing system contributed to the continued use of /ai/ in the Standard language. Literacy increased rapidly during the Edo period and spread to several social groups, such as the merchant class, which had traditionally only used the spoken language. As the number of literate people increased, written-language forms circulated more widely and may well have reinforced the retention of /ai/ and other conservative linguistic forms. In fact, acquaintance with the literary language may have even encouraged the merchant class to revert from the pronunciation of /ee/ back to that of /ai/, in emulation of the samurai class.

/Kwa/ vs /Ka/

In the specimen passage from *Ukiyoburo*, given above, /kwa/ was seen to be a Kyoto feature, and /ka/ to be from Edo-Namari. Other evidence in Shikitei Samba's works again confirms that speakers of Hon-Edo, the prestige dialect, said /kwa/ rather than /ka/. However, the fate of this pair was the opposite of that of /ai/ vs /ee/. That is, the sound which was ridiculed by the Kyoto woman overcame the prestigious pronunciation and established itself as a standard feature. *The Linguistic Atlas of Japan* shows some residue of /kwa/ in parts of Shikoku and Kyushu, but in most dialects, including that of Kyoto, only /ka/ is now used.

Since /kwa/ was a mark of the prestige dialect during the Edo period, explanations for the choice of /ka/ over /kwa/ must obviously be sought not in social conditions, but elsewhere. The explanation suggested below, therefore, is primarily of a linguistic rather than a sociological nature.

Historically this sound /kwa/, which occurred in /kwa/ /kwan/ /kwai/ /kwaku/ kwatsu/ and kwau/ (e.g. 火, 官, 回, 拡, 活 and 光 respectively), and the voiced counterpart /gwa/ /gwan/ /gwai/ /gwatsu/ and /gwau/ (e.g. 画, 元, 外, 月 and 業 respectively) were Japanese approximations for the Chinese pronunciations of certain characters. As the result of massive lexical borrowings from China the sound /kw/ and /gw/ had come to be established as distinctive phonemes in the Japanese language during the ninth and tenth centuries. Thereafter, a merger of /kwa/ with /ka/, and /gwa/ with /ga/ began to take place, the latter member of each pair being a part of the native Japanese phonological system. This sound change, /kwa>ka/ and /gwa>ga/, had completed its course in Edo by about 1750. In Kyoto, however, /kwa/ and /gwa/ remained, though there is some scattered evidence that a similar sound change may have begun in Kyoto at this time, too.

In the discussion above on the /ai/–/ee/ alternation, it was observed that the avoidance of homonym clash, which is often a strong counterbalance to the pressures of phonetic change, might have predominated in order to avoid many confusing homonyms. Chinese characters pronounced /kwan/ and /gwan/, however, lost their distinction from others voiced as /kan/ and /gan/. Table 5.5 shows a list of present-day general-use characters which originally had /kwan/ or

/gwan/ pronunciations. These are contrasted with other Chinese characters pronounced as /kan/ or /gan/. Similar contrastive lists could be made of characters with readings of /kwa/–/ka/, /kwai/–/kai/, /kwaku/–/kaku/, /kwatsu/–/katsu/, /kwau/–/kau/; /gwa/–/ga/, /gwai/–/gai/, /gwatsu/–/gatsu/ and /gwau/–/gau/.

Table 5.5   Present-day general-use characters which originally had /kwan/ or /gwan/ pronunciations

Sound	Character									
kwan	官	関	館	観	完	管	慣	勧	歓	冠	巻
	患	貫	喚	換	棺	款	閑	寛	緩	還	
kan	間	寒	感	漢	刊	幹	干	甘	甲	汗	肝	看
	陥	乾	勘	堪	敢	監	憾	簡	艦	鑑	
gwan	元	願	丸								
gan	岸	岩	顔	眼	含						

Because so many Chinese characters were involved in the change of /kwa/ and /gwa/ to /ka/ and /ga/, one may well wonder why the natural tendency to avoid homonym clash did not operate to avert this sound change. When we also take into account the fact that the original /kwa/ and /gwa/ were prestigous pronunciations, the reason for this sound change seems all the more puzzling. However, an explanation for this apparently unusual development can be suggested. (In order to simplify the explanations /kwa/ only will henceforth be used as the representative of all other combinations, /kwan/ /kwai/ /kwaku/ /kwatsu/ /kwau/ /gwa/ /gwan/ /gwai/ /gwatsu/ and /gwau/.)

Although the form /kwa/ had, as we have seen, a demonstrable importance in the language in its differentiating role, several factors taken together have prevented its demise from seriously disrupting intelligibility. Firstly, words containing /kwa/, like most Chinese loans, tended to have a rather literary flavour, and as such their occurrence was more frequent in the written than in the spoken language. It is also worth noting that the disappearance of /kwa/ caused a change only in the pronunciation of the Chinese characters, and not a change in the characters themselves. Furthermore, given that Sino-Japanese words usually occur as character compounds, the other characters forming the compound with what were originally /kwa/ characters offer contextual clues as to the intended meaning. For these reasons then, the merger of /kwa/ and /ka/ did not cause serious difficulties.

Having explained the reasons why this merger could take place without confusing effects on communication, we must now turn to the question of what actually encouraged the sound change in the first place. We can attribute its occurrence to two interrelated factors.

The first of these is the simple matter of ease of articulation. Compared with /ka/, the production of /kwa/ requires, of course, the assistance of lip rounding. Many sound changes which have taken place in the various languages of the world have been attributed to this 'law of least effort', and the change from /kwa/ to /ka/ can be explained in this way.

The second factor is more specifically related to Japanese. Prior to the massive wave of lexical borrowings from Chinese in the sixth century, the phonotactic structure of the Japanese language was basically restricted to the simple alternation of consonants with vowels or sequences of vowels. It was only under the influence of these foreign loanwords that more complex consonant-glide combinations, such as /kw/, came to be used. The replacement of these complex combinations with simple consonants resulted in sequences more familiar in the native phonotactic system, and these were naturally favoured.

That production played a more important role in this change than perception is evident. Ease of articulation and phonotactic regularity must have been a stronger motivation for this sound change than efforts to maintain distinctions and avoid homonym clash. These benefits also overcame the manifestly strong inclination to adopt features of the prestige dialect.

Conclusion

Comparing the linguistic pattern in Japan during and since the Edo period, we see that Standard Japanese has evolved on the foundations of the most prestigious dialect, whilst incorporating various features from other dialects, and finally replacing some of its own features with these.

In minor instances, there seem to have been many linguistic battles fought in Edo and Tokyo to determine the survival of the most apt linguistic forms, and specific groups among the Japanese people either win or lose according to the tide of popular will.

The examples given above clearly show that the choices were made, albeit subconsciously, by people who were conditioned by their social status, as well as by their physical and mental preferences and limitations. In certain cases some of these factors actually operated against each other; when one of them ultimately proved stronger than the rest, a change resulted that seems quite inexplicable on other grounds. Even so, such apparently unlikely developments were often the products of the interplay of both social and linguistic factors, and are not as random or unreasonable as they may at first seem.

Notes

1   See Matsumura Akira *Edogo, Tōkyōgo no kenkyū* Tokyo: Tōkyōdō, 1958, p. 207
2   See Inoue Fumio (ed.) *Shin-hōgen to kotoba no midare ni kansuru shakaigengogaku-teki kenkyū* Tokyo: Tōkyō Daiigaku Shuppan-kai, 1983
3   David Stampe 'On the Natural History of Diphthongs', *Papers from the Eighth Regional Meeting, Chicago Linguistic Society,* Chicago, 1973

References

Inoue Fumio (ed.) *Shin-hōgen to kotoba no midare ni kansuru shakaigengogaku-teki kenkyū* (A Sociolinguistic Study of New Dialect and Language Deterioration) Tokyo: Tōkyō Daigaku Shuppan-Kai, 1983
Kokuritsu Kokugo Kenkyūjo (ed.) *Nihon gengo chizu* (The Linguistic Atlas of Japan), Tokyo: The National Language Research Institute, 1966
Maeda Isamu, 'Renboin [ai] no onka ni tsuite (On the sound change of vowel sequence [ai]),' 21–30 in the *Kokugogaku* (Studies in the Japanese Language) No. 18, 1954
Matsumura Akira, *Edogo, Tōkyōgo no kenkyū* (Studies in the language of Edo and Tokyo) Tokyo: Tōkyōdō, 1958
Miller, Roy Andrew, *The Japanese Language,* Chicago: University of Chicago Press, 1967
Samuels, M. L. *Linguistic Evolution with Special Reference to English* Cambridge Studies in Linguistics 5, Cambridge: Cambridge University Press, 1972
Stampe, David 'On the Natural History of Diphthongs', *Papers from the Eighth Regional Meeting, Chicago Linguistic Society* Chicago, 1973
Sugimoto Tsutomu *Kindai Nihongo no shin-kenkyū* (Studies on Modern Japanese) Tokyo: Yōfūsha, 1967
Weinreich, Uriel, Labov, William and Herzog, Marvin J. 'Empirical foundations for a theory of language change', *Directions for Historical Linguistics* Winfred D. Lehman and Yakov Malkiel (eds) 95–195 Austin: University of Texas Press, 1968

Part III

HIGH CULTURE

6

Group portrait with artist:
Yosa Buson and his patrons

Mark Morris

Kitakaze Shōemon and Matsuoka Jin'emon were only two of many Kansai entrepreneurs who made their fortunes in the booming commercial centres that had grown up outside Kyoto and Osaka during the eighteenth century. They lived and worked in Hyōgo province. Jin'emon's Matsuya Brewery in Itami was well suited to take advantage of the increasing local demand for saké and to profit from reduced transportation costs and more dependable delivery of shipments which made accessible the juiciest market of all, Edo. Well before Jin'emon's time, Kansai brewers were supplying eleven million gallons of saké to Edo each year.[1]

Even amid the bustle of Itami commercial life, a number of successful merchants such as Jin'emon and Shōemon were interested in more than simply accumulating capital—once they had amassed a sufficient amount. People all over Japan may have drunk to one another's health with the product of Matsuya Jin'emon, but *haikai* poets, especially in western Japan, would have recognised the poems of Jin'emon in anthologies of *haikai* verse, where he traded under his poet's name, Shisen. And while we remain uncertain as to the exact nature of Kitakaze Shōemon's business, it must have been prosperous. He too had the leisure to study and compose *haikai* as a pastime. By at least the 1770s both wealthy townsmen had, in addition, become art collectors. Their money and their cultivated tastes earned each a place—alongside a number of other merchants, brewers, and professionals—within the circle of patronage that supported Yosa Buson (1716–83). Hence the following letter from Buson in Kyoto, sent to Shōemon using his poet's name *Kimuro*, dated Twenty-First of the Twelfth Month, An'ei 7 (1778).

Dear Kimuro,

How glad I am to know that in this terribly cold season you are as healthy as ever. Old man that I am, I have been cooped up for ages with my bowel complaint, although for the last few days I have been feeling much better. Please don't worry yourself on my account.

—As for the flounder and goby you were so kind to send the other day, they were delicious. How truly kind of you.

—Presently I will be sending along some paintings, as described below. Do give them your consideration.

Screen paintings, twelve panels.

Hung as *kakemono*, they would make six pair.

These paintings were prepared in response to a request from Aizu up north in Ōshū. Since that is so far away, there is no way of converting them quickly into funds. I am thinking, therefore, of sending something to Aizu in early spring. The fee agreed upon for the work was five silver *chōgin*.

Let me offer them first to you so close at hand. I would not be at all displeased if they were to find a place in your home. It is no longer easy for even myself to create such works; I cannot produce many. I would be most content to receive three gold *ryō* for them. I believe that you will certainly not be sorry if you accept them. This winter, before the end of the year, I have old debts falling due. Finding myself somewhat short of funds, I have thought to make ends meet with the above plan. Please give this matter your consideration, and act as you judge appropriate.

In addition, paintings on silk. These include one ordered previously by yourself. I have as well goods requested by Shisen and Riyu, so I will also send them along. Would you please see that each gets one painting or another. I have forgotten just what each requested—what did they ask me to do? I'm really not certain. If the price for the silk paintings is going to come to less than 200 silver *momme*, please send them back; I'll not be at all offended. Although I would generally expect to receive a remuneration of around one silver *chōgin* for a painting on silk, please do as you see fit according to your own judgement.

—What with Tairo's death and his affairs to be put in order, you must have been through a difficult time. Do take care of yourself. This spring I shall be visiting your way. I will stay in Tairo's old house. I trust you will allow me to call on you during my stay . . . In this busy season I am quite at my wits' end, busy at my painting day and night with never a moment to spare. I trust you will appreciate my predicament. I have therefore no poems to send you. It is also extremely unlikely that I will be able to write again before the New Year. I will have much to write in the spring.

Respectfully yours,
Buson.

P.S. Please send me your reply to the above matters by the 28th. My family send you their sincerest regards. (Letter No. 215)[2]

Yosa Buson left behind many different kinds of paintings and ink sketches, almost 2900 *hokku,* his contribution to over 100 linked-*haikai* sequences, and dozens of brief snatches of prose commentary and anecdote. We also have evidence of more than 350 letters, some of which must have taken a good deal of time and effort, that he wrote to fellow poets, friends and patrons; many of them were all three. Most letters date from relatively late in his life, when he was already in his sixties; the majority from between 1776 (An'ei 5) and 1783 (Temmei 3), the year of his death at the age of 68. He no doubt wrote many letters before these years, but it was in this last decade that his reputation as both poet and painter was firmly established and his correspondents realised that letters from Buson were worth hanging on to. And he was, after all, a superb calligrapher.

Aside from a half-dozen letters written to two men who studied painting with him, Ki Baitei and Matsumura Goshun (Gekkei), we have no evidence of Buson's correspondence with fellow artists. He had once collaborated on a set of small paintings with his famous contemporary Ikeno Taiga. But that had been business. A sense of professional rivalry and a considerable reserve of pride made casual contacts with competitors something Buson seems to have avoided.

It is not surprising that the largest group of letters addressed to a single invidivual, some 70 in number, was sent to Takai Kitō. Although by 1771 Kitō had become a professional *haikai* master with his own poetry circle, he continued to serve diligently as Buson's main disciple, his most trusted sounding-board for ideas about poetry, and de facto co-ordinator of Buson's *haikai* group.[3] Buson was so preoccupied with chasing down and completing painting commissions in his final decade that even the loyal student-friend-patrons that made up his small group might have drifted away if Kitō had not continued to organise their activities and sessions.

The bulk of the surviving letters are to patrons, customers for his paintings. These patrons were, almost without exception, themselves amateur *haikai* poets. Some were intimate members of Buson's inner circle, while others like Kimuro and Shisen were on the periphery. The letter to Kimuro cited above (Letter No. 215) is fairly typical. Unpacking its language and explicating the things talked about and how they are talked about within it may tell us a good bit about Buson's relations with his patrons and, more generally, about how a producer of culture survived in eighteenth-century Japan.

After the opening stock salutations and references to his own poor health (the letters give a fairly ache-by-ache account of the various minor ills that Buson, writing in the persona of aged and pitiable master, was careful to keep his correspondents informed of), the letter mentions some fresh fish sent to him several days before. For a wealthy Hyōgo merchant, sending a few flounder or goby (*haze*) up to Kyoto entailed no great expense. It might keep one in touch with an important Kyoto *haikai* master-cum-painter and was a sensitive, cultured way of sharing one's mercantile largesse with an artist whose calling was in theory something superior to and aloof from the kind of finger-on-the-abacus, nose-in-the-ledger wheeling and dealing that had produced that largesse.

Yosa Buson and many others in his era maintained, in their personal and professional lives, a rather precarious balance between the status of artisan and that of artist. *Haikai* teachers, painters, teachers of tea ceremony or of flower arrangement, teachers of Nō chanting or even of the recently revived sport-art of *kemari* football and various other teachers and craftsmen generally had to function outside the orbit of aristocratic or courtly patronage, within the mercantile bustle of the city. Yet most of their arts were sustained or justified by a structure of values that idealised the educated gentleman (*bunjin*) with leisure to engage in poetry, painting and other cultural pursuits as pure expressions of cultural refinement, not as means of making a living. The artisan-artist had to tread deftly through the social space of eighteenth-century urban Japan, on the one hand producing artefacts or providing lessons worth a determinable market value while presenting himself as a gentlemanly cultural arbiter who had chosen to dispense his knowledge or examples of his art to like-minded friends or acquaintances; the latter might choose to repay such kindness by casually dispatching in the direction of the former certain 'gifts', a few fresh fish perhaps. A painter such as Buson, who conceived his work to be an extension of the Chinese amateur-gentleman literati (*wenren*) tradition, was keenly aware that eighteenth-century Japanese realities could never support such aristocratic ideals.[4] Buson's letters show his attempts to negotiate a compromise that would allow him to be both artisan and artist.

Gifts of fish, saké, tobacco pouches, socks for his daughter, free passes to Kabuki, etc. that Buson received from admiring *haikai* amateurs were important to him. He was willing occasionally, however, to test his patrons' generosity. The following comments are from two letters sent to another Itami brewer-poet, Yamamoto Tōga.

Thank you for sending the barrel of saké. Let me ask you to keep me in mind and once again in future bestow upon me the favour of more such delicious mouthfuls. I will be sending the barrel back soon. (Letter No. 209)

—Saké, one barrel. Fish from the Inakawa River. The above goods reached Kyoto the evening of the Sixth. I was pleased that we received them in time for the Gion Festival. However, those Inakawa fish had gone completely off; they stank horribly and were absolutely no good. I had to have them thrown out. The maid who threw them away headed out with her face averted, holding her nose. Even the delivery man complained about having had to put up with the stink on the way here. Really, at this hot season of the year fish simply cannot last all the way to Kyoto. Please do not go to the trouble again of sending fresh-water fish in hot weather. (Letter No. 210)

Buson expected to receive such gifts or even to solicit them from patrons, who wanted above all his advice on their poems or a chance to appear in an anthology put out by his group, and who were at least willing to buy paintings. But they were luxuries; despite their delights as consumables, they were not enough to sustain Buson, wife, daughter and the occasional hired maid. Precisely because such gifts were luxuries, both parties to the transaction understood them as symbolic tokens of Buson's status as gentleman artist, and he shows little reserve in his letters about insisting that these tokens be of high quality.

While the gifts establish proper protocol and symbolic recognition, the actual negotiating over prices—usually described as 'remunerations', 'appreciations' or similar euphemisms—that occupies so much of the correspondence is fairly straightforward. As in the one to Kimuro, Buson's letters often come very close to looking like shipping invoices. In the Kimuro letter his opening gambit is one he used elsewhere as well: playing off one patron against another. Buson had been 'commissioned', as he put it, by someone up in Aizu province of northern Japan to do twelve paintings. Such a large set could be made into two six-panel screens or, as Buson suggests, used as hanging scrolls. His attitude is practical: he gives only the quantity and suggested uses of the products, not a word about what they are paintings of or their aesthetic value—Kimuro can judge that for himself. Buson is in a hurry. He is writing some ten days before the end of the year, in the midst of the dreaded bill-paying and debt-settling season which he once called 'my great enemy' (Letter No. 169). Still, rather than ask his price flat out, he insinuates: 'The fee agreed upon for the work was five silver *chōgin*', the large oblong silver coins known by that name. Even here there are protocols to be observed. When he writes that he 'would not be displeased if they were to find a place in your home', we, like Kimuro, understand that if he doesn't jump at the chance to buy them, they will be off to Aizu come spring. Of course, the patron might be nonplussed by the arrival of a dozen large, unsolicited paintings. As if to reassure Kimuro that he isn't out to flood the market, Buson next reminds him that he is, after all, getting on (he was 63) and 'cannot produce many' more works of such scale. Seemingly warmed by his own salesmanship, he optimistically lets fall another figure, three gold *ryō*, but with gentlemanly diffidence concludes this portion of the letter by leaving everything to Kimuro's wise judgement.

As the letter moves on to negotiate with Kimuro about the matter of silk paintings, Buson seems at once more frank and more wily than he was in offering the twelve unsolicited pieces. It is worth emphasising that a professional like Buson could not afford to paint simply what he might feel like painting, although such was the ideal of the scholar-gentleman in China or in Japan. A patron's taste and wishes, at least those generally favoured on the market, were inscribed in every painting Buson made, just as they were in the products of professional painters in China. Twentieth-century students of Japanese art are still at times tempted to interpret the works of a Buson or Taiga as only incidentally material products, but rather as lyric expressions of artistic genius. The myth of the artist-genius may have found its quintessential expression in European Romanticism, but it has its origins, as art historians have shown, in the struggle by which Renaissance painters forced their society, and especially their patrons, to recognise them as more than mere manual craftsmen.[5] Buson's letters reveal that while there are glimmers of pride and insistence that he is worthy of his wealthy patrons' respect, he was in no position to deal with them in the high-handed way of a da Vinci or Bellini.[6] An eighteenth-century Japanese artist was still at the stage of an average, commission-hungry Renaissance painter. When we look at a Buson painting or the work of such an Italian artisan, we are looking, as Michael Baxandall put it, at 'the deposit of a social relationship. On one side there was the painter who made the painting, or at least supervised its making. On the other side there was somebody else who asked him to make it, provided funds for him to make it, and after he had made it, reckoned on using it in some way or another.'[7] This is very much the picture painted by Buson's letters.

Clearly the paintings on silk that Buson was sending had been painted to suit the requests of Kimuro, Shisen and one other local poet, Riyu. Some of Buson's commissions were more specific than others; often they were relatively open-ended, within the range of available styles and limited knowledge of collectors. A patron would normally suggest the specific form desired—hanging scroll or screen, silk painting or paper scroll, depending on what uses he had in mind. He would often give some idea of what he would like to see on it— any landscape might do, or a scene with human figures, perhaps a 'portrait' of Bashō for the study, a painting based on a set theme from Chinese history such as a 'Roads to Shu', or perhaps something closer to home, such as a scroll or screen version of Bashō's *Narrow Road to the Deep North* (*Oku no hosomichi*). As Buson wrote to Kimuro (Shōemon) and Shisen (Jin'emon) five months before the letter cited above:

> I had heard from Tairo that you were interested in a scroll version of *Oku no hosomichi*. He told me to find the time to do one. I shall complete it soon and send it on. I believe that this will be one of the greatest works of my life. I trust you will give it your earnest consideration. (Letter No. 213)

Did the undertaking of a major work of calligraphy and *haiga* painting based on Bashō's famous travel diary actually begin with the request of an Itami brewer or did Buson intimate to his friend Tairo that he would like to be paid to tackle such a job? We cannot know but it is certain that around this time, 1777–78,[8] Buson began to produce his scroll and screen versions of *Narrow Road to the Deep North* and of Bashō's *Record of a Weathered Skeleton* (*Nozarashi kikō*), all of which rate as masterpieces. (see *Plates 14 & 15*, examples from this period)

So Buson is quite frank in his business-like fulfilment of painting commissions. However, he goes on to deploy the game-like tactic of more or less daring Kimuro to send him anything less than 200 silver *momme*, a minimum non-negotiable figure. It is interesting to compare this letter with one Buson wrote to two patron-poets in Nagoya around the same time. Buson is commenting on a large hanging scroll he had completed for them based on the historical topic of the T'ang Emperor Ming Huang's journey into exile along the 'Roads to Shu':

> This is one of my best works. There are any number of wealthy Kyoto people who would like to buy it, and I would be glad to get perhaps 1000 *momme*. Yet since I promised it to you long ago, you shall have it. Should you find the price excessive, please return it; I'll not be at all offended. I have not spoken before about painting fees, but, as they say, 'the stove's gone cold, the cupboard's bare', and especially with that demon, the end of the year, just ahead, fees are one way of keeping him at bay. (Letter No. 285)

Once again Buson takes aim at his patron's acquisitive instincts by a blunt reference to other possible customers, and offers his first price. At the same time, he explains any appearance of greediness by reference to his straitened circumstances at the close of the year. When Buson tells Kimuro that he should feel free to return paintings, especially commissioned ones, we can be certain that he is gently calling his bluff, daring him to do anything but the non-business-like, gentlemanly thing and fork out the money requested if not a little more. The game Buson plays here turns on a paradox quite familiar to present-day working artists and their patrons: only by acting success- fully as a businessman can the patron afford the generosity of not necessarily having to act like a businessman when it comes to culture; on the other hand, only by allowing the businessman to participate in the business of fine art and culture can the artist allow him a sense of transcending vulgar commercialism and still make a living.

In discussing the silk paintings in that first letter, Buson seems more wily than usual; he claims to have forgotten, once having accepted the commission for them, what the subject was to be. No apologies—here are the paintings, and here roughly is the cost. You have to admire the old codger. Of course he may have forgotten; but if so, we might expect some apology or some explanation as to why he had decided to go ahead and send these particular paintings. Given the overall tenor of the letters, it seems much more likely that Buson was here asserting a bit of independence. A true gentleman painter, in China or Japan, should be able to supply a friend with a painting conceived independently without anything so mean as an explicit commission; Buson's actions and words imply that even a hard- working literati artist (*bunjin*) might seek to preserve, albeit by sub- terfuge, the freedom of deciding for himself what a patron ought to accept and like.

Early in the New Year of 1779, Buson sent a short letter to Kimuro which included the following comments:

> Busy as you truly were at the end of last year, you promptly sent me
> 250 silver *momme* as payment for my paintings. The money arrived
> safely, and thanks to your benevolence, has proved a great help, tiding
> me over a difficult period. (Letter No. 216)

The Itami poet-merchants were obviously pleased to have their generosity put to the test, helping Buson out by adding 50 silver *momme* to his original minimum figure. Yet even their largesse seems to have had its limits, since there is no mention in Buson's note of any fee received for the twelve unsolicited pieces. Either Kimuro re- turned them, no doubt with a message of regret, or he passed them on to some other Hyōgo collector.

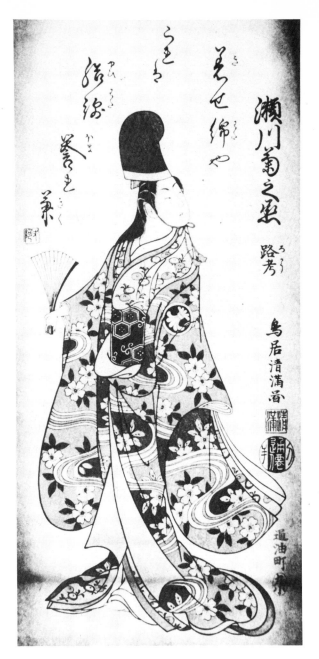

10 Segawa Kikunojō II, 1756, (Torii Kiyomitsu), Waseda
Theatre Museum

11 Woman's Bath, from the novel *Ukiyoburo* ('Bathhouse of the Floating World'), 1809

12 Woman's Bath, from *Ukiyoburo*

13 Ichikawa Danjūrō VIII as Sukeroku, 1850, (Utagawa Kuniyoshi), Waseda Theatre Museum

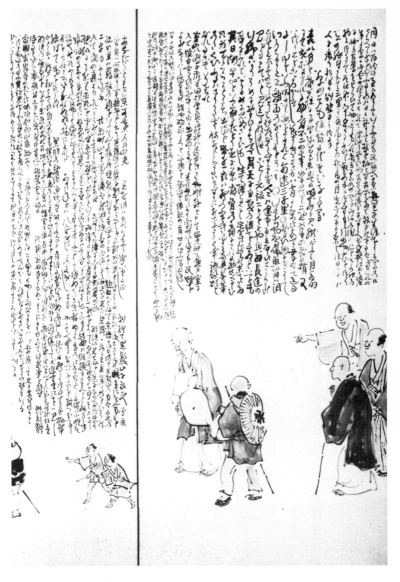

14 Oku no Hosomichi, 1779, by Yosa Buson, Yamagata Art Museum, Important Cultural Property

15 *Ravens in snow* by Yosa Buson, c. 1778,
Kitamura Art Museum, Important Cultural
Property

16 Motoori Norinaga Self-Portrait at the age of 61,
Motoori family collection

17 Portrait of Matsudaira Sadanobu, Matsadaira family collection

It was very much part of Buson's normal strategy to get even an outer-circle patron such as Kimuro to act as a middleman; Buson expected him to distribute paintings to Shisen and Riyu, to collect his fees and dispatch them to Kyoto. For all its long pre-eminence in arts and crafts and its commercial vitality, eighteenth-century Kyoto had yet to produce specialised art dealers. Buson and Ikeno Taiga were among the first successful *bunjin* painters; the market they helped to create would expand greatly after their time, to the benefit of painters such as Maruyama Ōkyo and Buson's own disciple Matsumura Goshun, founder of the Shijō school of painters.[9] It does seem that by about 1800 a more formal and public presentation of art works was being organised. From 1792 Minagawa Kien, a student of Ōkyo and an acquaintance of Buson, began a regular series of large-scale exhibitions presented at Kiyomizudera and other popular venues in the Higashiyama neighbourhood.[10] In Buson's time, however—the 1770s and 80s— an artist usually had to rely on personal contacts to market his paintings.

An interesting fact emerges from Buson's letters: it was through *haikai*, his primary vocation, that he made and maintained the personal contacts which permitted him to survive as a professional painter. For instance, in the case of the Hyōgo patrons, Buson's *haikai* disciple Tairo, mentioned in Letter No. 215, initially connected the merchants' money with his master's paintings. Yoshiwake Tairo was a former samurai who had come to Kyoto in 1766 in order to devote himself to the study of *haikai*, with an eye towards eventually supporting himself as a teacher.[11] He was a friend of Kitō, and when in 1770 Buson assumed leadership of their poetry circle as its recognised master, with Kitō as chief disciple and heir apparent, Tairo joined the group. In 1773 when Tairo moved to Osaka, Buson and Kitō encouraged their own Osaka students and acquaintances to support the poetry group being organised by the fledgling teacher. Soon, however, Tairo began to display his talent for alienating friends. In 1776 Buson heard first by way of his Osaka friend Ueda Akinari, then in a letter from Tairo, that the poetry group had broken down completely. Buson wrote a letter to one of the group, Tōshi, begging him to make it up with Tairo (Letter No. 158), but to no avail. Tairo left Osaka in 1777 and moved to Hyōgo; when he organised a new *haikai* circle there. The members included Kimuro, Shisen and other townsmen eager to study with a disciple of Yosa Buson. Buson and Kitō visited Tairo in Hyōgo that year and the next; this was no doubt an opportunity for both Buson and the Hyōgo poets to put relations heretofore mediated through Tairo on a more personal basis. In mid-1778, when Tairo spent a month back in Kyoto, seeking treatment for a nagging illness, Kimuro took advantage of his teacher's presence to visit Kyoto and call on Kitō. Buson wrote accepting the commission for 'Narrow Road to the Deep North' (Letter No. 213) soon after Kimuro's visit. It may even be that in promising to produce 'one of the greatest works of my life', Buson was, in addition to making the first move in the matter of negotiating a fee, also hoping to increase Tairo's stature in his patrons' eyes.[12] This may have assumed some urgency for Buson, because there is evidence that Tairo was again proving troublesome to the people upon whom he, and indirectly Buson, depended. Later the same year, 1778, Buson sent a joint letter to Kimuro, Shisen and two other members of Tairo's circle. Tairo was back in Kyoto, seriously ill. Buson wrote describing his declining condition and expressing sorrow that relations among the Hyōgo group were still severely strained. He told them to prepare for the worst (Letter No. 214). Buson's long letter to Kimuro (Letter No. 215) arrived after the Hyōgo poets had lost their teacher.

Useful as Tairo had been in providing contacts, Buson's attitude towards his difficult disciple was never merely instrumental or manipulative. While Tairo was alive, Buson was unstinting in his praise of his poetry (Letters No. 93, 100), and saw to it that he had every chance to establish himself in Osaka. As Tairo lay dying, he was cared for by Buson and his intimates. For all their money, and despite the shared devotion to *haikai*, men such as Shisen and Kimuro were on the outer circle of Buson's friends, students and patrons. For those on the inner circle—*haikai* students or his two apprentice painters— Buson was prepared to do all he could. For example, in a letter that seems mostly intent on bidding up the price of his 'Roads to Shu' (Letter No. 285), Buson also informed his patrons that his student Gekkei (Goshun) had painted a version of the subject. 'I will send it together with my own. You may reward him for his efforts as seems appropriate. The young lad certainly has a brilliant future ahead of him.' These Nagoya poet-patrons recognised an offer they were not meant to refuse; they sent Buson three gold *ryō* for his painting, and included an extra two *ryō* for the fortunate Goshun (Letter No. 286). In 1781 Buson used his own contacts to help Goshun set himself up in the town of Ikeda in Hyōgo, where his patrons included close friends of Buson, such as Kawata Dempuku, and yet another brewer-poet, Yamamoto Shōemon (Seifu).[13] Buson also made certain that the Itami group knew about Goshun. He wrote to Jin'emon (Shisen) a few months before his death in 1783, informing him that Goshun would be visiting those parts and asking Shisen to provide lodging. 'Goshun is of course at present unrivalled as a painter. You should allow yourself the pleasure of ordering some paintings from him. He is also extremely good at *haikai*, and even an accomplished flute player. All in all, an able fellow; as regards his skill at painting, the young man practically frightens me.' (Letter No. 219) Buson added, 'He's not at all like that unreliable Tairo', perhaps thinking that to help the living was more important than to honour the dead.

Obviously it helped Buson to have wealthy patrons who were in turn willing to play the part of middlemen and unpaid art brokers. Now and again, however, he seems to have lost track of his business arrangements. The result could be embarrassing. He wrote a long letter in 1776 to the poet-patron Ashida Kafu in Tajima. Buson thanks him for fees received and mentions a forthcoming delivery of paintings, some commissioned by Kafu and others for him to 'flog to the local yokels'. The letter then moves on to the ticklish matter of payment for screens he had done for Kafu's friend, an amateur poet known as Otofusa.

> I sent Otofusa's screens but I have not received any word as to whether or not they reached you. I feel a bit uneasy about what you may perhaps have in mind. I realise that, no doubt thinking of my prior debts to you, you may have decided to consider the screens a form of repayment. That would be most understandable. However, I have been suffering from a persistent illness, last year and on into this spring, an illness that left me feeling scarcely alive. This spring I have entirely abandoned painting; you can imagine the state of my finances, the hardships my family endures. Therefore, please give me a little more time to settle my debts, and I would be most grateful if you could send even a small portion of my fees. If not, I may not be able to hang on to my house (Letter No. 177).

One of Buson's modern editors, Ōtani Tokuzō, remarked that his letters rivalled in interest those of two other inveterate and intriguing correspondents, Rai San'yō and Natsume Sōseki.[14] There are times, though, when they seem more than just literary, when you can almost see the old man scribbling away and hoping desperately that his patrons won't simply be content to think that he's just painting away endlessly.

Was Buson as hard up as his letters frequently make him out to be? His friend Ueda Akinari, writing almost two decades after Buson's death, noted that 'the prices of Buson's paintings are now as high up as the cherry blossoms on Mt. Takama',[15] implying that his paintings did not command exceptionally high prices during his lifetime— something we might also infer from the sheer quantity he dispatched to favourite patrons. We know of course some of the prices he received for his works. The three silk paintings sent to his Hyōgo patrons (Letter No. 215) fetched 250 silver *momme*. One standard index of purchasing power for currency, in the Tokugawa period and even much later, is provided by the price of rice. The year Buson sold these paintings, 1778, the price of rice fluctuated on the Osaka market between 51 and 61 *momme* per *koku*; the Kyoto price averaged 66 *momme*.[16] Thus we can reckon that these three paintings earned Buson the equivalent of some three or four *koku* of rice. We can compare these figures and quantities with those given in one survey of Kansai standards of living. It is estimated that whereas the minimum maintenance stipend for a samurai was as low as 1.8 *koku* per year, a samurai family needed on average four to twelve *koku* of income to make ends meet.[17] Further, an extremely generous estimate of a farm labourer's earnings, both wages and payment in kind, is somewhere around 360 *momme* annually; a skilled worker in the city, a carpenter or mason for example, might earn three *momme* per day, even 1000 *momme* in a good year.[18] Compared with an unskilled labourer or a poor samurai, Buson would seem fairly well off, though we cannot be sure how many times a year he could raise 250 *momme* in one transcation.

He did, however, have considerable expenses connected with his profession; the letters are full of worries about how he will cover his debts to silk and paper shops. Unlike a farm labourer, he had to rent a house large enough to provide a studio. In his small family there was a daughter to be raised and prepared for marriage, and petit bourgeois standards then, as now, dictated that a yound lady had to have certain refinements: Buson's daughter played the *koto*. Similar standards made keeping one maid a necessity rather than a luxury. When his daughter did marry, Buson gave a reception that sounds fairly lavish: 'There were 34 or 35 guests, the finest *koto* artist in all Kyoto and 5 or 6 dancers to top it off—a marvellous party adorned with beautiful women, it went on until dawn, and now for four or five days I've been dragging myself about the house totally exhausted.' (Letter No. 163) His daughter had not married into the same class as Buson's patrons; her husband's occupation was cook for the Mitsui merchant family. When the marriage broke up and his daughter returned half a year later, the 62-year-old painter had nothing to show for his expenditure and as many mouths to feed as before.

All was not lower middle-class gloom, however. The letters give ample evidence of Buson's enjoyment of the good life. There were some wealthy men among the students of his poetry circle and, in addition to buying Buson's paintings and selling them to their own friends, they did what they could to see that the master shared some of the expensive pleasures they took for granted. Perhaps his favourite companion late in his life, next to Kitō, was Teramura Hyakuchi. The Teramuras had for three generations run a profitable business specialising in fine brocade; even before Buson had officially become a *haikai* master, the group forming around him had always been welcome at the Teramura mansion. Hyakuchi's father had studied *haikai* with Buson's master Hajin, and Hyakuchi quite naturally became one of the inner circle from the early 1770s. Judging from the many letters Buson sent to Hyakuchi, their relationship was relaxed and intimate:

> Dear Hyakuchi,
> As for that lantern you were kind enough to lend me the other day, I had meant to sent it right back. But yesterday I took my family for a nice leisurely day out of doors, and by the time we returned, it was already nightfall. Forgive me for the delay. Today again is such an incredibly lovely day, it seems a shame to stay shut up indoors. Should you happen to feel, as I do, like going to view the sunset on the cherry blossoms on Maruyama, I would gladly accompany you. I humbly await your response.
>
> Buson (Letter No. 142)

This was Buson's gentlemanly way of saying, 'please take me out for an evening on the town.' Hyakuchi and other prosperous intimates, like the bookseller Tanaka Katō, were always glad to oblige. And should they happen to forget to invite him, Buson could find other ways to join the fun. One of his briefest letters is the note he sent to the mistress (*kami-san*) of a favourite restaurant one chilly December evening: 'I suspect that Messrs Katō and Hyakuchi may be paying you a visit this evening. If they do, would you please send word to me.' (Letter No. 321)

Hyakuchi was on good terms with the Nagoya *haikai* master Katō Kyōtai.[19] This Nagoya connection seems to have proved quite profitable to Buson, yet he had enough pride as a poet to show some irritation when his wealthy young friend expressed admiration for a successful rival. Once Hyakuchi asked Buson to comment on criticisms that Kyōtai and his chief disciple Shiro had made of certain of Hyakuchi's poems. Buson made a grudging attempt to comply despite reservations that 'of course, the Nagoya style and my own are quite different, it really is difficult to suggest changes' to what the Nagoya group had recommended. He concluded the matter testily:

> Anyhow, please go ahead and alter the poems as Nagoya suggests. What a lot of fuss and prattle over *haikai*! The poems are not really worth all this nit-picking . . .
> P.S. In your correspondence please do not discuss our own method of *kireji* ['cutting words'] with those Nagoya people. Keep that to yourself. And don't for any reason show this letter to anyone or reveal its contents. Such a thing may turn good friends into bad. (Letter No. 102)

Another time, when Kyōtai and Shiro were on a journey to Kyoto and Osaka, they stopped for several days at a temple near Lake Biwa, at the site of Bashō's retreat Genjūan ('The Unreal Dwelling'). Buson and Hyakuchi joined them. The four men did compose poetry together, yet Buson and Hyakuchi seem to have been as interested in visiting the nearby red-light district of Ōtsu as in the reverential composition of *haikai* at Bashō's former dwelling. Buson sent a note to Hyakuchi soon after their return home to Kyoto:

> Well, how unfortunate that you are completely exhausted. Old me, I've been terribly busy all day. So the two gentlemen at the Genjūan will be paying you a call—do give them my very best. As to the idea of a visit to my house this evening, I'm afraid you must excuse me for the time being. Actually, what I said about being busy was a lie. I'm simply in no shape to talk to anyone today. Were you to take all the trouble of paying me a visit, I'd have nothing to offer but yawns. (Letter No. 101)

Although his letters show a predictable competitiveness tinged with crankiness directed at all his poetic rivals, Buson was glad for Hyakuchi to maintain his friendship with the Nagoya group. Through Hyakuchi, Buson's circle of patronage interesected with that of Kyōtai: Kyōtai and his wealthier students were among Buson's most important Nagoya customers. No doubt Kyōtai profited indirectly, becoming in his students' eyes the master who offered them access to one of the best *bunjin* painters in all Japan. In his dealings with the Kyōtai circle, Buson used Hyakuchi not only as an unpaid broker but also, as though seeking to keep as aloof as possible from his rival, a sort of secretary-cum-shipping agent:

> I am extremely grateful to have received from Nagoya the 300 *momme* in appreciation of my paintings. Do send them my sincerest thanks when next you write. Things here are hectic at the moment; please make an appropriate response on my behalf. (Letter No. 140)

> Since Kyōtai's request for *fusuma* screen paintings was an urgent one, I have completed them. Would you please send them on from your place right away. I've been terribly busy lately but did manage to put everything aside in order to do them. I would hate to see a delay in the dispatch of works I've taken so much trouble over. I hope you will understand. (Letter No. 148)

It is worth repeating that the personal contacts Buson established through friends and students such as Tairo and Hyakuchi were crucial for his economic survival. Professional painters had neither an organised marketing system nor the security that many other arts —flower arrangement, Nō chanting, *shakuhachi* music or tea ceremony, to name a few—were able to achieve in the eighteenth century by way of the *iemoto* (family corporation) system. Buson's poetic activities brought in very little income. There were fees one paid on joining the *haikai* group, others to have the master correct one's poems, and those for monthly meetings and subscriptions to anthologies, but these seem to have added up to very little.[20] Wealthier intimates would contribute seasonal gifts and donations and pay a special regular members' fee, yet Buson's group was always very small and he was not particularly interested in expanding it. Once in a while, he exploited poetry with the savvy he normally reserved for the painting business. One letter written to an old acquaintance in Tango province announces a forthcoming anthology of linked-verse sequences. 'Should you want to, perhaps you might enjoy composing a sequence together with me; that certainly is my own desire. Given the great distance that separates us, however, there is no way to do so. Forgive me, but what do you think—I would like to act as your stand-in, and publish a sequence with your name alongside my own poems.' (Letter No. 314) The price of this effortless fame would be 200 *momme*; alternatively, Buson would be willing to include, or invents, single *hokku* at two *momme* per poem.[21]

Buson occasionally expressed regret that he could not follow in Bashō's ascetic footsteps, that in place of wandering the highways and filling the landscape with poems 'I remain at home, labouring at my wearisome tasks, longing for one thing, fretting over another, with nothing I set my mind to amounting to anything'.[22] Dozens of letters record his complaints when painting commissions kept him from composing *haikai* and often made him miss sessions of what was supposed after all to be the Buson *haikai* circle. Conversely, when from time to time Buson personally had to take on chores for the poetry group, when poetry became not a vocation nor a source of patrons but more work, his complaints could sound just as bitter. In 1777 he wrote a letter to another close friend and student, Kuroyanagi Korekoma, lamenting the expenses and headaches he was suffering over the editing, publicising and delivery costs of one of the group's small publications:

> If I applied all the time I'm wasting on this to my painting, I could be making a considerable profit. *Haikai* is a delicate matter, and all I end up doing is making trouble for myself. I am so miserable: perhaps I should give it up. I'm grumbling like this because it is all too much. Please feel free to laugh at me. (Letter No. 292)

Buson was upset but not distraught: he had the presence of mind to ask Korekoma to meet the costs of the mini-anthology, and he signalled that he was bluffing about abandoning *haikai* by appending to the letter six of the finest *hokku* poems he ever wrote.

Although Buson always referred to himself as an old man in the years covered by the letters, they in turn reveal that he apparently didn't consider himself too old to make a fool of himself over a young woman. It was through another intimate, the prosperous bookseller Tanaka Katō, that Buson met the geisha Koito some time in the late 1770s. One day Katō treated Buson, Koito and two other geisha to a day at the Kabuki theatre.[23] The following day, Buson wrote an enthusiastic critique of the day's performances in a letter to his disciple Kitō; his mind had obviously concentrated on more than the stage.

It was an unbelievable crush, but the seats we finally found were just right of centre stage. I watched on with Kohina, Koito and Ishimatsu. Katō was tied up with business and only appeared later. Until then, there I sat, king of the mountain, looking on as brazen as old Tairo might have . . . Everything seemed so splendid, true Kyoto elegance—a scene rustics could not so much as dream of. (Letter No. 53)[24]

Kyoto elegance, as Buson learned, could prove to have surprising complications.

Dear Katō,
I have received a request from Koito—would I please paint a landscape on her white silk kimono. This I regard as being in abominable taste. If someone like myself were to do the painting, it would look terrible on such a beauty. My student Baitei should do it; he always knows how to handle a painting for some beautiful woman's kimono in such a way that the whole design works out quite nicely. I realise that Koito, with her awful taste, won't accept such logic. It truly is a shame to think how much she will regret it when she sees what I paint. But Koito is, after all, Koito, and I can't refuse her no matter what she asks, however dreadful her taste; I'll feel like I am tattooing [the legendary beauty] Hsi Shih. How painful that it is bound to detract from her beauty. She sends word that the kimono will be ready for me in a few days. Please go and see Koito and get her to understand my feelings. It is hard to put everything in writing. We can talk it all over when we meet next. (Letter No. 236)

The garrulousness of Buson on the topic of Koito contrasts with the brevity of the only surviving letter written to his wife Otomo. The errant husband had been off enjoying the good life with Katō for several days at one of his favourite haunts, a restaurant known as the Sangetsu.

To Otomo—Important:
I've stayed on since yesterday at Sangetsu and feel a bit hungover. Today we're off to Higashiyama but I'll definitely be home this evening.

Katō is sending a boy to pick up my coat, writing paper, inkstone, that notebook on my desk, black jacket, fan, tobacco and the like. Please send them on straight away. (Letter No. 294)

This pleasure-loving aspect of old Buson clashes with the aesthetic mystique accorded him by certain interpreters of his art. But it does seem accurate to conclude that one reason Buson wrote less poetry as he grew old was that, in addition to suffering the pressures of deadlines for painting commissions, he was, thanks to his patrons, able to savour the more expensive pleasures of Kyoto—banquets at patrons' homes, visits to tea houses and restaurants along the Kamo River or in Sanbongi and Gion, also to brothels like the Sumiya in Shimabara—all places which distracted him from the continued pursuit of that 'delicate matter', *haikai*.[25] Buson had worked long and hard, and apparently resolved to enjoy whatever of life was left to him.

There were, however, more moralistic spirits among Buson's inner circle to counteract Hyakuchi and Katō. Higuchi Dōryū, Confucian scholar and Chinese poet, son of the famous Emura Hokkai, did not approve of his master's relations with a young geisha. To him goes the dismal credit of having shamed Buson into giving up Koito. One of the final letters he wrote, a few months before his death, was in response to a scolding from his straight-laced disciple:

Dear Dōryū,
I agree with your opinion on the pleasure quarters. Your letter was most appropriate, also your poems—as of today, my passion for Koito is at an end. My unseemly behaviour only brings shame upon an old man. Never again. And yet, here is a poem of mine, do give me your opinion.
     There by my love's hedge
     there grow the shamisen flowers
     now all abloom.
The sentiment is that of finding a rare jewel in the mud. It is merely a poem I've found some pleasure in lately, seated here at my desk. I am most grateful for all your concern on my behalf.
                                        4th Month, 25th Day, 1783.
                                        Buson (Letter No. 283)

When Buson's health failed during the winter of 1783, he summoned his closest disciples, not his patrons. Takai Kitō and the two painting students Ki Baitei and Matsumura Goshun helped his wife and daughter care for him. They listened to his worries about work left undone, his regrets about being far from achieving a valedictory poem as powerful as Bashō's final poem on dreams wandering through winter fields, his recollections of the past and his fears for what would become of his daughter. They recorded the final three poems he did manage to recite and watched him slip peacefully away during the night. When they sent word of their master's passing, first on the scene the next morning were the intimate patron-students mentioned above, men such as Hyakuchi, Dempuku and Katō. On the following day Kitō organised a memorial poetry session at Buson's house in which 72 poets close to Buson contributed one verse each to a linked *haikai* sequence. Kitō had the honour of presenting the opening link (*hokku*), then followed Hyakuchi, Dempuku, Goshun, with Katō and then Baitei following soon after—a poetic pecking order that reflects well Buson's degree of intimacy with the disciples and patrons concerned. It seems a sort of justice that next to last came Dōryū.[26]

Notes

1 Susan B. Hanley and Kozo Yamamura *Economic and Demographic Change in Preindustrial Japan, 1600–1868* Princeton: Princeton University Press, 1977, pp. 95–6

2 Ōtani Tokuzō (ed.) *Busonshū, Koten haibungaku taikei* Vol. 12, Tokyo: Shūeisha, 1972, pp. 472–3. All citations of Buson's letters follow the numbering of this standard edition.

3 Yamazaki Shōji 'Takai Kitō', *Buson, Issa, Nihon bungaku kenkyū shiryō sōsho* Tokyo: Yūseidō, 1975, pp. 211–29

4 On Buson and *wenren/bunjin* aesthetico-ethics, see my 'Buson and Shiki: Part One' *Harvard Journal of Asiatic Studies* 44 (Dec. 1984), pp. 381–407

5 See Margot and Rudolf Wittkower *Born Under Saturn* London: Weidenfeld & Nicolson, 1963, especially pp. 1–44, 253–80

6 ibid. pp. 34–8

7 Michael Baxandall, *Painting and Experience in Fifteenth Century Italy* Oxford: Oxford University Press, 1972, p. 1

8 An earlier letter, from 1776, to the Kyoto poet Kiyū describes in uncharacteristic detail and with genuine enthusiasm the *Oku no hosomichi* scroll Buson had made for Kiyū: see Letter No. 298

9 Imaizumi Atsuo et al. (eds) *Kyōto no rekishi* (10 vols) (Tokyo: Gakugei Shorin, 1973, 6:160–76

10 ibid. 6:182–3.

11 For a sketch of Buson's relations with Tairo, see Kuriyama Riichi 'Buson no sekai: sono seikatsu to geijutsu' *Haikai no keifu* Tokyo: Kadokawa Shoten, 1980, pp. 226–35

12 ibid. p. 232

13 *Kyōto no rekishi*, 6:173

14 *Busonshū*, Introduction, p. 23

15 Nakamura Yukihiko (ed.) *Ueda Akinarishū, Nihon koten bungaku taikei*, Vol. 56, Tokyo: Iwanami Shoten, 1959, p. 265

16   Endō Motoo *Kinsei seikatsushi nempyō* Tokyo: Yūzankaku, 1982,
     p. 241
17   Hanley and Yamamura, pp. 122–3. Note that these estimates are based
     on nineteenth-century materials.
18   ibid. pp. 122–4
19   For relations between Buson and Kyōtai, see Ōtani Tokuzō 'Tegami ni
     miru Buson' *Biburiya* No. 76 (April 1981), pp. 139–51; Maruyama
     Kazuhiko 'Buson to Kyōtai to no kōshō' *Buson, Issa* (see No. 3),
     pp. 175–84
20   Kuriyama 'Buson no sekai', pp. 196–7
21   It is not known how prevalent the practice of surrogate composition
     (*daiku*) may have been in Buson's time, but it did exist and could pro-
     vide a mercenary teacher with an important source of income; a fair
     amount of caution may be required when assessing the texts of a given
     school of *haikai* poets. Concern for professional standards amid the in-
     creasingly competitive area of *haikai* teaching in Buson's years may also
     have been involved. For example, in a letter to Kitō, Buson once sug-
     gested that the two of them compose a proxy sequence to represent the
     inner circle of their school. 'We should compose it together then add the
     names of the others. The lot of them are hardly likely to have anything
     to complain about.' (Letter No. 18)
22   *Busonshū*, p. 327
23   On Buson's love of Kabuki, see Moroi Yasuko 'Buson to Kabuki' *Tenri
     Daigaku gakuhō* No. 90 (April 1974), pp. 42–57; on Kyoto Kabuki in
     the eighteenth century, see *Kyōto no rekishi* 6:201–10
24   Buson seems to use Tairo's name to evoke an image of the Kyoto *tsū*
     (connoisseur), a rake parading his geisha friends in public. Ironically this
     would appear to be an image that Tairo and others had of old Buson.
     Kyōtai visited Tairo once in 1772 during a trip through the Kansai area.
     Once back in Nagoya, Kyōtai wrote Tairo thanking him for his hospital-
     ity and travel guidance.

>   I took your advice and headed over the Washū Pass into Yamato, and
>   from the crest of Mt Ikomo I was awestruck by the most beautiful view
>   in all Japan. To think that Kansai poets make no effort to sing the
>   praises of such a scene made me feel all the more ill at ease, even bitter
>   towards their notion of refinement. I had to accept that, as you yourself
>   said, their definition of refinement and sensitivity would have it that
>   where there is no partying and banqueting, there is nothing of in-
>   terest.

But Kyōtai appends a kind of tag ending frequent in Buson's more
strongly worded letters: 'I should not want others to hear this. Please be
certain to toss this letter into the fire.' See Kuriyama, 'Buson no sekai' p.
240
25   ibid., p. 210
26   'Karaeba', *Buson ichidaishū* (Vol. 2), *Nihon haisho taikei* Tokyo:
     Shunjūsha, 1928, 8:3–8

7

The Tale of Genji *in the eighteenth century: Keichū, Mabuchi and Norinaga*

Thomas J. Harper

There seems never to have been any doubt in anyone's mind that the eighteenth century was a great moment in the history of *The Tale of Genji*. Certainly the authors of the massive commentaries of the century regarded their work as radically different from that of the past—'as different as clouds and mud'.[1] Their successors in the nineteenth century not only ratified the assessment of their forebears, they decided that new nomenclature was needed to make the distinction unambiguous: all works prior to and including Kitamura Kigin's *Genji monogatari Kogetsushō* (1673) would be called the 'Old Commentaries'; those from Keichū's *Genchū shūi* (1696) forward would be the 'New Commentaries'. In our own century these designations remain in common use, and the principal pioneers of the New— Keichū (1640–1701), Kamo no Mabuchi (1697–1769) and Motoori Norinaga (1730–1801)—are seen not simply as remarkable for their time but as patriarchs of modern *Genji* studies. As an agenda for research, '*The Tale of Genji* in the Eighteenth Century'[2] seems absolutely clear-cut: compare a sample of clouds with one of mud and the accomplishments of this age of wonders should stand revealed.

Yet when one turns to the texts themselves, and actually begins to compare Old and New, assurance soon gives way to doubt. At a cursory glance, the New Commentaries look very like the Old Commentaries with but minor modifications. Most of the subject headings at the beginning of Norinaga's *Genji monogatari Tama no ogushi* (1796), for instance, could have been taken from Nakanoin Michikatsu's (1558–1610) *Mingō nisso*[3] completed two centuries earlier. There are short dissertations on the author, her life, how she came to write the novel, when it was written, the title, the historical basis of the plot and previous commentaries, all of which are discussed by Michikatsu and others before him. Not until the reader comes to Norinaga's general discussion of the novel (*ōmune*), in which he sets forth his famous theory of fiction (*mono no aware ron*), is there any hint of change that is other than incremental. Moving on into the body of the commentary, one finds the same format—consecutive citation followed by explication—that had been in use for some five centuries.

An equally cursory glance at the last of the Old Commentaries, Kigin's *Kogetsushō* (1673), only strengthens one's suspicions. This work really does look new. It is the first commentary to incorporate a complete text of the *Genji*. It also provides a battery of extremely useful reading aids—*furigana, furi-kanji,* punctuation, voicing marks and interlinear glosses in modern (seventeenth-century) Japanese. The headnotes include not only Kigin's own annotations, but a rich sampling drawn from the best of the earlier commentaries going back as far as Teika's *Okuiri* (ca. 1236).[4] At this point in the project, one might well wonder why *Kogetsushō* should not be counted as one of the New Commentaries, perhaps even the newest of the New.

But these are first impressions. Further investigation leaves little doubt that the eighteenth-century commentaries, despite their outward resemblance to earlier works, *are* genuinely and dramatically new. Still, the initial reservations cannot be ignored; they should suggest to the researcher that a simple comparison in terms of clouds and mud will not suffice to explain *all* that is new in the New Commentaries. The Old Commentators, too, had corrected the errors of their predecessors and made impressive contributions of their own, but always in tones of great modesty, acknowledging their debts and denigrating the value of their own work. Why should there now be such loud claims of novelty and superiority? Why for the first time in the critical history of *Genji* should progress be proclaimed as revolutionary rather than evolutionary? If we are to appreciate fully the newness of the New Commentaries, we must ask not only what was new but why it was seen as new.

Perhaps the clearest indication of where one might look for answers to both of these questions is found in the preface to Hagiwara Hiromichi's (1813–63) *Genji monogatari hyōshaku* (1854) in a passage where he explains his reasons for drawing a distinction between Old and New Commentaries:

> *Genchū shūi,* by the monk Keichū, is a fascinating and magnificent work. On the basis of extensive investigation of ancient texts, the author demonstrates the failings of the aforementioned Old Commentaries and rectifies their errors. The author is an extraordinarily learned

man. In his interpretations of the poetic anthologies he is never bound by the views of [previous] commentaries; he ascertains the facts by direct reference to the ancient texts. He makes not a single unfounded assertion; indeed he is the pioneer scholar of modern 'Critical Philology'[5] (*kōshōgaku*). His *Genchū shūi* totally changed the nature of commentary on this novel. For this reason I set it and those that follow it apart and call them the New Commentaries.[6] (pp. 36–37)

Unfortunately Hiromichi's discussion of Mabuchi is concerned mainly with textual discrepancies in the various editions of his work and reveals little of what he thinks its distinguishing qualities might be. When he moves on to Norinaga, however, the expansive tone returns:

> And then there is the venerable Motoori's *Tama no ogushi*. This work discusses in great detail every aspect of the [genre] *monogatari*. There has never before been anything like it. The way he picks out those passages where the author hints obliquely at her intentions, then brings them all together and explicates their significance—this in particular is an unprecedented piece of scholarship. His [conclusion], too—that sensitivity to emotion (*mono no aware o shiru*) is the whole point of the novel—is not to be found in any previous commentary. (p. 37)

The body of Norinaga's commentary, Hiromichi goes on to say, is as original as his general discussion of the novel. It treats such minute but important matters as syntactic flow and function (*kotoba no utsurizama, hatarakizama*) and the correlation of particles (*tenioha no kakari musubi*), and is informed throughout by a deep understanding of the workings of human feeling—all of which Norinaga sets forth in a 'calm and reasoned manner' which persuades readers to assent with whole heart to the logic of his argument.

Philological rigor and a sensitivity to the inner workings of the novel, both on a scale unknown to previous ages, are, in Hiromichi's view, the principal elements of newness in the New Commentaries. And when we turn a second time to the texts, we find that these qualities do indeed characterise all three of the great eighteenth-century commentaries.

Philological rigor is difficult to illustrate succinctly, but it is worth the risk of some tedium to demonstrate why Hiromichi regards this as so important an element of the New. In Keichū the most immediately noticeable sign of this rigor is a changed attitude to the commentaries of the past. The polite tentativeness with which commentators of the past questioned the theories of their predecessors has given way to impatience, even exasperation, with error. Where once it was

'The logic of this theory is a bit unclear',[7] 'I have my doubts about this',[8] or simply a new theory offered without mention of earlier error,[9] we now find 'this is close but not quite right',[10] 'this is not really wrong but it misses the point',[11] or more directly, 'the old commentaries are wrong'.[12] And in setting right these errors he invariably appeals to philological rectitude rather than established authority, as in this brief explication of the adverb *yaora*:

> *Yaora yoritamaite.*[13] The commentaries say this means 'immediately', *yagate*; or again that it means 'quietly', *shizukanari*. On present consideration: *yaora* is the same as *yawara*, as in *yawaraka nari*. In other works of fiction there are passages where it appears unchanged as *yawara*, which is equivalent to vernacular *sorori to*. This means 'softly', and therefore 'quietly' is the correct meaning. To say it means 'immediately' is wrong.[14]

Here the evidence cited is etymological; in another passage we find an example of the 'extraordinary learning' mentioned by Hiromichi. Near the beginning of the 'Hahakigi' chapter is a sentence which sets the scene of the famous 'rainy night discussion' of women: '*naga-ame harema naki koro, uchi no on-monoimi sashitsuzukite*' (the long rains continued without a break, and the court remained in retreat). As Keichū points out, the *Kakaishō* (1363), the oldest extant full-scale commentary on the *Genji,* annotates the word *monoimi* in this sentence with a long quotation in Chinese that traces the origin of this term to Indian legend. Here is Keichū's response:

> The *Kakaishō* here cites the *Giki* ('Rites and Rules'). The *Giki* are so named because they are collections of excerpts from the esoteric scriptures describing rites and rules for the conduct of worship of the Buddhas and Bodhisattvas. They are Buddhist scriptures. Amongst the scriptures brought from China by the eight patriarchs of Shingon, there are numerous *Giki*, but not one of them has anything to say about matters of this sort. The text cited is probably a forgery by some Japanese master of Ying–Yang divination.[15]

Keichū is perhaps too harsh on the *Kakaishō*. Modern printed editions of the commentary do not in fact state that this quotation is drawn from the *Giki*, but only that it is translated by the Chinese monk Gijō [I-Ching; 635–713]. The attribution which seems to have found its way into Keichū's text may not have been put there by the author. Moreover the *Kakaishō* citation is repeated in substantially the same form in the *Ainōshō*,[16] a Muromachi period miscellany containing a number of Buddhist texts, which suggests that Ying–Yang diviners and gullible noblemen were not the only ones to accept it as authentic. But whether or not the attack is precipitate, the grounds upon which it is based are significant: instead of simply repeating the earliest comment on this matter, as every scholar before him had done, Keichū—a Shingon monk who claims to have read the *Giki*—denounces the text upon which the original comment depends, thus undercutting the authority of the previous 300 years on the matter of *monoimi*. This is not of much help to anyone reading the second chapter of *Genji*, but as a style of scholarship it is startlingly new. As Hiromichi says, Keichū is mainly concerned to 'rectify the errors of the Old Commentaries; his work is seldom of use in dealing with the text'.[17]

Moving on to Mabuchi's *Genji monogatari shinshaku* we notice a marked shift in emphasis, away from denigration of scholars of the past and towards 'user friendliness'. Compare, for example, Mabuchi's annotation of the same occurrence of *monoimi*:

> The '*mono*' is the *mono* of *mono no ke*, *bakemono*, and such—i.e. it means 'spirits'. In the *Man'yōshū* the character 鬼 'spirit' is often used to render the word '*mono*'. '*Imi*' is the same as *imitsutsushimu*, to practice abstention. In times of natural disasters, and even against minor mishaps and bad dreams, people would shut their gates and write *monoimi*, 'abstention against spirits', on slips of paper which they would attach to blinds and screens and such, and then go into retreat. These practices were dictated by Ying–Yang diviners, and seem to have extended to even the most insignificant mishaps.[18]

This is unmistakably the work of another practitioner of 'Critical Philology' grounded in etymology and textual evidence, but here the aim is to help rather than condemn. The tendency is even more marked in his explications of poetry, where the reader stands in greatest need of help. Here, for instance, is his explanation of the teasing poem with which Oborozukiyo no Naishi no Kami replies to Genji when , on the morning after their first night together, he asks her name:[19]

> *ukimi yo ni [yagate kienaba tazunetemo kusa no hara oba towaji to ya omou.]* (were I, unfortunate one, simply to perish from this earth, inquire though you may, would you yet not come to the grassy moor in search of me?) That she speaks of perishing suggests how thoroughly infatuated she is. The grassy moor is the graveyard, the world of the dead. Therefore, when she says 'would you not come to the grassy moor?', she is reproaching him: 'even though henceforward I put all my trust in you, for you this is no bond to last into worlds beyond, but only a fleeting whim of the present world. If you cared for me at all deeply, surely you would show some sign that you wished to come in search of me; but instead you only say, if I do not tell you my name how can you inquire after me?'[20]

No previous commentary gives anywhere near as helpful an explication of both the meaning and intent of this poem. Nor, for that matter, has any subsequent edition improved upon it.

In Norinaga, it is as if the critical correctiveness of Keichū and the
philological friendliness of Mabuchi are combined, and in the process
the compass of both expanded and their quality exhanced. As Hiromichi notes, this extends even to brief but extremely useful notes on
syntax and usage; here for instance is a random sampling found within the space of two pages:

> *Omoitamaeru* is always used to show deference to another. When
> speaking of oneself, one said *omoitamauru*. Scholars of later ages were
> ignorant of the distinction and carelessly took them to mean the same
> thing. One sees this error frequently.[21]

> When the syntax of a sentence seems jarring, one should read on and
> work out the relationship [of the various clauses]. When you persist in
> puzzling over a passage without achieving this sort of understanding
> you will usually go wrong.[22]

> *Nari keri* is an ending that is always attached to a word explaining the
> reason for some previously described situation.[23]

> The particle *mo* here corresponds to vernacular *maa*; it adds a dimen-
> sion of depth to the overall sense of the poem.[24]

In correcting the earlier commentaries, he may point not only to specific error but to failings in method as well; as in this note on the word
hanayaka naru:

> The *Kakaishō*, citing *Hakushi monjū*, renders this word with the char-
> acters 声花. In many of its notes on the novel it cites some compound
> found in a Chinese text or else the *Nihongi*. On rare occasions, they
> are correct and we learn something from them. But often its render-
> ings are dubious and irresponsible. Hence, when one follows uncriti-
> cally the renditions in these notes, one will misconstrue the meaning.
> As a rule it is best not to depend upon any of them. 声花, in the
> *Hakushi monjū* is read *hanayaka*; in this sense it is correct. But to take
> *hanayaka* as meaning only 声花 is quite mistaken. One may read 声花
> as *hanayaka*, but one must not take *hanayaka* to mean 声花. One
> must be aware of this in using any of these notes.[25]

Or Norinaga may point out some contextual determinant to the
meaning of a word:

> In the *Kakaishō* we find, '*nazusai* means *naremutsubu*'. This word,
> when it occurs in prose fiction (*monogataribumi*) invariably means

this. It also occurs frequently in the *Man'yōshū*, and its meaning as used there in poetry is quite different. . . .[26]

Elsewhere, comment on a word or phrase may lead into a discussion not of its meaning but of its role in the larger structure of the narrative, as in this disquisition on one of Uma no Kami's remarks in the Rainy Night Discussion of women in 'Hahakigi':

> *Ue ga ue wa uchiokihaberinu* ('And so I leave them where they are, the highest of the high.') This entire discussion, from beginning to end, deals exclusively with the middle rank of women. This particular phrase follows a passage that begins 'those who have just arrived at high position', and proceeds, point by point, down to the present phrase. This same phrase also governs all sections that follow, down to the very end [of the discussion]. It is this phrase, then, by which we know that the discussion deals only with the middle rank, and not the highest of the high or the lowest of the low.
>
> At the beginning, To no Chūjō speaks of 'those born to high rank', 'the middle rank', and 'the lowest rank'. This passage, too, when you consider the wording, seems meant to suggest a discussion of the middle rank alone, in the course of which something is suggested of the character of the high and low.
>
> Then again, the aforementioned passage, beginning 'those who have just arrived at high position' and proceeding on to 'when a woman has the highest rank and a spotless reputation', has as its main concern the categorizing of women by rank, while the several sections that follow discuss the character and behaviour of these women. That which comes before [this division] and that which follows it form, so to speak, the warp and weft of the discussion.
>
> To read the novel careless of such detail slights the care lavished upon it by the author.[27]

Fortunately it is neither so difficult nor so necessary to demonstrate the second element of Newness of which Hiromichi speaks—sensitivity to the inner workings of the novel. Norinaga's *mono no aware ron* is too well known to require elaboration here. From the foregoing samples we can see that the same sensitivity that characterises his famous preface informs his commentary as well. What may perhaps need to be pointed out is that Norinaga is not the only one of the New Commentators to possess this sensitivity. The refutation of the Buddhist interpretations of the Old Commentaries upon which Norinaga grounds his treatise is to be found in germinal form in Keichū; and the larger view of the *Genji*, as a member of the genre *monogatari*, which forms the framework of Norinaga's treatise, is foreshadowed by Mabuchi. Just as all three of our New Commentators are 'Critical Philologists', all three are sensitive readers. Their work is refreshingly replete with all that Hiromichi claims for them in proclaiming them pioneers.

And yet—one feels almost ungrateful to ask—and yet, is their work so radically different that it marks a distinct rupture with all that goes before it? Anyone who has used the Old Commentaries, learned from them, and found some of their revelations exciting, is bound to wonder why there should be such fanfare about the advances of the eighteenth century. Philological rigor is not utterly unknown in the Old Commentaries, nor was Norinaga the first scholar to detect structural pattern in 'Hahakigi'. One need not demean the erudition and perspicacity of the New Commentators to suspect that something more than a passion for Truth lies behind the fervour of these scholars and the acclaim with which their work was met. As to what this something else might be, Hagiwara Hiromichi is again our best guide. Here is the passage in his preface where he explains why he relegates all that precedes Keichū to the catetory of 'Old Commentaries':

Now, *Kakaishō, Kachō yosei*, and the other [early] commentaries were most of them written by ranking gentlemen of the court nobility (*kumo no ue haruka naru onkatagata no arawashitamaeru mono nite*), and they date from an age nearer to antiquity than our own. One might well wonder, therefore, how they could be [so inaccurate]. But let us consider the reasons. These learned gentlemen of the past had one unfortunate failing—whatever they learned they kept secret. Even the most insignificant bits of knowledge were kept secret. As a result, these commentaries would be transmitted secretly to no more than one or two persons. Not only was there no custom of sharing their work, they were lax about the collection and collation of ancient texts and the study of evidence (*koto no akashi o kangauru nado no manabi*, i.e. *kōshōgaku*, 'Critical Philology'). In many cases they would simply conclude that such-and-such was the case and compose their annotation from memory. Consider too the matter of court customs and ceremonies, clothing and furnishings. Since these commentaries were written by persons of such exalted lineage, we would expect that surely *they* would not be in error. And yet when we compare their work with the ancient texts, we sometimes have our doubts. This, I think, is because as the years passed, court customs and ceremonies developed into something quite different from those of the regin of the Ichijō emperor, when the novel was written. After the Jokyū and Kemmu disturbances (1219 and 1333) even the palace was quite changed from what it had been in the past. Moreover, the age in which the commentators themselves lived was a troubled one. Now of course, if we know all there is to know about something, there is no need for anyone to write a commentary about it; but the amount of detail that remains unknown, even with these commentaries, is extraordinary; which makes it difficult to trust anything they have to say. For this reason, the *Kogetsushō* and all commentaries prior to it I call the 'Old Commentaries', and I do not as a rule cite them.[28]

There is more than a hint here that Hiromichi is drawing a social as well as an academic distinction between the Old and the New Commentators. His language is almost excessively deferential, but his verdict is clear: the Old Commentators were aristocrats (or those who for one reason or another had entreé to aristocratic society), and the characteristic attitudes of that class had a deleterious effect upon their scholarship. Their possessiveness precluded any extensive investigation of sources; their smugness led them to false conclusions; their secretiveness deprived them of the benefits of argumentative scrutiny by other scholars.

This of course is Hiromichi's retrospective view of the social situation of the New Commentaries, but when we check to see whether the New Commentators themselves would draw such a distinction, we find that all three of them do indeed associate the failings of the Old Commentaries with the aristocratic lineage of their authors. Here are the very first words of Keichū's *Genchū shūi*:

> The first of the major commentaries on this novel is the *Kakaishō*. However, whether due to lapses in memory or scribal errors in transcription, not a few citations said to be drawn from the *Nihongi, Man'yōshū*, and such are not to be found in the original texts. Subsequent commentaries, compiled by noblemen of later ages (*nochi ni yoki hitobito no tsuzukite tsukuritamaeru shōdomo*) built upon this work, and, on the assumption that the author was a man to be trusted, repeated his errors without checking the sources. Nor is this true of this one work alone. Hardly any commentary on any work of prose fiction (*kana monogatari*) fails to perpetuate these errors. Caution is called for. The saying 'if the start is in disorder, the finish can not be well ordered'[29] applies to all things.[30]

Mabuchi is more diplomatic in assigning the blame for these shortcomings, but he too traces them to aristocratic origins.

> It is not that these gentlemen of quality (*yoki atari*) would knowingly have put false information in their commentary. It is more likely that some ardent enthusiast (*sukigoto no mono*) has added these citations interlinearly; or that someone who knew nothing of ancient studies (*kogaku*) had the good fortune to be summoned to lecture (*tokikiko* [yu]) to some gentleman of quality, which nobleman (*kijin*), in good faith (*shōjiki ni oboshite*), noted down (*shirushitamau*) these citations without reference to the original texts—hence the great number of errors.

Norinaga, in *Genji monogatari Tama no ogushi*, seems even more circumspect than Mabuchi in his treatment of the Old Commentators. His discussion of earlier commentaries does mention the errors of the *Kakaishō* and *Kachō yosei*, but nonetheless concludes that these works are 'indispensible'.[32] Were we to look no further than this, we might think him quite unconcerned by matters of lineage. Yet we know from other sources that his condemnation of the secret teachings of the aristocratic schools of poetry can be at least as harsh as Hiromichi's. Would he take a different view of their studies of the *Genji*? Indeed he does not. As it happens he has only deleted his discussion of this matter from the final draft of *Tama no ogushi*. In an earlier work, *Shibun yōryō* (1763), which with minor alterations and excisions he used as the preface to *Tama no ogushi*, he has a great deal to say about the scholarship of the aristocracy:

There are those, in all walks of life, who will accept uncritically any theory propounded by a gentleman of high birth (*yangotonaki hito*). 'This,' they will say, 'is the secret theory of such-and-such a great house.' 'This is the honoured theory of Lord so-and-so.' In scholarship (*gakumon*), however, in whatever field, worth is not determined by rank. The [work] of someone of a certain [noble] family may be of no worth whatever; while it often happens that someone of the most humble birth will produce surpassingly fine work. It goes without saying that the Way of Poetry originates in our innate feelings and is shaped by the individual's knowledge and devotion to the art. The same is true of poetic scholarship. One must not, therefore, believe uncritically [a theory] because it is [the property of] a certain house or [the work of] a certain [noble]man. This is a matter to be decided only on the basis of merit. The rank beginner will not, of course, be able to distinguish what is good and what is bad. Nevertheless, precisely because such knowledge is needed, it would be unutterably foolish to conclude categorically that [the work of] the noble families (*kika*) is superior. Some good may well come of the fact that the various polite arts (*shogei*) are preserved in these families. But scholarship is not one of the polite arts. Here we have a canon of ancient texts, and there can be nothing more correct than what is propounded on the basis of them. What then are we to think of those modern scholars who ignore the truth as it is propounded in the ancient texts and subscribe to the notions of this house or that person, as if [scholarship] were the same as those polite arts that have no written sources of any sort. The so-called secret teachings of the noble houses of the recent past are for the most part formulated arbitrarily, without any deep study of the ancient texts. When one does consult the ancient texts, therefore, their errors are apparent. One should not accept uncritically these erroneous theories.

simply because it is 'the secret theory of such-and-such a great house' or 'the honoured theory of Lord so-and-so'. One must always consult the ancient texts and draw one's conclusions upon careful considera- tion of what is good and bad, correct and incorrect. This is the essen- tial key to understanding this novel, just as it is the essential key to understanding in poetic scholarship.[33]

And at the very end of the same work, we find this impassioned postscript—also excised from the revised version:

This work, *Shibun yōryō*, volumes 1 and 2, is the product of my own ideas of recent years, the result of repeated thoughtful reading of the novel. It owes nothing to the teachings of my mentor; it is as different from previous commentaries as are clouds and mud. Those who may read it, pray do not regard it not with suspicion. Savour first the spirit of the novel, and against it weigh this work; then decide whether what I say is right or wrong. Pray reject not these words for the condition of the man who wrote them! My writing, moreover, is poor; as this is only a draft, I have paid no attention to style. I trust judgement will be withheld until it is revised and re-copied. Pray reject not the man for the condition of his words![34]

From this it should be clear that all three of our New Commenta- tors are animated by more than just a zeal for Truth. Were getting it right their only concern, they could easily have afforded to be more magnanimous to those they criticise, and more modest about their own contributions to what by then was a critical tradition of seven centuries' standing. Yet, throughout the rhetoric of Critical Philology runs a clear descant of protest—protest not simply against ideological blindness, methodological laxity and outright error, but against the smug exclusivity of the aristocratic class that produces such blemished scholarship.

To a twentieth-century sensibility, accustomed to a more strident and aggressive style of scholarship than was once usual, this may seem comfortably familiar and 'modern'. But if we make some attempt to situate the New Commentaries in an eighteenth-century setting, we find there is more to their tone than just a forgivable excess of confidence.

The 'National Studies' (*kokugaku*) movement, of which Keichū, Mabuchi and Norinaga were all central figures, is now rightly seen as one of the most important schools of scholarship of the Edo period. In the eighteenth century, however, it was by no means a part of the mainstream of scholarship. If scholars of Neo-Confucianism had difficulty gaining recognition—and patronage—for their studies,[35] the problems were vastly more difficult for scholars of *Kokugaku*.

Keichū, as a monk, derived most of his living from his temple. Only in middle age (1743) did Mabuchi obtain his position as tutor/adviser to Tayasu Munetake (1715–71). Norinaga, almost until his death, earned his living as a physician. He lectured to his students in the evening, and studied and wrote late at night. The degree to which scholars of this sort could feel slighted and excluded is movingly revealed in Norinaga's diatribes against those scholars of things Chinese who would be mortified to be found ignorant of even the most obscure point of Chinese history or literature, and yet would cheerfully, almost proudly, confess to total lack of knowledge of their own country[36]; or against the injustice of using the word 'scholarship' (*gakumon*) to refer to Chinese studies while a special designation, 'national studies' (*kokugaku*), was needed to refer to the study of Japan.[37] Surely, too, there is some significance in the fact that Keichū, Mabuchi, and some of their predecessors in the *Kokugaku* school are among the biographies of the *Kinsei kijin den*, 'Lives of Modern Eccentrics', where their lives are encapsulated along with those of the rich man who lay in a ditch all day reading borrowed books (*Kinsei kijin den*, pp. 122–23), the calligrapher whose hut was in such a shambles he had to suspend a tub over his table to keep the rain off his paper (224–26), and the samurai whose greatest delight was to lie down for a nap on his money (296–98). Apparently only a bit of an odd fellow would take up the study of things Japanese.

In such a situation, one might imagine that scholars of things Japanese would have found interested colleagues, and perhaps even political allies, among the old court families, who had themselves maintained, under considerable adversity, a long tradition of Japanese literary studies. Yet here too the *Kokugakusha* were shut out, at least from entry on their own merits. 'Poetry is the exclusive domain of the court,' the *Taiheiki* reminds us;[38] and the court was not anxious to share the lore that constituted such a large part of its own claim to a share of Bakufu patronage. It was, of course, common enough for the court poet/scholars to accept disciples of less than noble birth—at first from the ranking military clans, as in the case of Taira no Tadanori (1144–84), but later from the most obscure origins, as with Sōgi (1421–1502), the renga master. But to be accepted as a disciple, pledged to total subservience, was one thing; to be recognised as a colleague, purely on the merit of one's work, was quite another, for which the indispensible prerequisite was high birth. A *Kokugakusha* might apprentice himself to a nobleman as a student of poetry and the classics, as Norinaga did for a time while a student in Kyoto; for their own ideas they could expect no hearing whatever, and possibly even expulsion from disciplehood should they be so bold as to express them. It is no coincidence that all of the Old Commentators who were not of noble birth (e.g. Sōgi, Kigin) were nonetheless initiates in the Secret Teachings of the *Kokinshū* (*Kokin Denju*) that Hiromichi so reviles.

Unfortunately for the researcher, snobbery of this sort is more likely to be expressed in significant silences than in words, and thus is even more difficult to document than the fruits of Critical Philology. Every now and again, though, one does catch hints of it, not from the aristocrats themselves, but in the writings of their awed disciples. Probably the most famous is Matsunaga Teitoku's own description of the silent fury of Nakanoin Michikatsu upon learning that Teitoku had disseminated his knowledge of the classics, acquired from his noble master, in lectures to the rabble.

> He [Nakanoin Michikatsu] was furious with me for ignoring the counsel of the ancients 'not to tell at the roadside what one has learned along the way'.[39] My crime was inexcusable. Even now, when I recall it, I am helpless with grief. Had he been a base commoner like myself, he would have summoned me and struck me; but because he was of the highest ranking nobility, he showed not a sign of his anger, even when we sat face to face. Oh, the shame! What a thoughtless fool I was when I was young![40]

Another renga master, Okanishi Ichū (1639–1711), holds forth in his *Ichiji zuihitsu* on the importance of knowing the authors of the great scholarly works of the past. He begins with a list of these works, all by aristocratic and imperial authors, and then goes on to speak of *Genji* scholarship:

> There are a great many commentaries on the *Genji*. The *Kakaishō*, in 20 fascicles, is by Lord Yotsutsuji. *Kachō yosei*, in 20 volumes, is the commentary of Lord Gojōonji [Ichijō Kanera]. *Rōka* [*shō*] in 8 volumes, is from the brush of Muan Rōjin [Sōgi]. *Sairyū shō*, in 20 scrolls, is by Lord Shōyōin [Sanjōnishi Kin'eda]. *Myōjōshō* is by Lord Sankōin [Sanjōnishi Saneeda].
>
> *Bansui Ichiro*, in 54 fascicles, is by someone called Noto no Eikan, a disciple of the monk Sōken. This commentary enjoys wide popularity in the world at large, but Lord Karasumaru Mitsuo (1647–1690) this spring mentioned that in the honoured houses of the nobility they do not deign to use it. It was a great privilege to learn of this.[41]

Yet another renga master, Wada Sonō, writing in the early eighteenth century, has this to say in his *Genji monogatari tai'i*:

> Since the *Kogetsushō*, a great many commentaries on the *Genji* have been written by commoners. For the most part their grasp of the language is adequate, but often the spirit of the work escapes them. By

this I mean that the author Murasaki Shikibu was deeply imbued with
the teachings of the Buddha. If one is ignorant of Buddhism one can
hardly understand Murasaki's meaning. (p. 16)

The evidence is slight, and none of it comes from the court scholars
themselves; we have only the word of their devoted (and apparently
deeply grateful) disciples. Still it does give some sense of the atmosphere in which the New Commentators of the eighteenth century
worked. As far as the nobility were concerned, the notion of what we
now call Japanese Literature did not exist. The literature of Japan
was not a national heritage. It was the family property of the nobles
whose ancestors had written it—or at best the cultural heritage of the
aristocratic class. They might deign to initiate certain underlings in its
mysteries; what anyone else might have to say about it was not only
irrelevant but presumptuous.

In this setting, the sharp words and shrill tones of the New Commentaries begin to seem less the cries of over-sensitive egos than part
of a strategy to discredit the Old Commentators as incompetent
custodians of classical tradition, and thus to gain a hearing for their
authors' views on a subject normally closed to outsiders. There was
more to the strategy, of course, than bold rhetoric. In this 'age of
commentary', when scholars customarily demonstrated their learning
and expressed their opinions through comment on some canonical
text, there could be no more effective way of making a point than to
demonstrate that previous commentators had misread or misinter-
preted the text—hence, no doubt, the eagerness of the New Commentaries to point a finger at error. Their methodology, too—*kogaku/
kōshōgaku*—served political as well as epistemological ends. As the
favoured method of several of the newer schools of Confucian
studies, it would have lent some of the authority of the mainstream
to their cause. More importantly, however, it legitimised a direct appeal to ancient texts as the final authority, in the process bypassing
the court nobles and rendering their family traditions irrelevant.
What need to be privy to the secrets of the Three Great Genji Questions if one can answer them more authoritatively by citing the
Nihongi or *Man'yōshū*, as Keichū and Mabuchi do repeatedly? Norinaga, for his part, is a particular beneficiary of *kogaku/kōshōgaku*.
The attempt to purge what were seen as Buddhist distortions from
Chu Hsi Neo-Confucian thought provided an extremely useful prece-
dent for his attempts to do the same with *Genji* scholarship.

Conversely, the stridency was not all strategy; a significant portion
of it was sheer emotion. This component of the mix is much more
difficult to analyse, but we can perhaps grasp something of its power
from a more recent—and more overt—instance.

In 1980 the Reizei family of Kyoto, direct descendents of the great court poet Fujiwara Teika and owners of a treasure trove of documents passed down in his line, announced that they would open up their storehouses to the inspection of scholars and transfer their contents to the custodianship of a foundation, the Shiguretei Bunko. In doing so they relinquished, if not ownership itself, the right to sell these manuscripts as private property and the right to deny access to them to serious scholars who wished to consult them. The reaction of the mass media to the announcement was tumultous and sustained. Most of the reportage dwelt upon the riches of the storehouses and the high-minded generosity of the Reizei family. However, tucked away in the pages of a special issue of *Asahi gurafu* devoted to full-page colour photographs of the documents, was an interview with the eminent textual scholar, Kyūsojin Hitaku, which struck a slightly different note. Professor Kyūsojin was asked to comment on the significance for scholarship of the new archive. He replied, 'The first thing to be said is that an archive of this sort must be regarded as a repository of the 'property of the Japanese people' (*Nihonjin no zaisan*).' (p. 63) Then, to illustrate his point, he told of an experience his own teacher had some years earlier:

> Sasaki Nobutsuna [1872–1963] was once shown the Genryaku Kōhon
> Text of the *Man'yōshū*, now ranked as a National Treasure, at the
> home of its owner, Baron Furukawa. On that occasion, when the
> Baron brought in the manuscript, he was smoking a cigar. Professor
> Sasaki fairly exploded with indignation. 'You may think of this as your
> very own,' he bellowed at the Baron, 'but in fact it is the property of all
> mankind (*jinrui no zaisan*), and you are nothing more than its custo-
> dian.' (p. 63)

The confrontation here is direct and the provocation more dramatic—and hence the reaction more explicit than that of the New Commentators. But the difference, surely, is only one of degree. Keichū's uncharacteristic railing, Mabuchi's occasional testiness, Norinaga's almost melodramatic protests of absolute originality, and even Hiromichi's insistence upon the epoch-making quality of their work rise, I think, from the same source as Professor Sasaki's indignation against the Baron Furukawa. They are bent not simply upon getting the facts straight; they are claiming property rights to *The Tale of Genji*, if not for 'all mankind', at least for all Japanese.

Happily, this view of the New Commentaries, as the products of partisan strategies and self-righteous ire, need not undermine our appreciation of the work of these eighteenth-century scholars or discredit the assessment of it by their successors. Rather, it helps us to see why the New Commentaries are so very new. If plebeian scholars of things Japanese had been welcomed by the Confucian and aristocratic establishments, if the only impetus to change had been the changing needs of readers yet further removed from the world of the *Genji* than those of previous centuries, it is hard to imagine that anyone would have proclaimed a break between Old and New. Without the goad of wounded pride and the strategies it inspired, there probably would have been no New Commentaries, only more and better versions of what had gone before—valuable, no doubt, but lacking the sharp edges of relentless accuracy and new ideas aggressively argued.

Notes

1   *Motoori Norinaga zenshū* (*MNZ*) Ono Susumu and Ōkubo Tadashi (eds), Tokyo: Chikuma Shobō, Vol. 4, p. 133
2   The one hundred years here called the eighteenth century actually begins in 1696, the year in which Keichū's *Genchū shūi* was published, and ends in 1796 with Motoori Norinaga's *Genji monogatari Tama no ogushi*.
3   1598; *Genji monogatari kochū shūsei* (*GMKS*) Tokyo: Ōfūsha, Vol. 11, p. 15
4   The version of Kigin's work currently in print, edited by Arikawa Takehiko, also contains quotation marks and a sampling of notes from the New Commentaries. The original edition can be consulted in *Kitamura Kigin Kochūshaku shūsei (KKKS)* Tokyo: Shintensha, Vol. 7, p. 17.
5   'Critical Philology' is Paul Demiéville's translation of *k'ao-cheng* [*hsüeh*], the Chinese antecedent of *kōshōgaku*. See Paul Demiéville 'Chang Hsüeh-ch'eng and his Historiography in W. G. Beasley and E. G. Pulleyblank (eds) *Historians of China and Japan* London: Oxford University Press, 1961, p. 168
6   So far as I can determine, Hiromichi is the first person to draw this distinction between *shinchū* and *kyūchū*. Keichū occasionally refers to earlier commentaries as *kochū* (e.g. *Keichū zenshū* (*KZ*) Hisamatsu Sen'ichi (ed.) Tokyo: Iwanami Shoten, Vol. 9, p. 252) but never suggests that his own work should be called 'new'. Probably the distinction was suggested by the *shinchū/kochū* of Confucian studies, where the terms were used to distinguish the new commentaries of the Sung Dynasty from the old of the Han and T'ang.
7   *GMKS*, Vol. 1 p. 13
8   ibid., p. 172
9   ibid., p. 23; s.v. *osaosa*; cf. *Kokobun chūshaku zensho* (*KCZ*) Muromatsu Iwao (ed.) Tokyo: Kokugakuin Daigaku Shuppanbu, Vol. 3, pp. 32–3
10 *KZ*, Vol. 9, p. 252
11 ibid., p. 277
12 ibid., p. 250

13 *Nihon koten bungaku taikei* (*NKBT*) Tokyo: Iwanami Shoten, Vol. 14, p. 90; 'he quietly drew near'
14 *KZ*, Vol. 9, p. 243
15 ibid.
16 1445; *Nihon koten zenshū* (*NKZ*) Masamune Atsuo (ed.) Tokyo: Nihon Koten Zenshū Kankōtai, Series 5, no vol. no., p. 67
17 *KCZ*, Vol. 12, p. 37
18 *Kamo no Mabuchi zenshū* (*KMZ*) Hisamatsu Sen'ichi (ed.) Tokyo: Zoku Gunsho Ruijū Kanseikai, Vol. 13, p. 62
19 *NKBT*, Vol. 14, p. 307
20 *KMZ*, Vol. 13, p. 282
21 *MNZ*, Vol. 4, p. 323
22 ibid., pp. 323–4
23 ibid., p. 324
24 ibid.
25 ibid., p. 318
26 ibid., p. 329
27 ibid., p. 430
28 *KCZ*, Vol. 12, p. 36
29 '*Moto midarenureba sue osamarazu*'; after *Ta hsüeh*. *Chūgoku koten sen* (*CKS*) Yoshikawa Kōjirō (ed.) Tokyo: Asahi Shimbunsa, Vol. 4, pp. 52–3
30 *KZ*, Vol. 9, p. 223
31 *KMZ*, Vol. 13, p. 32
32 *MNZ*, Vol. 4, p. 180
33 ibid., pp. 14–15
34 ibid., p. 113
35 W. J. Boot *The Adoption and Adaption of Neo-Confucianism in Japan*. Leiden: Rijksuniversiteit Leiden, 1982, particularly Chapter IV.
36 *MNZ*, Vol. 1., pp. 40–41
37 ibid., pp. 47–8
38 *NKBT*, Vol. 34, p. 63
39 '*Michi ni kikite michi ni toku koto nakare*'; after *Lun yü* 17. *CKS* Vol. 3, pp. 274–5
40 *Taionki*; *NKBT*, Vol. 95, p. 60
41 *Nihon zuihitsu taisei* (*NZT*) Hayakawa Junzaburō (ed.) Tokyo: Nihon Zuihitsu Taisei Kankōkai, 1st series, Vol. 1, p. 734

References

Arikawa Takehiko (ed.) *Zōchū Genji monogatari Kogetsushō* (3 vols) Osaka: Yukawa Kōbunsha, 1953
Asahai gurafu 3092 (1 July 1982)
Boot, W. J., *The Adoption and Adaptation of Neo-Confucianism in Japan: The Role of Fujiwara Seika and Hayashi Razan* Leiden: Rijksuniversiteit Leiden, 1982

Chūgoku koten sen Yoshikawa Kōjirō (ed.) (20 vols) Tokyo: Asahi Shimbun-sha, 1965–66 [*CKS*]

Demiéville, Paul, 'Chang Hsüeh-ch'eng and his Historiography' in *Historians of China and Japan*, W. G. Beasley and E. G. Pulleyblank (eds) London: Oxford University Press, 1961

Genji monogatari kochū shūsei (15 vols) Tokyo: Ōfūsha, 1978–84 [GMKS]

Genji monogatari tai'i, Takatani Mieko and Fujikawage Toshiaki (eds) Honkoku Heian bungaku shiryō kō, 2. Hiroshima: Hiroshima Heian Bungaku Kenkyūkai, 1968

Kamo no Mabuchi zenshū Hisamatsu Sen'ichi (ed.) (27 vols) Tokyo: Zoku Gunsho Ruijū Kanseikai, 1977–   [*KMZ*]

Keichū zenshū Hisamatsu Sen'ichi (ed.) (16 vols) Tokyo: Iwanami Shoten, 1973–76 [*KZ*]

Kinsei kijin den, Zoku Kinsei kijin den, Munemasa Isō, (ed.) Tōyō Bunko 202, Tokyo: Heibonsha, 1972

Kitamura Kigin Kochūshaku shūsei (50 vols) Tokyo: Shintensha, 1977–83 [*KKKS*]

Kokubun chūshaku zensho Muromatsu Iwao (ed.) (20 vols) Tokyo: Kokugakuin Daigaku Shuppanbu, 1908–10 [*KCZ*]

Motoori Norinaga zenshū, Ono Susumu and Ōkubo Tadashi (eds) (22 vols) Tokyo: Chikuma Shobō, 1968–   [*MNZ*]

Nihon koten bungaku taikei (100 vols) Tokyo: Iwanami Shoten, 1957–68 [*NKBT*]

Nihon koten zenshū Masamune Atsuo (ed.) (266 vols) Tokyo: Nihon Koten Zenshū Kankōkai, 1925–44 [*NKZ*]

Nihon zuihitsu taisei Hayakawa Junzaburō (ed.) (41 vols) Tokyo: Nihon Zuihitsu Taisei Kankōkai, 1927–31 [*NZT*]

8

The role of traditional aesthetics

Nakano Mitsutoshi

The eighteenth century falls neatly into the middle of the nearly 300 years of the Tokugawa era. It is now common practice to designate this period as the 'middle early modern', but since this term has only become established in the last ten years, I feel it would be useful to begin with a discussion of this periodisation.

In earlier histories of Tokugawa literature, the most common periodisation was a division into two: early and late. The early period was said to have centred in Kansai (Kyoto–Osaka) and the late in Edo, with their respective representative writers such as Matsuo Bashō (1644–94), Ihara Saikaku (1642–93) and Chikamatsu Monzaemon (1653–1725) listed for the early period, and Santō Kyōden (1761–1816), Shikitei Samba (1776–1882), Jippensha Ikku (1765–1837) and Takizawa Bakin (1767–1848) for the late. This periodisation was also generally applied in cultural histories. Recently, however, scholars have become aware of, and accepted the necessity for, three divisions: namely, early, middle and late. The first spans 1603 to 1715, ending with the famous government reforms of Kyoho (1716–35); the second spans 1716 to 1800, ending with the Kansei reforms (1789–1800); and the final period ends in 1868. The reason for this new periodisation lies, I believe, in a reappraisal of the art and culture of the eighteenth century by modern historians. In the former two-phase division, this century was treated simply as transitional, during which the centre of culture moved from Kansai to Edo, and was termed 'The Period of Gradual Eastward Transition of Culture'. It was not considered necessary to treat it as a separate era in its own right. Obviously, this judgement of the 1700s was supported by the advocates of the view that Tokugawa culture was essentially popular in nature. The eighteenth century, therefore, was seen simply as transitional, and as producing no writer of the stature of the great names listed for the centuries before and after it. This 'two-period' appraisal was widely accepted in the so-called 'post-war democratic era', and though its wide acceptance is understandable, this view has become patently anachronistic. It has become evident that the culture of the eighteenth century has to be recognised as worthwhile in its own right and is, in fact, perhaps even superior to the cultures of the earlier and later centuries. This reappraisal also challenged the hitherto prevalent view that Edo culture was primarily popular in nature. The new view of the Edo period is an attempt to present the culture of the Bakufu feudal system from a more rigorously accurate historical perspective, without the distortions of previous simplistic views. And this approach has, at last, provided us with a more accurate picture of Tokugawa culture, giving the eighteenth century its due importance in the cultural history of the nation. In fact the Middle Period can be seen as the time of its apogee, and the best representative of the Edo Period as a whole.

The social system during the Tokugawa era was authoritarian and hierarchical, and a rigid class structure dominated the lifestyles of all the social classes. It goes without saying that upper-class culture was considered superior. Certainly there was a lively townsmen's culture, but it was always in an inferior position *vis à vis* the upper-class culture, which it constantly sought to imitate. It never became upper-class in its own right; indeed, the most fascinating feature of the eighteenth century is the fact that during this time 'high' culture provided active leadership and functioned as a refining influence on popular culture. The historians who first began to re-evaluate the Edo period focused on the eighteenth century; they must be congratulated for opening up the possibility for a more accurate view of this era. Literary historians, too, will no doubt be stimulated to review their own interpretations of this century.

The terms most often used to describe Tokugawa aesthetics are essentially connected with pleasure-seeking: *sui* (elegance), *tsū* (connoisseurship), and *iki* (refinement). I have described these terms in a recent paper,[1] and will content myself with presenting only its conclusion here. The terms *sui* and *tsū* had their origins in the licensed pleasure quarters at a time when they had an aesthetic life and a vigorous, creative culture; they were the ideals of the sophisticated customers who frequented them. This particular form of 'aspiring' culture can only be maintained as long as a well-defined class system exists. At first, the culture of the pleasure quarters was sustained by the daimyo aspiring to aristocratic culture. Then it was taken up by wealthy townsmen who aspired to the aesthetic experiences of daimyo, and finally it became the domain of the ordinary town-dweller who longed to feel, if only for one night, like a daimyo. At this point, culture expired. In chronological terms, the 'high-culture' of the pleasure quarters lasted into the 1800s, but by the time of the Tempō Reforms, in the 1840s, had lost its vigor. The terms *sui* and *tsū*, while still in use, had lost all their cultural and aesthetic connotations, and had become simply descriptions of certain kinds of behaviour in the pleasure quarters. *Iki*, as 'refinement', denoted the mental or spiritual qualities associated with the terms *sui* and *tsū* when they were aesthetic terms. Even when *sui* and *tsū* lost such aesthetic connotations, *iki* continued independently to express a certain attitude towards the actual shapes, colours and sounds of everyday life, imbuing them with a spiritual, aesthetic dimension.

Thus only *iki* remained in use as an aesthetic term by the 1850s. *Sui* and *tsū* had lost this dimension at least 50 years earlier and so cannot be applied to the aesthetics of the Edo period as a whole. This mistake arose because of the misconception of Tokugawa culture as being primarily popular. The cultural vigor and creativity of the pleasure quarters in fact completely disappeared when the upper classes were replaced as customers by the common people, a change that took place shortly after 1800. From that time the pleasure quarters became what they have remained in living memory: merely marketplaces for sex.

Present-day depictions of Yoshiwara and Shimabara so popular in TV dramas and films are precisely those of such degraded times; the ugly decadence underlying the superficial glamour of such dramas is a far cry from the aesthetic values of their heyday. Until quite recently, scholars applied the terms *sui, tsū* and *iki* to the aesthetics of the pleasure quarters in the 1800s in the same way as earlier, thereby making popular culture the standard for the aesthetics of the Edo period as a whole.

However, if we adopt the more recent approach to the eighteenth century and abandon the idea that Edo culture is solely popular culture, then it follows that *sui, tsū* and *iki* are inappropriate as terms applying to the aesthetics of the whole society of that century. The words I would like to propose as the more correct terminology are *ga* (elegance, refinement) and *zoku* (vulgarity, coarseness). Obviously, these terms seem similar to *sui, tsū* and *iki*; in fact, they are the conceptual fundamentals from which the concepts of *sui, tsū* and *iki* are derived. In other words, the universal concept of *ga zoku* found its particular expression in the pleasure quarters of the eighteenth century as *sui, tsū* and *iki*: the principle was *ga zoku*, and the practice was *sui, tsū* and *iki*.

Ga zoku was originally a concept of Chinese poetics. It appears first in *The Book of Songs* as the term *fūga* (aesthetic elegance and refinement), *zoku* being its opposite. *Ga* applied to traditional classical literature whose values were considered supreme, while any innovative creations were considered inferior and pejoratively termed *zoku*. Thus *ga* referred to superior, high-class literature, while *zoku* denoted vulgar writings. Gentlemen were those who, finely conscious of the distinction between *ga* and *zoku*, strove to make the former the model for their behaviour, while the commoner remained content in the world of *zoku*, taking no interest in *ga*. So popular culture was by definition *zoku*, and in the hierarchical society of the time, it was always clearly in a position of inferiority, destined to look up to *ga* as the highest aesthetic ideal. Popular culture was by no means the sole repository of aesthetic taste. On the contrary, the dominant aesthetic concept of the eighteenth century was *ga*, to which all levels of society aspired.

Next, we might consider some of the particular characteristics of the concept of *ga zoku* in the 1700s. The remarkable development of *ga* culture during the first third of the eighteenth century is described thoroughly by Nakamura Yukihiko in *Fūgaron teki bungakukan*.[2] Here let me cite one or two examples of the consciousness of *ga* prevalent at the time. The first example is from Gion Nankai's (1676–1751) *Shiketsū* (1787) in a section entitled *Shihōgazokuben*:[3]

When we contrast *ga* and *zoku*, *ga*, as I have said previously, is a concept used by aristocrats, scholars and gentlemen. It has nothing to do with the lower classes. Only elevated and gentle words come in this category. *Zoku* originally referred to the popular, common things in society, Among such things, there are the good and the bad, and we do not have to despise everything common. In contrasting *zoku* with *ga* we should first consider *zoku* in its Japanese reading of *iyashi*. For example all the vulgar, coarse, low language and jokes in popular stories, the crass language of commerce and everyday life, the crude language of farmers and housewives, prostitutes and actors are all *zoku*. Only literary language is *ga*. Furthermore there are various kinds of *zoku* words: some are Chinese and some ancient *ga* words have now become *zoku* and vice versa. Although poetry and prose do not belong to the world of *zoku* in every collection there will be some *zoku* poems. Some poets devote their life's work to *zoku*. Factual accounts may be *zoku*. Simply put, *ga* is neatness, propriety, elegance; *zoku* is vulgarity. Poetry cannot be written without an understanding of how *ga* and *zoku* differ.

The distinction between *ga* and *zoku*, therefore, lies in the tone of the language used and in changing usages over time. The aspiring poet must, at the outset, make a determined effort to grasp this point.

Nankai emphasised this principle, quoting the following passage from Yen Yu's *T'sang-lang Shih-hua*,[4] the chief textbook of the Ken'en poets:

> The aspiring poet must rid himself of the five vulgarities (*zoku*) on the first day, of form; on the second day, of meaning; on the third day, of expression; on the fourth day, of vocabulary; and on the fifth day, of sound.

It was not only poets of the time who made the distinction between *ga* and *zoku*; the entire artistic world adopted the principle of avoiding *zoku*. The following is a passage from *Avoiding Vulgarity* from the Chinese treatise *Chieh-tzu-Yuan hua-chuan*,[5] the most widely read work in the eighteenth-century art world.

> When you paint, simplicity is preferable to complexity, boldness to caution. Complexity is lifeless, caution vulgar. Vulgarity must be avoided, and the only way to avoid it is by reading. With reading, one's mind is elevated and uncouthness diminished. Scholars, take heed!

According to the *Hakusai Shomoku*[6] the *Chieh-tzu-yuan huan-chuan* first appeared in Japan in 1719, and immediately commanded high respect, but it achieved widespread circulation only after a woodblock impression, the so-called Kana version, was produced in 1748. There is evidence however that Nankai was acquainted with the Chinese original.[7] The encouragement of reading here is probably directly drawn from the saying 'Read ten thousand books, walk ten thousand miles' found in T'ung Ch'i-chang's (1555–1636) *Hua-ch'an shih sui-pi*. By reading one absorbs the superior cultural mentality of the ancients, and by travelling one is exposed to the influences of pure beauty in nature, thus refining the spirit and avoiding *zoku*. These ideas were widely accepted in eighteenth-century Japan. Yosa Buson's famous *ga zoku* theory, which he expounded to his disciple Shōha, and Ayatari's theory appearing in his *Kanga Shinen* (Manual on Chinese painting) were both virtual plagiarisations of 'Avoiding Zoku', which appeared in a Japanese translation of the *Chieh-tzu-yuan huan-chuan* by Kashiwagi Soki (1763–1819) in 1818.

Another related though different concept was initiated by Bashō's theory of *fūga*. As Shiraishi Teizō points out in his excellent essay, *Ga no Makoto* (The truth about *ga*),[8] Bashō raised haikai poetry, traditionally a *zoku* form, to the world of *ga*, thereby confounding the traditional distinctions of *ga* and *zoku*.

Bashō's innovative theory is briefly expressed in the admonition to his disciples: 'After raising your mind to an enlightened state, return to *zoku*', recorded by his disciple Dōhō in the *Sanzōshi* (Three note-books, 1704). The *Sanzōshi* is not a record of Bashō's actual words, but presents Bashō's ideas as interpreted by Dōhō. Nevertheless, it is the authoritative voice of the influential Bashō School of poets. By 'raising your mind' Bashō means 'practising *ga* while remaining in the ordinary *zoku* world of haikai'. This can only be done by 'reading ten thousand books and travelling ten thousand miles'. Bashō makes this point again in the opening paragraph of his *Oi no kobumi* (Manuscript in my knapsack, 1709): 'Saigyō's *waka*, Sōgi's *renga*, Sesshū's paintings and Rikyū's tea all have one thing in common.' Bashō believed that one should attain the mental level of these ancient artists and then return to the world of haikai—not lowering *ga* to the level of *zoku*, but lifting haikai progressively into the world of *ga* until it reaches the level of these masters. Thus *zoku* gradually rises and impinges on the world of *ga*. Whether the haikai poets of the Bashō style fully understood this theory is debatable. In any case, it was hardly possible to gain wide acceptance for a theory putting *zoku* on the same level as *ga* in such a rigidly hierarchical society. Nevertheless, it was a significant and well known variation on the predominant *ga zoku* theories of the time.

From around 1750, a subtle change came over the accepted theory of *ga zoku*. Influenced, more than likely, by the haikai written according to Bashō's *fūga* theory, *ga* and *zoku* became blended, with *zoku* almost rivalling the superiority of *ga*. The poet Yanada Zeigan (1672–1757) bemoaned this fact as early as the 1730s: 'The writing of the whole country has fallen into the hands of the common people.' Poetry, hitherto the preserve of the upper classes, was gradually opened to the common people, departing from the philosophical canons of traditional *fūga* theory. The *Komaya Sūgen* also records: 'After the 1730s literature declined into the realm of the common people.' In other words, class barriers to literary composition were dissolving, making the traditional concern of writers with the distinction between *ga* and *zoku* a thing of the past. Thus Kinryū Michihito (1712–1782) in his preface to Ayatari's *Nishiyama Monogatari* (Tale of Nishiyama, 1768) praises Ayatari for his great success in 'handling *zoku* according to the rules of *ga*, using it to create *ga*.' Thus the supreme artist does not despise *zoku* or avoid it at all costs, but on the contrary actively seeks *ga* in *zoku*. Ōta Nampo (1749–1823) says in his *Kana Sōsetsu* (Kana preface, 1824), 'The refined person who sports with *zoku* is the master of *ga*.' So authors who would formerly have devoted themselves entirely to *ga* were becoming fascinated with the world of *zoku*, or perhaps more accurately, were beginning to discover considerable value in toying with *zoku*.

Of course, this development coincided with subtle changes in class consciousness. However, on a more superficial level, and perhaps according to the perceptions of the intelligentsia at the time, it was greatly influenced by current trends in China, always the leader in matters of taste. The years 1716 to 1763 coincided with the flowering of the Chinese colloquial novel, edited and praised by the eminent scholars, Li Cho-wu (1527–1602) and Chin Sheng-tan (1610–61). Thus in China it was *ga* persons who actually compiled and published these novels, so it is not surprising that a similar phenomenon occured in Japan.

This confusion of *ga* and *zoku* did not, however, supersede traditional *ga zoku* theories, or produce a brand new aesthetics, since *ga* always remained supreme, and *zoku* always subordinate. Ayatari's *zoku* was praised *after* it had changed to *ga*, and Nampo's *zoku* became *ga* only because it was handled by a refined person. Thus, from the very beginning, *zoku* was only valued after it had been transformed into *ga*; it was never valued in itself, and so never became a real threat to the traditional superiority of *ga*. Had this happened, the traditional *fūga* aesthetic might have met its end and a new sense of values emerged. But this could never happen while a rigid social hierarchy prevailed: only a fundamental change in the structure of society could have given rise to such a revolutionary change in aesthetics.

Fūga is thus the dominant artistic value of the eighteenth century and the representative aesthetic of the Edo period as a whole. *Gesaku* (popular satirical) literature, traditionally seen as the most characteristic example of Edo popular culture, is, in fact, a late artistic development arising from the current trend of blending *ga* and *zoku*. At first a form of esoteric entertainment for writers, its *fūga* foundation is indisputable. In fact, to understand the parody in *gesaku*—and parody is essentially what it is—requires a clear knowledge of the distinction between *ga* and *zoku*. Only sophisticated people can appreciate the subtle interplay between *ga* and *zoku*. Knowing *ga* they can appreciate *zoku*, but the reverse is more difficult. For parody to be successful it must have a serious intent, namely *dō* or the Way. The entertaining element, then, became the *ridō* (back street). Without a proper understanding of the main highway, the back streets cannot be appreciated, and the more highways there were, the more back streets proliferated. With the spread of the principle of *dō* came an increase in interest in the *ridō*. Of course a perfect balance between the *dō* and *ridō* was not always maintained (although the ideal was to be able to do so): there was always some shifting of emphasis, but when the *ridō* element became extensive, sophisticated writers often became ashamed of themselves and made an effort to raise the tone of their works.

The above is only a brief, very general description of eighteenth-century aesthetics, on which much further work needs to be done, particularly on its role in the various styles of literature and painting in the Edo period.

(*Translated by Maria Flutsch*)

Notes

1 '*Sui, tsū, iki*—sono seisei no katei' (The process of the development of elegance, connoisseurship and refinement) in *Kōza Nihon Shisō* (Lectures on Japanese Thought) Vol. 5, Tokyo: Tokyo University Press, 1984, pp. 109–41

2 In 'Kinsei bungei shichōron' *Nakamura Yukihiko Chojutsushū* Tokyo: Chūōkōronsha, 1982, Vol. 1, pp. 339–78

3 Reprinted in *Nihon Shiwa Sōsho* Tokyo: Bunkaidō Shoten, 1920, Vol. 1, pp. 14–15

4 Reprinted in *Chokyōsen, Seishū Shōsō* Vol. 8 Tokyo: Kohakkan Inmusho, Year 25, Vol. 8, p. 29

5 The author is Wang Kai of the Ch'ing dynasty (exact dates unknown). The work was written in 1679 and is reprinted under the full title *Kaishi Engaden Shoshū Sansuijuseki* (2 vols), Tokyo: Chikuma Shobō 1975. The quotation is from Volume I, entitled *Ching-chai-t'ang hua-hsueh ch'enshua* pp. 24–5, and is the first of eighteen rules of his theory of art.

6 Published in 1810 by the Imperial Household Publishing Office and is a catalogue of T'ang books imported into Japan through Nagasaki between 1699 and 1754. It is republished by the Kansai Daigaku Tōzai Gakujutsu Kenkyūsho, 1972.

7 See Tsuruta Takeyoshi 'Kaishiengaden ni tsuite', *Bijutsu Kenkyū*, Tokyo: Tōkyō Kokuritsu Bunkasai Kenkyūsho, 1972, Vol. 3, No. 283.

8 *Koza Nihon Shisō*, pp. 83–108

9

Matsudaira Sadanobu and Samurai education

Robert L. Backus

Although Matsudaira Sadanobu (1758–1829) contributed nothing to the evolution of Confucian thought, he illustrated in his public life the Confucian ideal of nobility of mind in selfless devotion to the commonweal. We should not expect to find in Sadanobu a humanistic significance that may at times transcend history and culture as can be found in Confucius, or even a personality for which we might feel a certain congenial attraction; the values he embodied were adapted to an elitist, static conception of society, and the commonweal he served was mediated by a government in principle autocratic. But Sadanobu lived a Confucian life, which means a life oriented to some notion of the common good, and he possessed an intelligence and sense of mission that enabled him, indeed compelled him, to articulate the ideals of Confucianism along with his own experience of putting them into practice, and to present his thought systematically in the cause of moral enlightenment. In short, he had the commitment and, it must be admitted, the disquieting certitude of a teacher of the Truth.

Teaching was but one aspect of his career, however, for birth and circumstances dictated that Sadanobu would be a ruler. That he was also a teacher illustrates the Confucian tenet that rulership is essentially a responsibility to lead rather than coerce, to serve as an exemplar encouraging the willing compliance of the ruled. As the daimyo of Shirakawa from 1783 to 1812 and as chief councillor (*rōjū shuseki*) and regent (*hosa*) of the Bakufu from 1787 to 1793, Sadanobu exercised an active personal rule which was informed by the Confucian ideal of humane government (*jen cheng*), which justified the possession of power by representing it as a commission from Heaven to order society in such a way that all its members conducted themselves properly and received their due in accordance with prescribed social role and status.

This was a static order. It rested on an economic policy of regulating consumption at the top and encouraging agricultural productivity below; it required a public-spirited bureaucracy which would carry out directives impartially, keep itself informed of the condition of the people, and communicate information and advice to the top honestly; and it presupposed a morality which taught all men from the ruler down their place and duties in relation to each other, curbing ambition in conformity to the rules and expectations of each status in the network of human relationships.

Such a conception of order was at the heart of the Tokugawa polity, and when Sadanobu assumed the leadership of the Bakufu, he did so with the express purpose of actualising that ideal anew after the corruption and laxity of the preceding regime under Tanuma Okitsugu. His renovation of the Tokugawa government—strengthening its finances, disciplining its bureaucracy, and standardising its educational system—prompted similar movements in the domains and, lasting beyond his departure from office, closed the eighteenth century with a conservative revival of such magnitude in politics and education as to distinguish the 1790s in history as the period of the Kansei Reform.

Indeed, Sadanobu appears to be the last prominent defender of the old order, its polity and the moral authority underpinning it, who could act with confidence in his beliefs; for the accelerating crises of Bakufu politics in the next century, due to its inability to accommodate mounting social stresses and impotence in the face of foreign pressure, undermined samurai faith in the rule of the shogun; all official actions thereafter were a defensive series of embattled stands ending in humiliating concessions. Therefore Sadanobu justly stands as a model of eighteenth-century political leadership and the embodiment of what he aspired to be: the conscience of the ruling elite. Accordingly, his Confucian thought may be seen as exemplifying the moral ethos of the military-administrative establishment (the samurai) not only in the eighteenth century, but back through the seventeenth as well.[1]

It needs to be pointed out, however, that Sadanobu's Confucianism was not the only form prevalent in Japan, nor the only form that laid claim to the souls of the samurai. To put this complication into context, let us backtrack to the beginning. Since the death of Confucius in 479 B.C., his teachings had undergone immense elaboration of what was implied or thought to be implied between the lines of his recorded sayings. Nevertheless, his original vision of a co-operative world in which the selfish interests of men are brought into harmony through self-discipline and moral awareness remained intact; as did an optimistic belief in the educability of men, with the possibility of achieving social transformation by the moral transformation of individuals. Confucius's teaching started with the cultivation of character and envisioned a diffusion of exemplary conduct whereby the mutually supportive behaviour within families, together with the dignity and mutual respect characteristic of the performance of communal and family rites, would extend outward to pervade the impersonal and competitive sphere of interaction among strangers.

Accordingly, it was character that occupied Confucius's attention, and he honoured the integrity and moral courage of the educated man by dignifying him with the aristocratic title of *chün tzu* 'nobleman', now to be taken as a designation of personal worth dissociated from pedigree—a noble man. Only high aspiration and the strength to achieve it by moral striving qualified one to enter the circle of noble men; consequently the circle was necessarily small, because few men had the time or inclination (or the capacity either, according to some Confucians) to make the effort for self-transformation. These lesser mortals were the *hsiao jen* 'common men', or plebeians. The social role of the noble man was to teach those who could be taught, guide the others by moral example, counsel the great, and take office if possible. Thus the co-operative world of Confucius's vision was not an egalitarian one, but a community of different orders of men working together harmoniously under the benign influence of the virtuous.[2]

The unavoidable distinction between the noble and the common man gave rise to an elitist bias in later Confucianism, which was only partially compensated by some teachers making it their business to bring education to the masses. In Japan, this distinction appears during the eighteenth century and it is certainly true that, in the seventeenth century, most Confucian teachers addressed themselves primarily to samurai, although this did not inhibit them from instructing commoners who gave promise of good character and capacity for learning; while some of them, usually at the behest of their daimyo patrons, even preached occasional homilies on obedience, frugality and industry to the countryfolk. At the same time, an important strain of Confucian thought appeared among the commonality, which articulated an ethic affirming the dignity of labor and commerce as worthy pursuits in the service of family and community. This movement, known as Shingaku (the Learning of the Mind), was energised by an earnest spirit of introspection to rid the mind of selfishness, and did much to enhance the self-respect of craftsmen and tradespeople by equating their occupations to the public service of the samurai.[3]

We thus discern two general kinds of Confucianism: an elite form addressed to men who were destined to exercise public responsibilities, along with some others from the wealthier levels of the commonality, who might choose a scholarly career or hold a position of authority in local government; and a popular form addressed to common men who spent their time in making a living. Both forms shared the same values; the former provided a morality of leadership and made a point of intellectual content, while the latter cultivated communal virtues and moralised in a simple idiom within the reach of everyone. Of course, Sadanobu's Confucianism belonged to the elite form; he spoke exclusively to samurai and discoursed in the style of a lord teaching his retainers the central importance of a Confucian life to the success of their mission as defenders and administrators of the country.

The lifetime of Sadanobu coincided with the climax of a long process of diversification of Japanese Confucianism into contending schools of thought—a process which to a considerable degree was stimulated by similar developments in China. Such diversity was inevitable given the propensity of original minds to react to changing circumstances and light upon integrative insights in the wake of uncertainties. But the contention was exacerbated because of an assumption on the part of all Confucian thinkers that their goal was to recover and actualise in the present a unitary truth, or Way of the Sages, which had prevailed in the high antiquity of China. Whereas Confucius avowed a reverence for antiquity but relied implicitly on common sense to underpin his philosophy, his followers came to give priority to the authority of canonical texts. The diversification of Confucian thought involved disagreements over which texts were to be taken as authoritative and how they were to be interpreted, and since these issues cast a doubt on the assumed reality of a single truth, they gave a superficial appearance of strident controversy that distracted attention from a remarkable degree of consensus.

Nevertheless, some divisions were substantive. Perhaps the most important of these, because it affected the cultivation of character, arose with the development of a new practice of mind control (*hsin fa*), an inward grappling with mental processes to cut off the source of evil before it expressed itself in thought and action. This came to be recommended in addition to traditional reliance on the external approach through schooling, example and scholarship. The purpose of mind control was to regulate the emotions and eliminate selfishness, manifested most conspicuously in excessive desire. The two approaches, outer and inner, were meant to coexist in a balanced system of edification and praxis, but in the event they were too often seen as opposites, with the traditionalists accusing those who practised mind control of an unnatural asceticism, a fussy exactitude that stultified the capacity for large-mindedness, and an introversion that discouraged scholarship and social action.

Sadanobu practised mind control, and in his old age wrote an account of some of his experiences with it under the title of *Sugyō roku* (A Record of Self-Training).[4] In the light of the above criticisms of the practice it is clear that he maintained a realistic balance. He was in no sense introverted, being committed to a scholarship of ethics and social utility, and actively involved himself in government and teaching. With regard to the matter of exactitude, he was strict with those whom he admitted to his friendship, but pragmatically tolerant of human foibles in his retainers and the people at large. With himself, however, he was rigorous. According to his account, he succeeded in training himself to dismiss and call back at will any desire, except for one which he never mastered—the desire for reputation. The training consisted in denying himself until he was satisfied that he could control each desire: dismiss it into oblivion and recall it whenever he pleased. An especially striking instance of this discipline is recorded for his late twenties when, after a year of sexual abstinence, he took a female attendant to bed to see whether he could dismiss prurience at will. He proved the efficacy of his training all right, but it is doubtful whether the girl, despite the fact that he lectured her on wifely duties against the day when she would marry, took much away from the encounter except her bewilderment.

Such practices are foreign to classical Confucianism, which approves desire as natural and seeks only to regulate its antisocial excesses by instilling habits of conduct that conform to objective standards of propriety. Mind control, on the other hand, interiorised discipline and laid it open to subjective eccentricities in which the line between naturalness and vice shifted arbitrarily or disappeared altogether. Still, Sadanobu seems to have gotten around this subjectivity by framing his discipline as one of mastering desire rather than rejecting it either in whole or in part. Moreover, he does not seem to have urged his practice upon others, but instead expounded another aspect of mind control, that of self-examination, in which the subject searched his mind to expose ulterior motives, the fruits of self-interested calculation that merge deceptively with goodness and dilute it.

The new emphasis on mind control was part of a Confucian revival in China during the eleventh and twelfth centuries which both reacted against Buddhism by reaffirming the value of the workaday world and took some hints from it to construct an ontology that identified the essential nature of man with a rational-moral order of the universe. Among the scholars who contributed to this movement, the brothers Ch'eng Hao (1032–1085) and Ch'eng Yi (1033–1108) were pre-eminent in the eleventh century, and their thought, with that of their spiritual predecessors, was synthesised in the twelfth century by Chu Hsi (1130–1200) to constitute an identifiable school, which is called by various descriptive terms and also, most conveniently, by the simple name Ch'eng-Chu.[5]

Ch'eng-Chu ontology conceives of 'being' as formed from the condensations of a rarefied, invisible material force or ether (*ch'i*), which take place spontaneously according to a universal reason or principle (*li*) inherent in the ether. Principle is both natural and normative, and as such is identified with the traditional concepts of Heaven, the Tao or Way, and the nature (*hsing*) of man; by principle a thing is what it is and by principle a man can be what he ought to be. Since Confucian thought centres on man, the normative import of principle takes precedence in Ch'eng-Chu discourse, and the names for the traditional Confucian values come to designate aspects of principle. But actually this system of thought draws no distinction between the natural and the normative, for a man is what he is—a perfectly moral being, a sage—when he perfectly manifests principle in his physical existence.[6]

By Sadanobu's time Ch'eng-Chu still enjoyed a close association with the Bakufu owing to the fact that the first shogun, Ieyasu, had taken the Ch'eng-Chu scholar, Hayashi Razan (1583–1657), into his service as a hereditary retainer. Razan commended himself to Ieyasu for his classical erudition and command of historical and administrative precedents. His service to the Bakufu ensured official patronage of his scholarly and educational enterprise as well as that of his descendants, who succeeded him in what eventually became the office of rector of education (*daigaku no kami*). Their common endeavours, especially those of the first three Hayashi, combined with their exalted position to secure the dominance of Ch'eng-Chu Confucianism in Edo and in samurai education, while in Kyoto another major centre of Ch'eng-Chu scholarship was making similar if less spectacular progress. Thus, during the seventeenth century, Ch'eng-Chu was almost synonymous with Confucianism in Japan.

This position markedly deteriorated in the eighteenth century, however, as a reaction against Ch'eng-Chu metaphysics and mentalism set in and expanded into a varied movement that had as its common objective a return to the original and simple truth. In Sadanobu's day it appears that only slightly more than half of the domain scholars, those who were most involved in samurai education, belonged to the Ch'eng-Chu persuasion. Sadanobu, of course, followed Ch'eng-Chu and saw to it that the samurai school in his own domain did likewise. At the same time he was also engaged in launching the 1790s Kansei Reform, which included the standardisation and expansion of education for Bakufu retainers, and it was here that he took action which radically altered the fortunes of Ch'eng-Chu in the nineteenth century.

Naturally considering Ch'eng-Chu to be the proper standard for Bakufu education, he issued in 1790 a directive to that effect to the rector of education—the so-called Kansei prohibition of heterodoxy. Then, with the help of like-minded scholars whom he appointed to the Hayashi school, he began a program of enlarging its facilities and converting the whole institution into a government academy. Although he was out of office before the project reached completion, his appointees carried it forward, until by the end of the century they had furnished the Bakufu with the biggest educational establishment in the country, which was officially committed to teaching Confucianism according to the Ch'eng-Chu commentaries. As the domains increasingly followed Bakufu example and restricted their samurai schools to the teaching of Cheng-Chu, that tradition recovered lost ground and entrenched itself in the early nineteenth century as the major Confucian influence in samurai education.[7]

This excursion into the vicissitudes of Ch'eng-Chu is intended to point out the importance of that school in Tokugawa Japan and clarify the grounds on which it may be treated as typical of the intellectual content of samurai education. In addition, some mention of Ch'eng-Chu metaphysics, such as was made earlier, is necessary to appreciate the implications of Sadanobu's Confucian thought. In 1784, at the age of 26, Sadanobu undertook to expound this thought for the benefit of ranking officials of his household in a series of lectures delivered twice a month at his castle at Shirakawa. He chose for his text the Ch'eng-Chu recension of the *Ta hsüeh* (Greater Learning).[8] In doing so he was following a secular practice in Neo-Confucianism; for the thesis of the *Greater Learning*, laconic and methodical, gave more than enough room for edifying expatiations on the part of countless teachers and at the same time imposed an orderly development that started from the mind and ended with the pacification of the realm.[9] The key passages are as follows:

> The Way of the Greater Learning consists in beaming the light of shining virtue, renewing the people, and resting in the highest good. Only after we know where to rest is our purpose fixed; only after our purpose is fixed can we be calm; only after we are calm can we be settled; only after we are settled can we deliberate; only after we deliberate can we attain the Way. Things have a base and top; affairs have a

beginning and end. When we know what to put last, we are close to the Way.

The ancients who wished to beam the light of shining virtue in the realm first put their countries in order. Those who wished to put their countries in order first regulated their households. Those who wished to regulate their households first cultivated their persons. Those who wished to cultivate their persons first rectified their minds. Those who wished to rectify their minds first made their thoughts sincere. Those who wished to make their thoughts sincere first perfected their knowledge. The perfection of knowledge consists in understanding things.

The thesis next goes on to recapitulate these steps from the bottom up, adding an eighth step at the top: 'Only after the country is put in order is the realm pacified.' Chu Hsi designated these steps as the 'eight particulars' (*pa t'iao mu*), and the three constituents of the greater learning—beaming the light of shining virtue, renewing the people and resting in the highest good—he called the 'three axioms' (*san kang ling*).

The eight particulars specify the action necessary to realise the three axioms. They begin with (1) encountering things and (2) the perfection of knowledge. The perfection of knowledge through encountering things is identified with knowing the highest good, and thus it is here made explicit that the concern is with moral knowledge acquired by scrutinising the affairs of man for the principles that inform them. The next three particulars—(3) making the thoughts sincere, (4) rectifying the mind and (5) cultivating the person—together with the first two, make up the process of beaming the light of shining virtue, inasmuch as all five have to do with the transformation of the self. The last three particulars represent an expanding field of the individual's moral influence over others, and are therefore subsumed under 'renewing the people'. They are: (6) regulating the household, (7) putting the country (a feudal state) in order and (8) pacifying the realm (the totality of countries). Finally, as the first two particulars—encountering things and perfecting knowledge—constitute the process of knowing the highest good, so the remaining six, from making the thoughts sincere, are identified as the sequence of accomplishments leading to the attainment of the highest good; and thus the whole process is seen on this plane as beginning with knowing the highest good and ending with its attainment.[10]

Much of the Ch'eng-Chu interpretation of the thesis rests on the denotation of the phrase *ko wu*, here translated as 'encountering things', and on the implication drawn from it. Although the denotation of *ko wu* is now ambiguous, it could not have been so at the time the *Greater Learning* was written, because there is nothing in the commentary to explain it. Ch'eng Yi took one of the possible senses of *ko*, which is 'to arrive at', and from it drew the implication that the phrase means 'to arrive at the principles of things exhaustively'; hence James Legge's rendering 'the investigation of things', which has become standard. This implication is so important to the Ch'eng-Chu conception of scholarship that it is worth quoting in full Chu Hsi's development of it, which he interpolated as section five of the commentary on the assumption that the original explanation had been lost in the transmission of the text:

> What is meant by saying that the perfection of knowledge consists in encountering things is this: If we wish to perfect our knowledge, it consists in putting ourselves in contact with things and exploring their principles fully. For certainly the numinous intelligence of the human mind in no case lacks the faculty of knowing and no thing under heaven lacks a principle. The problem is that principles are not always fully explored and therefore knowledge of them may not be complete. For that reason the first instruction of the greater learning requires the student to put himself in contact with all things under heaven, explore every one of them more fully from the principles he already knows, and in this way try to reach their limit. After exerting himself for a long time, he will one day perceive them throughout in full view; then the numerous things in their several aspects and various qualities will be totally apprehended, and our mind in its perfect substance and great functioning will be entirely lucid. This is described as things encountered. This is described as knowledge perfected.

The thesis of the *Greater Learning* and its Ch'eng-Chu interpretation provided Sadanobu with the pattern for his lectures; his task was to fill in the generalities with explanatory and illustrative material that made sense to samurai laymen in terms of their own lives and careers, not as items of intellectual interest.[11] 'To rest in the highest good,' says Sadanobu, 'means to know the culmination of principle and rest without shifting off centre in conformity with the Way of the Sages wherever it may stretch a bit here or contract a bit there'. (p. 20) This is the condition proper to man; it distinguishes his mind from that of a bird or beast. Since scholarship is essential to attaining it, the samurai has no excuse for neglecting booklearning:

> Besides, is scholarship really so difficult? If it were a case of creating something outside ourselves, naturally I can see that that would be hard to do; but . . . man receives the rightness of Heaven and Earth when he is born, and therefore his nature is good, so that, as regards the wondrous and unfathomable power of his mind, there is no need to consider whether a man is a Sage or like ourselves. It is only a matter of recovering what we were born with. (p. 6)

If scholarship is a pleasure, ignorance is a sin. An ignorant man betrays his parents. After their many years of travail and self-sacrifice to bring up a son as a human being, the least he can do for them is to develop his mind:

> To be brought into existence, raised from infancy, and taught and guided is a beneficence truly deeper than the sea and higher than the mountains; how can we repay it! Therefore is it not said that the filial son has a lifetime of care? Even if he cannot repay that beneficence, at the very least, since his parents have bestowed life on him, it is imperative that he grows up to possess a mind appropriate to his existence as a person. (pp. 7–8).

Accordingly, an ignorant samurai fails his lord, although it may appear at first sight that learning need not greatly concern a man of action.

> The fashion nowadays is to say that we need not pursue scholarship; but every bowl of rice we eat and every piece of clothing we wear comes from the beneficence of our lord, and that we support a wife and children and succeed to our ancestral house is also thanks to our lord. Anyone who has done well by his lord's beneficence and that of his father and grandfather and yet does not discipline himself to pursue scholarship does not merit even cursory consideration as a human being. (pp. 24–25)

For knowledge or principle means to know the essence of things; which in practice is to know the difference between right and wrong, between true principle and what merely resembles it in the workaday world. For example, everyone thinks he knows what loyalty is, but when it comes to achieving, it without the benefit of having studied its exemplification in real life, one cannot be certain how to act:

> There is a story that once long ago, when Lord Taiyū-in [the shogun Iemitsu (1640–1651)] was scheduled to go on a hawking excursion in the fifth hour [between 7.00 and 9.00 a.m.] and the proclamation had been issued, the appointed hour arrived in the middle of His Lordship's breakfast, with the result that he set out leaving it half-eaten. Somebody had suggested that they postpone the hour of departure and inform him after he had finished because it would be bad for his health to interrupt him. But the late Director of Housekeeping Naotaka scolded that person roundly: 'A shogun must not for one moment lose his credibility even if he does not eat for a whole day,' he said; and so the hour came even in the middle of His Lordship's breakfast, he informed him of his prior appointment.
> Here we see that the person who raised the issue of His Lordship's

health had a loyalty concerned with the well-being of mouth and belly, and the one who saw to it that the did not lose his credibility had genuine loyalty. Unless a person pursues scholarship, he cannot know that a mere hairsbreadth lies between loyalty and disloyalty . . . while at the same time they are miles apart. (p. 4)

Fulfilment of principle is not simply a matter of good intentions; it depends on knowledge applied to differing circumstances. Again in the case of loyalty:

. . . in serving a humane lord, one endeavors to influence that human-ity to flow further downward so as to allow the rule of country and household to approach the good order of [the Sage Kings] Yao and Shun; toward a lord who lacks humanity, one starts by offering one's life to admonish him so that he will conform to the Way, and does one's best to see that country and household are not disturbed; as to loyalty in personal service to the lord, one praises what is excellent in him and, passing over what is bad, dissuades him in all his activities, including eating and drinking, from improper actions. (p. 37)

The correct fulfilment of principle in action is an instance of attain-ing the highest good, and the process leading to that attainment is one of freeing the mind of consciousness of self. What this process means for the samurai is quite clear in the martial arts: in fencing, for exam-ple, where the self-conscious man 'closes his eyes when he sees the sword and, heedless of its direction, gets hit. Anticipating it to come from the left or the right, he concentrates on one or the other direc-tion, and he ends being wrong.' (p. 23) By contrast, a mind which has risen above consciousness of self abides in a serenity like still water as it reflects the image of the moon back upon its source instantaneously and with perfect objectivity. 'When the sword strikes and the mind is utterly blank and tranquil, all is clear to the swordsman: never reflec-ting whether the blow is aimed at the left or the right, his sword strikes home of itself. Even though his mind does not consider where to strike, he hits the exact spot unconsciously.' (p. 17)

Important as mastery of the martial arts certainly is, it is only a preparation for the samurai's mission; in performance of this mission a disciplined and selfless mind grounded on scholarship distinguishes itself as dependable or incompetent:

They say that the warrior need not know scholarship; even so, if I may take up the subject of the warrior's performance, let me start by point-ing out something which is relevant to going into battle. If at that mo-ment your heart overflows with such passions and desires as anxiety to spare your body and save your life, together with love for wife and children, worry that you might lose your stipend, and a wish to make a name for yourself and be praised, how can you get a chance to thrust the first spear or lead the first charge? When one acts as I have just described in mere fencing practice, what performance can he give, what principles can he know when this selfish desire arises under the pressure of a real life-or-death situation? Thus, even if we view the warrior as performing only on the battlefield, unless he reaches these four stages where his mind is fixed in its purpose, is calm, is settled, and deliberates, he cannot even begin to fulfil his duty. Much less when we consider that the warrior is not only a fighter, that the warrior's performance is precisely to render loyal service to his lord, to keep order by governing the country without varying from principle in administrative affairs, and to give a long and lasting peace to the realm by retaining the services of the men whom he appoints to office; therefore we cannot say that the warrior has only a military role. And even if that were true, he would fail as a warrior unless capable of these four rules. Such capability means only one thing, that our minds have a clear knowledge of the highest good which is principle, and to know this is impossible to attain unless one pursues scholarship. (p. 23)

But the effects of goodness are not to be considered only in respect of the samurai's mission. Goodness brings prosperity and long life, whereas evil results in ruin and an early death. This is the justice of Heaven. There is nothing mysterious about it. For Heaven and Man share the same principle, and 'since all under Heaven are equally human beings, what the people hold to be good, Heaven holds to be good, and what they hold to be bad, Heaven holds to be bad.' (p. 97) Therefore:

As the good man does good therefore people respect and appreciate him; they give him his status and appointment in accordance with his character, and consequently he is certain to gain a stipend, reputation, and office, so is certain to flourish. The evil man declines and perishes because he acts contrary to this. Moreover, as the good man does good therefore people respect him, appreciate him, make friends with him, and become attached to him, and accordingly they will help him out if he suffers a reverse and raise him up if he comes down in the world; consequently he always flourishes and his good fotune extends to his descendants. The evil man does not flourish but goes to ruin because he acts contrary to this. Then too, the good man leaves his fate to heaven and does his best on earth, so he never suffers in mind and, with nothing to be ashamed of before Heaven above or Man below, he feels easy in mind and is never depressed; he cares for his health without tormenting his mind with selfish desire; consequently he has a long life. The evil man has a short life because he acts contrary to this. (p. 28)

True, there are seeming exceptions to this rule. Some evil men prosper and live long, and some good men fail and die young. But these anomalies are few, and in any case they are compensated for by the fact that the reputation for goodness or evil lives on in the memory of its owner and affects the fate of his decendants accordingly. Nevertheless, since Heaven's justice 'differs from human justice in that it is not as swift as the punishment following the crime, the petty man in his artfulness comes to believe that the retribution of Heaven does not exist because he escapes it for the time being'. (p. 29) But such skepticism is dangerously wrong; and what is more, it misses the point:

> Now, to put the matter more precisely, it is not that we do good and refrain from evil because of the penalties and rewards of Heaven; we ought to develop the mind proper to a man and consequently, regardless of reward and punishment, to do good and refrain from evil; we set aside human desire and become perfect in principle, because that is simply the way we should act. Such being the case, we do not act because of others, but in order to avoid being men with minds like that of birds or beasts. So we discipline our minds . . . and reflect when we are alone; that is, we discipline ourselves by ordering our minds, unknown to others. (p. 45)

The discipline of the mind starts with making the thoughts sincere. One uses knowledge of the principle to examine the mind for ulterior motives, arising from self-interest.

Sincerity of the thoughts forms the basis on which to rectify the mind. To 'rectify' in this instance means 'so to place the mind that it leans neither to one side nor to the other, at the point which lies between going too far and not going far enough' (p. 50). It means to restore the objectivity of the original mind, and to do that it is necessary first of all to regulate the emotions and eliminate bias.

Emotion tends to linger on in the mind after the stimulus for it has passed, resulting in capricious behaviour because successive emotions do not correspond with the events that stimulate them:

> It is in the nature of things that the mind, being originally perfectly void and tranquil, is like a blank mirror or a level balance, free from outside influence; and it is in the nature of things that whenever 'fear' 'sorrow,' or 'anger' enters our mind, or remains there from previously, like a form reflected in a mirror that blots out all other images, the mind cannot correctly respond to anything else.[12]

To illustrate the foregoing, when a person is in a good humour, he may not be offended very much even if you say something likely to offend him, but on the contrary may be good-humoured about it.

When he is in a bad humour, you may not say anything so offensive, you may even say something that ought to please him, but he still takes offense because of it. (p. 51)

Bias constitutes a further impediment to the mind's objectivity. It comes in many guises; all insidious and hard to recognise, an 'intangible foe' that attacks from within and overthrows the mind before we are even aware of it (p. 60). When the mind is so affected by an emotion towards an object that it cannot distinguish right from wrong, bias result, as when an indulgent father spoils his child, or a man dislikes another so intensely that he cannot bear even the good in him. 'Much worse when the ruler of men is moved even a little in this respect by partiality and prejudice, so that he hates good things and applauds the bad, or advances the men he favours and removes ones he hates; when he gets so carried away by anger that he condemns too harshly, or so swayed by joy that he rewards too lavishly. (p. 71)[13]

Given progress in the perfection of knowledge, the problem of the emotions and bias becomes amenable to two countermeasures: the internal discipline of seriousness (*ching*) and the external influence of propriety (*li*). When the subject keeps the workings of his mind attentive and concentrates completely upon the task at hand, be it self-examination or a piece of business, he is practising the discipline of seriousness. The commentary of the *Greater Learning* (Section 7) says; 'When the mind is not attentive, we look but do not see, listen but do not hear, eat but do not know what it tastes like'; to which Chu Hsi adds: 'Whenever the mind is distracted, we have no means of controlling the person. For that reason the noble man is always exact in this matter and remedies it by seriousness; only then is the mind constantly attentive and the person never left uncultivated'.

Seriousness is vigilance that maintains a constant respectfulness in the sense of 'giving particular attention', and its object is the mind:

Now mark this: Master K'ung [Confucius] said that if you hold it, it stays with you, and if you let it go, it is lost [*Meng-tzu* (Book of Mencius), 6, pt. 1: 8: 4]; which means that the seriousness I mentioned checks this absent-mindedness. When the mind loses its voidness and clarity . . ., when what is supposed to be the master of one's person takes flight, the retainers who are left behind, who function as the eyes, the ears, and the mouth become useless and lose their purpose; therefore the first effort necessary for cultivating our person is to make sure that our mind remains attentive. (p. 52)

Some 50 years earlier Muro Kyūsō (1658–1734) summed up his discussion of seriousness in the following words: 'Seriousness consists in having the mind present when you are alone, so that you constantly keep watch over yourself. Here it is the watchman of your person. Seriousness consists in having the mind present when you are called upon to act, so that you constantly scrutinise your action. Here it is the inspector of your actions.' The discipline of seriousness, then, calls for unremitting attention to the quality of one's thoughts and acts.[14]

As seriousness controls the mind from within, it is complemented by the influence of propriety from without. The concept of propriety is expanded from the rites of ancient China to include all the ritual acts of civilised behavior from the stateliest ceremonial down to combing the hair and rinsing out the mouth when one gets up in the morning. Whatever one habitually does influences the mind:

> For that reason every townsman who deals in weaponry has something of a martial tinge to his character, while booksellers are a bit inclined to a fondness for things Chinese. Each activity penetrates the inner mind, as when, to give other examples, a pharmacist becomes a physician or a hauler becomes a wrestler, and consequently he finds both his appearance changed and his mind transformed by that activity. (pp. 68–9)

When this rule is applied to the cultivation of the person, observance of the proprieties becomes a matter of disciplining the mind by selective conditioning.

In its subtle working upon the mind through the formation of good habits, propriety is 'the Way of the Sages as it tacitly assists the way of man' (p. 67). Its effects on men's lives can be compared to the benefit which the merchant enjoys thanks to the unsung labours of the farmers and girl silkweavers: They toil through the year to produce rice and cloth, while 'at market the townsman will turn over a hundred or two hundred bolts of cloth in the time it takes to puff a pipe, and a thousand or two thousand bales of rice just while he is clearing his throat'.

'No one is as muddleheaded as a farmer': so the townsman scoffs in boastful ignorance of his dependence on agriculture. Similarly:

> we complain that propriety and righteousness are bothersome, yet by the grace of the Sages and Heaven and Earth, before we know it each of us enters upon that path unconsciously, and we practise the virtues of piety toward parents, loyalty toward our lord, tenderness for our children, and respect for our elder brother; so in like manner are we unaware that prostration, obeisance, bowing at the waist, and bending the knee, which we do nowadays, all arise in the spontaneous course of nature and are due to the influence of the Sages acting within.' (pp. 65–6)

How grateful we should be for this influence from the Way of the Sages! The Way of the Sages works just like a potter making earthenware on a wheel; within it ourselves and others are transformed unconsciously, as a tea bowl or wine jug takes shape before we know it, and neither the clay nor the jug is conscious of the transformation. Now, as all human creatures, under the influence of Heaven and Earth and the Sages, all unknowingly grow into filial children, loyal vassals, and virtuous women on that potter's wheel, they are unaware of the hidden benefit they enjoy; and though they do not admit that scholarship or the Sages have anything to do with it, they are after all like the townsman laughing at the farmer. (p. 66)

Samurai education was summed up in the phrase *bun bu* 'letters and arms', which was much bruited during Sadanobu's administration. It projected an ideal figure of raw courage tempered to meet the demands of leadership, integrating moral culture through scholarship and mastery of weapons through training in the martial arts. This balance was difficult to achieve since both of its constituents required sustained effort, and hard to maintain when it was not at all apparent how scholarship and moral discipline related to the practicalities of government service and the psychology of military training. That is why Sadanobu took pains to demonstrate its usefulness, while at the same time not neglecting to point out its importance for one's personal life and its value as an end in itself.

If these benefits were not enough to elicit effort, then the samurai's sense of indebtedness and gratitude could propel it from within. When Sadanobu spoke of requiting the beneficence of parents and lord, he drew upon a powerful source of energy latent in the clannish families and closed communities of early modern Japan. In a world where even the spirits of the dead were believed to be watching benevolently close at hand, the child grew up acutely aware of his dependence on the people around him, and was easily imbued with gratitude toward his ancestors, parents and superiors. None of this was due to influences from China except insofar as the Chinese language supplied a word to articulate the feeling and introduce it into moralistic discourse. That word is *on* (from Chinese *en*), which denotes the benefits received and, in Japan, stresses the indebtedness and gratitude of the recipient. *On* was a feeling of unredeemable debt; the recipient strove to meet the expectations of those to whom it was felt, and if he detected in himself any failure to do so he suffered the torments of guilt. Therefore it was inevitable that Sadanobu appealed to it in order to motivate his retainers. In his role as a ruler, it was probably his strongest card.

There is no doubt that Confucianism nurtured a sense of public duty and provided a powerful rationale for government; but in these excerpts from Sadanobu's lectures on the *Greater Learning* we see an additional role for Confucianism perhaps unique in its history: that of justifying a military regime. The best of the Tokugawa samurai never lost sight of the close association between letters and arms, and if, as may be supposed under the cumulative weight of over two centuries of peace, the balance often tilted in favour of letters, it is also true that when the sword came into play again in the civil war of the 1860s, there was no lack of exemplars to display the integrity of the Confucian character on the battlefield.

Notes

1   See Herman Ooms for a biography of Matsudaira Sadanobu. This book ought to be read in conjunction with John Whitney Hall's monograph on Tanuma Okitsugu.
2   This synopsis of Confucius's thought is based on the works of H. G. Creel and Herbert Fingarette.
3   Shingaku was a popularisation of Ch'eng-Chu, discussed below, which began in the early eighteenth century and continued well into modern times, with echoes even today. Robert N. Bellah has a chapter on this movement in his study of Tokugawa religion.
4   The *Sugyō roku* was written during 1822–23. It gives the picture of a man in his mid-sixties who has transcended desire and is at peace with himself. The incident with the female attendant is recounted on pp. 184–5.
5   Ch'eng-Chu philosophy is comprehensively presented in A. C. Graham's monograph on the Ch'eng brothers and Carsun Chang's history of the revival of Confucianism from Han Yü to Chu Hsi.
6   The ramification of Neo-Confucianism and its interaction with Buddhism and with other forms of Confucian thought after the Sung dynasty are being explored in a co-operative effort of scholars under the general co-ordination of William Theodore de Bary. Four volumes of essays—*Self and Society in Ming Thought, The Unfolding of Neo-Confucianism, Principle and Practicality* and *Yüan Thought*—contain the fruits of this research to date.
7   Maruyama Masao analyses the process of diversification of a dissolution of the Ch'eng-Chu doctrine of natural order which accompanied the stresses and gradual disintegration of the actual Tokugawa order. Sagara Tōru covers the same ground, discussing the ramifying currents of Confucianism in terms of polarities such as formalistic thought in support of the polity versus individualistic adaptations, the external and internal approaches to character, and the samuraisation of Confucianism versus its generalisation; and he sees a decline from the late eighteenth century evidenced by loss of confidence in the existence of a unitary truth of Confucianism which proved inadequate to solving the problems of a changing society.

8 The *Ta hsüeh* is an anonymous treatise of the Confucian school which appears as Chapter 42 of the *Li chi* (Records of Rites), compiled in the first century B.C. For translations of the *Ta hsüeh*, see James Legge, E. R. Hughes, Wing-tsit Chan, and Daniel K. Gardner. Legge and Chan follow the Ch'eng-Chu recension, and Gardner's work is both a translation and an in-depth study of that recension. Hughes follows the *Li chi* text. Akatsuka gives both versions annotated separately, with a Japanese translation.

9 For the importance of the *Greater Learning* in Ch'eng-Chu education, see de Bary, *Neo-Confucian Orthodoxy and the Learning of the Mind-and-Heart*, pp. 83ff.

10 Although Chu Hsi's interpretation of the thesis, not to mention his attribution of it to Confucius, fell short of being universally accepted, his attention to the *Greater Learning* was symptomatic of a new appreciation of that work in the Sung Dynasty (960–1279) and did much to commend it to Confucians thereafter, whether Ch'eng-Chu or otherwise. Expressions from it occur everywhere in the subsequent literature, and the structure of the thesis pervades Confucian discourse generally.

11 There are two editions of the lectures: *Daigaku kōgi* (Lectures on the *Greater Learning*), 104 pp. in *Haru no kokoro*; and *Daigaku keibun kōgi* (Lectures on the Canonical Text in the *Greater Learning*), 188 pp. in *Rakuō Kō isho*, Vol. 3. Items in these two anthologies of Sadanobu's works are paginated separately. Page references are to the *Daigaku kōgi*.

12 Sadanobu adheres throughout to the proposition that 'When speaking of good and bad, even though there seem to be various kinds, there are but two things: the principle of Heaven and the desire of man.' (p. 42) Thus, for Sadanobu, at least in these lectures, human desire is synonymous with bad.

13 Sadanobu's discourse on bias, which has been much abbreviated here, starts from a passage in section eight of the *Ta hsüeh* commentary: 'Few in the world know what is bad in those whom they like and what is good in those whom they hate.'

14 See Kyūsō's *Sundai zatsuwa* (Conversations at Suruga Heights, 1732), *Iwanami bunko* series, 1383–1384, Tokyo: Iwanami, 1936, p. 101. *Ching* denotes respectful attention and is ordinarily given to spirits, parents, elders, and business at hand. It is cognate with *ching* in a different tone meaning 'take warning', 'watch out'. The underlying connotation of both words, then, is one of tense alertness. I have opted for 'seriousness', because that seems to be the only word that corresponds generally to the technical meaning of *ching*; though it will help if the reader also notes the connotation of mental concentration and attentiveness.

References

Akatsuka Tadashi (editor and commentator) *Daigaku Chūyō* (The *Ta hsüeh* and *Chung yung*). *Shinshaku kambun taikei* series Vol. 2, Tokyo: Meiji Shoin, 1967

Aoki, Michiko Y. and Margaret B. Dardess 'The Popularization of Samurai Values: A Sermon by Hosoi Heishū', *Monumenta Nipponica* Vol. 31, No. 4 (Winter, 1976), pp. 394–413

Ashikaga Tomoo *Kamakura Muromachi jidai no jukyō* (Confucianism in the Kamakura and Muromachi Periods) Tokyo: Nihon Koten Zenshū Kankōkai, 1932

Backus, Robert L. 'The Relationship of Confucianism to the Tokugawa Bakufu as Revealed in the Kansei Educational Reform', *Harvard Journal of Asiatic Studies*, Vol. 34 (1974), pp. 97–162; 'The Kansei Prohibition of Heterodoxy and Its Effects on Education', ibid. Vol. 39, No. 1 (June 1979), pp. 55–106; 'The Motivation of Confucian Orthodoxy in Tokugawa Japan' ibid. Vol. 39, No. 2 (Dec. 1979), pp. 275–338

Bellah, Robert N. *Tokugawa Religion: The Values of Pre-Industrial Japan* Glencoe, Ill.: The Free Press, 1957

Chan, Hok-lam, and William Theodore de Bary, (eds) *Yüan Thought: Chinese Thought and Religion under the Mongols* New York: Columbia University Press, 1982

Chan, Wing-Tsit (translator and compiler) *A Source Book in Chinese Philosophy* Princeton, N.J.: Princeton University Press, 1936

——(ed.) *Chu Hsi and Neo-Confucianism* Honolulu: University of Hawaii Press, 1986

Chang, Carsun *The Development of Neo-Confucian Thought* New York: Bookman Associates, 1957

Chu Hsi, and Lü Tsu-ch'ien *Reflections on Things at Hand: The Neo-Confucian Anthology Compiled by Chu Hsi and Lü Tsu-ch'ien*, a translation, with notes, of the *Chin ssu lu* by Wing-Tsit Chan, New York and London: Columbia University Press, 1967

Creel, Herrlee G. *Confucius: The Man and the Myth* New York: John Day, 1949; London: Routledge and K. Paul, 1951. Reprinted as *Confucius and the Chinese Way* New York: Harper and Row, 1960

de Bary, William Theodore *Neo-Confucian Orthodoxy and the Learning of the Mind-and-Heart* New York: Columbia University Press, 1981

de Bary William Theodore and the Conference on Ming Thought *Self and Society in Ming Thought* New York and London: Columbia University Press, 1970

de Bary William Theodore and the Conference on Seventeenth-Century Chinese Thought *The Unfolding of Neo-Confucianism* New York and London: Columbia University Press, 1975

de Bary William Theodore and Irene Bloom (eds) *Principle and Practicality: Essays in Neo-Confucianism and Practical Learning* New York: Columbia University Press, 1979

Fingarette, Herbert *Confucius—The Secular as Sacred* New York and London: Harper and Row, 1972

Gardner, Daniel K. *Chu Hsi and the Ta-hsüeh: Neo-Confucian Reflection on the Confucian Canon* Harvard East Asian Monographs 118, Cambridge, Mass. and London: Harvard University Press, 1986

Graham, A.C. *Two Chinese Philosophers: Ch'eng Ming-tao and Ch'eng Yi-ch'uan* London: Lund Humphries, 1958

Hall, John Whitney *Tanuma Okitsugu (1719–1788): Forerunner of Modern Japan* Harvard-Yenching Institute Monograph Series, No. 14, Cambridge, Mass: Harvard University Press, 1955

Hughes, E. R. *The Great Learning and the Mean in Action: Newly Translated from the Chinese, with an Introductory Essay on the History of Chinese Philosohy* New York: E. P. Dutton, 1943

Legge, James *The Chinese Classics, Vol. 1: Confucian Analects, The Great Learning, The Doctrine of the Mean* first edition, 1861, Hong Kong: Hong Kong University Press, 1960

Maruyama Masao *Studies in the Intellectual History of Tokugawa Japan,* a translation by Mikiso Hane of *Nihon seiji shisō shi kenkyū* (Studies in the History of Japanese Political Thought), 1952, Princeton, New Jersey and Tokyo: Princeton University Press and the University of Tokyo Press, 1974

Matsudaira Sadanobu *Rakuō Kō isho* (The Surviving Works of Lord Rakuō) (3 vols), Ema Seihatsu (ed.), Osaka: Seibunkan, 1893

—— *Haru no kokoro* (The Heart of Spring) Kodera Seijirō (ed.), Kuwana: Chinkoku Shukoku Jinja, 1928

—— *Uge no hito koto* (Someone is Speaking under the Eaves), *Sugyō roku* (Record of Self-Training) Matsudaira Sadamitsu (ed.), *Iwanami bunko* series, No. 2990–2991. Tokyo: Iwanami, 1942. *Uge no hito koto* is Sadanobu's autobiography. Its ghostly title is derived from a graphic pun; combine the four characters to make two and they spell out 'Sadanobu'.

Ooms, Herman *Charismatic Bureaucrat: A Political Biography of Matsudaira Sadanobu (1758–1829)* Chicago and London: University of Chicago Press, 1975 Sagara Tōru *Kinsei Nihon ni okeru jukyō undō no keifu* (The Filiations of the Confucian Movement in Early Modern Japan) Tokyo: Risōsha, 1975

Glossary

bun bu　文武
Ch'eng Hao　程顥
Ch'eng Yi　程頤
chi　機
ch'i　氣
Chin ssu lu　近思録
ching 'canon'　經
ching (seriousness)　敬
ching (watchful)　警
Chu Hsi　朱熹
chün tzu　君子
Chung yung　中庸
Daigaku keibun kōgi　大學經文講義
Daigaku kōgi　大學講義
daigaku no kami　大學頭
Haru no kokoro　春の心
Hayashi Razan　林羅山

hosa   輔佐
Hsiao hsüeh   小學
hsiao jen   小人
hsien   賢
hsin fa   心法
hsing   性
jen cheng   仁政
ko wu   格物
Kodera Seijirō   小寺鉎次郎
li (principle)   理
li (propriety)   禮
Li chi   禮記
Liu Tzu-ch'eng   劉子澄
Lu Chia   陸賈
Lü shih ch'un ch'iu   呂氏春秋
Lü Tsu-ch'ien   呂祖謙
Matsudaira Sadamitsu   松平定光
Matsudaira Sadanobu   松平定信
Muro Kyūsō   室鳩巣
on   恩
pa t'iao mu   八條目
pen t'i   本體
Rakuō Kō isho   樂翁公遺書
rōjū shuseki   老中主席
Sagara Tōru   相良亨
san kang ling   三綱領
sheng   聖
Shih chi   史記
Shih ching   詩經
Shingaku   心學
Shu ching   書經
Sugyō roku   修行録
Sundai zatsuwa   駿臺雑話
Ta hsüeh   大學
Ta hsüeh chang chü   大學章句
Tanuma Okitsugu   田沼意次
Tseng Shen   曾參
Uge no hito koto   宇下人言

Index